Washington Irving

Sunnyside Dec. 15th 1851.

THE WORKS
OF
WASHINGTON IRVING

LONGRIVER

PRESS
Secaucus, N. J.

Published by Longriver Press
A Division Of Book Sales, Inc.
Secaucus, New Jersey 07094
1976

ISBN-0-89009-076-9

Library Of Congress No. 76-20218

Manufactured In U.S.A.

CONTENTS

WASHINGTON IRVING.

BIOGRAPHICAL SKETCH.

IRVING may be named as the first author in the United States whose writings made a place for themselves in general literature. Franklin, indeed, had preceded him with his autobiography, but Franklin belongs rather to the colonial period. It was under the influences of that time that his mind and taste were formed, and there was a marked difference between the Boston and Philadelphia of Franklin's youth and the New York of Irving's time. Politics, commerce, and the rise of industries were rapidly changing social relations and manners, while the country was still dependent on England for its higher literature. It had hardly begun to find materials for literature in its own past or in its aspects of nature, yet there was a very positive element in life which resented foreign interference. There were thus two currents crossing each other: the common life which was narrowly American, and the cultivated taste which was English, or imitative of England. Irving's first ventures, in company with his brothers and Paulding, were in the attempt to represent New York in literature upon the model of contemporary or recent presentations of London. "The town" in the minds of these young writers was that portion of New York society which might be construed into a miniature reflection of London wit and amusement. His associates never advanced beyond this stage, but with Washington Irving the sketches which he wrote under the signature of *Jonathan Old Style* and in the medley of *Salmagundi* were only the first experiments of a mind capable of larger things. After five or six years of trifling with his pen, he wrote and published, in 1809, *A History of New York, by Diedrich Knickerbocker*, which he began in company with his brother Peter as a mere *jeu d'esprit*, but turned into a more determined work of humor, as the capabilities of the subject disclosed themselves. Grave historians had paid little attention to the record of New York under the Dutch; Irving, who saw the humorous contrast between the traditional Dutch society of his day and the pushing new democracy, seized upon the early history and made it the occasion for a good-natured burlesque. He shocked the old families about him, but he amused everybody else, and the book, going to England, made his name at once known to those who had the making there of literary reputations.

Irving himself was born of a Scottish father and English mother, who had come to this country only twenty years before. He was but little removed, therefore, from the traditions of Great Britain, and his brothers and he carried on a trading business with the old country. His own tastes were not mercantile, and he was only silent partner in the house; he wrote occasionally and was for a time the editor of a magazine, but his pleasure was chiefly in travel, good literature, and good society. It was while he was in England, in 1818, that the house in which he was a partner failed, and he was thrown on his own resources. Necessity gave the slight spur which was wanting to his inclination, and he began with deliberation the career of an author. He had found himself at home in England. His family origin and his taste for the best literature had made him English in his sympathies and tastes, and his residence and travels there, the society which he entered and the friends he made, confirmed him in English habits. Nevertheless he was sturdily American in his principles; he was strongly attached to New York and his American friends, and was always a looker-on in England. His foreign birth and education gave him significant advantages as an observer of English life, and he at once began the writing of those papers, stories, and sketches which appeared in the separate numbers of *The Sketch Book*, in *Bracebridge Hall*, and in *Tales of a Traveller*. They were chiefly drawn from material accumulated abroad, but an occasional American subject was taken. Irving instinctively felt that by the circumstances of the time and the bent of his genius he could pursue his calling more safely abroad than at home. He remained in Europe seventeen years, sending home his books for publication, and securing also the profitable results of publication in London. During that time, besides the books above named, he wrote the *History of the Life and Voyages of Christopher Columbus;* the *Voyages and Discoveries of the Companions of Columbus; A Chronicle of the Conquest of Granada;* and *The Alhambra*. The Spanish material was obtained while residing in Spain, whither he went at the suggestion of the American minister to make translations of documents relating to the voyages of Columbus which had recently been collected. Irving's training and tastes led him rather into the construction of popular narrative than into the work of a scientific historian, and, with his strong American affections, he was quick to see the interest and value which lay in the history of Spain as connected with America. He was eminently a *raconteur*, very skilful and graceful in the shaping of old material; his humor played freely over the surface of his writing, and, with little power to create characters or plots, he had an unfailing perception of the literary capabilities of scenes and persons which came under his observation.

He came back to America in 1832 with an established reputation, and was welcomed enthusiastically by his friends and countrymen. He travelled into the new parts of America, and spent ten years at home, industriously working at the material which had accumulated in his hands when abroad, and had been increased during his travels in the West. In this period he published *Legends of the Conquest of Spain; The Crayon Miscellany*, including his *Tour on the Prairies, Abbotsford and Newstead Abbey; Astoria;* a number of papers in the *Knickerbocker Magazine*, afterwards published under the title of *Wolfert's Roost;* and edited the *Adventures of Captain Bonneville, U. S. A., in the Rocky Mountains and the Far West.*

In 1842 he went back to Spain as American minister, holding the office for four years, when he returned to America, established himself at his home, Sunnyside on the banks of the Hudson, and remained there until his death in 1859. The fruits of this final period were *Mahomet and his Successors*, which, with a volume of posthumous publication, *Spanish Papers and other Miscellanies*, completed the series of Spanish and Moorish subjects which form a distinct part of his writings; *Oliver Goldsmith, a Biography;* and finally a *Life of Washington*, which occupied the closing years of his life, — years which were not free from physical suffering. In this book Irving embodied his strong admiration for the subject, whose name he bore and whose blessing he had received as a child; he employed, too, a pen which had been trained by its labors on the Spanish material, and, like that series, the work is marked by good taste, artistic sense of proportion, faithfulness, and candor, rather than by the severer work of the historian. It is a popular and a fair life of Washington and account of the war for independence.

Irving's personal and literary history is recorded in *The Life and Letters of Washington Irving*, by his nephew, Pierre M. Irving. His death was the occasion of many affectionate and graceful eulogies and addresses, a number of which were gathered into *Irvingiana: a Memorial of Washington Irving.*

Rip Van Winkle is from *The Sketch Book.*

Washington Irving was born in New York April 3, 1783, and died at Sunnyside on the Hudson, November 28, 1859.

THE SKETCH-BOOK

OF

GEOFFREY CRAYON, GENT.

"I have no wife nor children, good or bad, to provide for. A mere spectator of other men's fortunes and adventures, and how they play their parts; which, methinks, are diversely presented unto me, as from a common theater or scene."—BURTON.

To

SIR WALTER SCOTT, BART.,

THIS WORK IS DEDICATED, IN TESTIMONY

OF THE

ADMIRATION AND AFFECTION

OF

THE AUTHOR

ADVERTISEMENT

FIRST AMERICAN EDITION

—————————

THE following writings are published on experiment; should they please, they may be followed by others. The writer will have to contend with some disadvantages. He is unsettled in his abode, subject to interruptions, and has his share of cares and vicissitudes. He cannot, therefore, promise a regular plan, nor regular periods of publication. Should he be encouraged to proceed, much time may elapse between the appearance of his numbers; and their size will depend on the materials he may have on hand. His writings will partake of the fluctuations of his own thoughts and feelings; sometimes treating of scenes before him, sometimes of others purely imaginary, and sometimes wandering back with his recollections to his native country. He will not be able to give them that tranquil attention necessary to finished composition; and as they must be transmitted across the Atlantic for publication, he will have to trust to others to correct the frequent errors of the press. Should his writings, however, with all their imperfections, be well received, he cannot conceal that it would be a source of the purest gratification; for though he does not aspire to those high honors which are the rewards of loftier intellects, yet it is the dearest wish of his heart to have a secure and cherished, though humble corner in the good opinions and kind feelings of his countrymen.

London, 1819.   11

ADVERTISEMENT

TO THE

FIRST ENGLISH EDITION

THE following desultory papers are part of a series written in this country, but published in America. The author is aware of the austerity with which the writings of his countrymen have hitherto been treated by British critics; he is conscious, too, that much of the contents of his papers can be interesting only in the eyes of American readers. It was not his intention, therefore, to have them reprinted in this country. He has, however, observed several of them from time to time inserted in periodical works of merit, and has understood that it was probable they would be republished in a collective form. He has been induced, therefore, to revise and bring them forward himself, that they may at least come correctly before the public. Should they be deemed of sufficient importance to attract the attention of critics, he solicits for them that courtesy and candor which a stranger has some right to claim who presents himself at the threshold of a hospitable nation.

February, 1820.

THE AUTHOR'S ACCOUNT OF HIMSELF

"I am of this mind with Homer, that as the snaile that crept out of her shel was turned eftsoones into a toad, and thereby was forced to make a stoole to sit on; so the traveler that stragleth from his owne country is in a short time transformed into so monstrous a shape, that he is faine to alter his mansion with his manners, and to live where he can, not where he would."—*Lyly's Euphues*

I WAS always fond of visiting new scenes, and observing strange characters and manners. Even when a mere child I began my travels, and made many tours of discovery into foreign parts and unknown regions of my native city, to the frequent alarm of my parents, and the emolument of the town crier. As I grew into boyhood, I extended the range of my observations. My holiday afternoons were spent in rambles about the surrounding country. I made myself familiar with all its places famous in history or fable. I knew every spot where a murder or robbery had been committed, or a ghost seen. I visited the neighboring villages, and added greatly to my stock of knowledge, by noting their habits and customs, and conversing with their sages and great men. I even journeyed one long summer's day to the summit of the most distant hill, from whence I stretched my eye over many a mile of terra incognita, and was astonished to find how vast a globe I inhabited.

This rambling propensity strengthened with my years. Books of voyages and travel became my passion, and in devouring their contents I neglected the regular exercises of the school. How wistfully would I wander about the pier-heads in fine weather, and watch the parting ships, bound to distant climes—with what longing eyes would I gaze after

13

their lessening sails, and waft myself in imagination to the ends of the earth!

Further reading and thinking, though they brought this vague inclination into more reasonable bounds, only served to make it more decided. I visited various parts of my own country; and had I been merely influenced by a love of fine scenery, I should have felt little desire to seek elsewhere its gratification; for on no country have the charms of nature been more prodigally lavished. Her mighty lakes, like oceans of liquid silver; her mountains, with their bright aerial tints; her valleys, teeming with wild fertility; her tremendous cataracts, thundering in their solitudes; her boundless plains, waving with spontaneous verdure; her broad deep rivers, rolling in solemn silence to the ocean; her trackless forests, where vegetation puts forth all its magnificence; her skies, kindling with the magic of summer clouds and glorious sunshine:—no, never need an American look beyond his own country for the sublime and beautiful of natural scenery.

But Europe held forth all the charms of storied and poetical association. There were to be seen the masterpieces of art, the refinements of highly cultivated society, the quaint peculiarities of ancient and local custom. My native country was full of youthful promise; Europe was rich in the accumulated treasures of age. Her very ruins told the history of times gone by, and every mouldering stone was a chronicle. I longed to wander over the scenes of renowned achievement —to tread, as it were, in the footsteps of antiquity—to loiter about the ruined castle—to meditate on the falling tower—to escape, in short, from the commonplace realities of the present, and lose myself among the shadowy grandeurs of the past.

I had, beside all this, an earnest desire to see the great men of the earth. We have, it is true, our great men in America: not a city but has an ample share of them. I have mingled among them in my time, and been almost withered by the shade into which they cast me; for there is nothing so baleful to a small man as the shade of a great one, particularly the great man of a city. But I was anxious to see the great men of Europe; for I had read in the works of various philosophers that all animals degenerated in America, and man among the number. A great man of Europe, thought I, must therefore be as superior to a great man of America as a peak of the Alps to a highland of the Hudson; and in this idea I was confirmed, by observing the comparative importance and swelling magnitude of many English travelers among us, who, I was assured, were very little people in their own country. I will visit this land of wonders, thought I, and see the gigantic race from which I am degenerated.

It has been either my good or evil lot to have my roving passion gratified. I have wandered through different countries, and witnessed many of the shifting scenes of life. I cannot say that I have studied them with the eye of a philosopher, but rather with the sauntering gaze with which humble lovers of the picturesque stroll from the window of one print-shop to another; caught sometimes by the delineations of beauty, sometimes by the distortions of caricature, and sometimes by the loveliness of landscape. As it is the fashion for modern tourists to travel pencil in hand, and bring home their portfolios filled with sketches, I am disposed to get up a few for the entertainment of my friends. When, however, I look over the hints and memorandums I have taken down for the purpose, my heart almost fails me, at finding how my idle humor has led me aside from the great objects studied by every regular traveler who would make a book. I fear I shall give equal disappointment with an unlucky landscape-painter, who had traveled on the Continent, but, following the bent of his vagrant inclination, had sketched in nooks, and corners, and by-places. His sketch-book was accordingly crowded with cottages, and landscapes, and obscure ruins; but he had neglected to paint St. Peter's or the Coliseum; the cascade of Terni, or the Bay of Naples; and had not a single glacier or volcano in his whole collection.

THE SKETCH-BOOK

THE VOYAGE

"Ships, ships, I will descrie you
    Amidst the main,
I will come and try you,
What are you protecting,
And projecting,
    What's your end and aim.
One goes abroad for merchandise and trading,
Another stays to keep his country from invading,
A third is coming home with rich and wealthy lading,
Hallo! my fancie, whither wilt thou go?"—OLD POEM

To an American visiting Europe, the long voyage he has
to make is an excellent preparative. The temporary absence
of worldly scenes and employments produces a state of mind
peculiarly fitted to receive new and vivid impressions. The
vast space of waters that separates the hemispheres is like
a blank page in existence. There is no gradual transition by
which, as in Europe, the features and population of one country blend almost imperceptibly with those of another. From
the moment you lose sight of the land you have left all is
vacancy until you step on the opposite shore, and are launched
at once into the bustle and novelties of another world.

In traveling by land there is a continuity of scene and a
connected succession of persons and incidents that carry on
the story of life, and lessen the effect of absence and separation. We drag, it is true, "a lengthening chain" at each
remove of our pilgrimage; but the chain is unbroken; we
can trace it back link by link; and we feel that the last of

17

them still grapples us to home. But a wide sea voyage severs us at once. It makes us conscious of being cast loose from the secure anchorage of settled life, and sent adrift upon a doubtful world. It interposes a gulf, not merely imaginary, but real, between us and our homes—a gulf, subject to tempest, and fear, and uncertainty, that makes distance palpable, and return precarious.

Such, at least, was the case with myself. As I saw the last blue line of my native land fade away like a cloud in the horizon, it seemed as if I had closed one volume of the world and its concerns, and had time for meditation, before I opened another. That land, too, now vanishing from my view, which contained all that was most dear to me in life; what vicissitudes might occur in it—what changes might take place in me, before I should visit it again! Who can tell, when he sets forth to wander, whither he may be driven by the uncertain currents of existence; or when he may return; or whether it may be ever his lot to revisit the scenes of his childhood?

I said that at sea all is vacancy; I should correct the expression. To one given to day dreaming, and fond of losing himself in reveries, a sea voyage is full of subjects for meditation; but then they are the wonders of the deep and of the air, and rather tend to abstract the mind from worldly themes. I delighted to loll over the quarter-railing or climb to the maintop, of a calm day, and muse for hours together on the tranquil bosom of a summer's sea; to gaze upon the piles of golden clouds just peering above the horizon; fancy them some fairy realms, and people them with a creation of my own; to watch the gentle undulating billows, rolling their silver volumes, as if to die away on those happy shores.

There was a delicious sensation of mingled security and awe with which I looked down, from my giddy height, on the monsters of the deep at their uncouth gambols: shoals of porpoises tumbling about the bow of the ship; the grampus, slowly heaving his huge form above the surface; or the ravenous shark, darting, like a specter, through the blue waters.

My imagination would conjure up all that I had heard or
read of the watery world beneath me: of the finny herds that
roam its fathomless valleys; of the shapeless monsters that
lurk among the very foundations of the earth, and of those
wild phantasms that swell the tales of fishermen and sailors.

Sometimes a distant sail, gliding along the edge of the
ocean, would be another theme of idle speculation. How
interesting this fragment of a world hastening to rejoin the
great mass of existence! What a glorious monument of
human invention; that has thus triumphed over wind and
wave; has brought the ends of the world into communion;
has established an interchange of blessings, pouring into the
sterile regions of the north all the luxuries of the south; has
diffused the light of knowledge, and the charities of cultivated life; and has thus bound together those scattered portions of the human race between which nature seemed to
have thrown an insurmountable barrier.

We one day descried some shapeless object drifting at a
distance. At sea, everything that breaks the monotony of
the surrounding expanse attracts attention. It proved to be
the mast of a ship that must have been completely wrecked;
for there were the remains of handkerchiefs, by which some
of the crew had fastened themselves to this spar to prevent
their being washed off by the waves. There was no trace
by which the name of the ship could be ascertained. The
wreck had evidently drifted about for many months; clusters
of shell-fish had fastened about it, and long sea-weeds flaunted
at its sides. But where, thought I, is the crew? Their
struggle has long been over—they have gone down amid the
roar of the tempest—their bones lie whitening among the
caverns of the deep. Silence, oblivion, like the waves, have
closed over them, and no one can tell the story of their end.
What sighs have been wafted after that ship; what prayers
offered up at the deserted fireside of home! How often has
the mistress, the wife, the mother, pored over the daily news,
to catch some casual intelligence of this rover of the deep!
How has expectation darkened into anxiety—anxiety into

dread—and dread into despair! Alas! not one memento shall ever return for love to cherish. All that shall ever be known, is, that she sailed from her port, "and was never heard of more!"

The sight of this wreck, as usual, gave rise to many dismal anecdotes. This was particularly the case in the evening, when the weather, which had hitherto been fair, began to look wild and threatening, and gave indications of one of those sudden storms that will sometimes break in upon the serenity of a summer voyage. As we sat round the dull light of a lamp, in the cabin, that made the gloom more ghastly, every one had his tale of shipwreck and disaster. I was particularly struck with a short one related by the captain:

"As I was once sailing," said he, "in a fine, stout ship, across the banks of Newfoundland, one of those heavy fogs that prevail in those parts rendered it impossible for us to see far ahead, even in the daytime; but at night the weather was so thick that we could not distinguish any object at twice the length of the ship. I kept lights at the masthead, and a constant watch forward to look out for fishing smacks, which are accustomed to lie at anchor on the banks. The wind was blowing a smacking breeze, and we were going at a great rate through the water. Suddenly the watch gave the alarm of 'a sail ahead!'—it was scarcely uttered before we were upon her. She was a small schooner, at anchor, with a broadside toward us. The crew were all asleep, and had neglected to hoist a light. We struck her just amidships. The force, the size, the weight of our vessel, bore her down below the waves; we passed over her and were hurried on our course. As the crashing wreck was sinking beneath us, I had a glimpse of two or three half-naked wretches, rushing from her cabin; they just started from their beds to be swallowed shrieking by the waves. I heard their drowning cry mingling with the wind. The blast that bore it to our ears swept us out of all further hearing. I shall never forget that cry! It was some time before we could put the ship about, she was under such headway. We returned as nearly as we could guess to the place where the smack had anchored. We cruised about for several hours in the dense fog. We fired signal-guns, and listened if we might hear the halloo of any survivors; but all was silent—we never saw or heard anything of them more."

I confess these stories, for a time, put an end to all my fine fancies. The storm increased with the night. The sea was lashed into tremendous confusion. There was a fearful, sullen sound of rushing waves and broken surges. Deep called unto deep. At times the black volume of clouds overhead seemed rent asunder by flashes of lightning that quivered along the foaming billows, and made the succeeding darkness doubly terrible. The thunders bellowed over the wild waste of waters, and were echoed and prolonged by the mountain waves. As I saw the ship staggering and plunging among these roaring caverns it seemed miraculous that she regained her balance, or preserved her buoyancy. Her yards would dip into the water; her bow was almost buried beneath the waves. Sometimes an impending surge appeared ready to overwhelm her, and nothing but a dexterous movement of the helm preserved her from the shock.

When I retired to my cabin, the awful scene still followed me. The whistling of the wind through the rigging sounded like funereal wailings. The creaking of the masts; the straining and groaning of bulkheads, as the ship labored in the weltering sea, were frightful. As I heard the waves rushing along the side of the ship, and roaring in my very ear, it seemed as if Death were raging round this floating prison, seeking for his prey: the mere starting of a nail, the yawning of a seam, might give him entrance.

A fine day, however, with a tranquil sea and favoring breeze, soon put all these dismal reflections to flight. It is impossible to resist the gladdening influence of fine weather and fair wind at sea. When the ship is decked out in all her canvas, every sail swelled, and careering gayly over the curling waves, how lofty, how gallant, she appears—how she seems to lord it over the deep! I might fill a volume with the reveries of a sea voyage; for with me it is almost a continual reverie—but it is time to get to shore.

It was a fine sunny morning when the thrilling cry of "land!" was given from the masthead. None but those who have experienced it can form an idea of the delicious throng of sensations which rush into an American's bosom when he first comes in sight of Europe. There is a volume of associations with the very name. It is the land of promise, teeming with everything of which his childhood has heard, or on which his studious years have pondered.

From that time, until the moment of arrival, it was all feverish excitement. The ships of war that prowled like guardian giants along the coast; the headlands of Ireland, stretching out into the channel; the Welsh mountains, towering into the clouds; all were objects of intense interest. As we sailed up the Mersey, I reconnoitered the shores with a telescope. My eye dwelt with delight on neat cottages, with their trim shrubberies and green grass-plots. I saw the mouldering ruin of an abbey overrun with ivy, and the taper spire of a village church rising from the brow of a neighboring hill—all were characteristic of England.

The tide and wind were so favorable that the ship was enabled to come at once to the pier. It was thronged with people; some idle lookers-on, others eager expectants of friends or relatives. I could distinguish the merchant to whom the ship was consigned. I knew him by his calculating brow and restless air. His hands were thrust into his pockets; he was whistling thoughtfully, and walking to and fro, a small space having been accorded him by the crowd, in deference to his temporary importance. There were repeated cheerings and salutations interchanged between the shore and the ship, as friends happened to recognize each other. I particularly noticed one young woman of humble dress, but interesting demeanor. She was leaning forward from among the crowd; her eye hurried over the ship as it neared the shore, to catch some wished-for countenance. She seemed disappointed and agitated; when I heard a faint voice call her name.—It was from a poor sailor who had been ill all the voyage, and had excited the sympathy of every one on board. When the weather was fine, his messmates had spread a mattress for him on deck in the shade, but of late his illness had so increased that he had taken to his hammock, and only breathed a wish that he might see his wife before he died. He had been helped on deck as we came up the river, and was now leaning against the shrouds, with a countenance so wasted, so pale, so ghastly, that it was no wonder even the eye of affection did not recognize him. But at the sound of his voice, her eye darted on his features; it read, at once, a whole volume of sorrow; she clasped her hands, uttered a faint shriek, and stood wringing them in silent agony.

All now was hurry and bustle. The meetings of acquaintances—the greetings of friends—the consultations of men of business. I alone was solitary and idle. I had no friend to meet, no cheering to receive. I stepped upon the land of my forefathers—but felt that I was a stranger in the land.

ROSCOE

"—In the service of mankind to be
A guardian god below; still to employ
The mind's brave ardor in heroic aims,
Such as may raise us o'er the groveling herd,
And make us shine for ever—that is life."—THOMSON

ONE of the first places to which a stranger is taken in Liverpool is the Athenæum. It is established on a liberal and judicious plan; it contains a good library, and spacious reading-room, and is the great literary resort of the place. Go there at what hour you may, you are sure to find it filled with grave-looking personages, deeply absored in the study of newspapers.

As I was once visiting this haunt of the learned my attention was attracted to a person just entering the room. He was advanced in life, tall, and of a form that might once have been commanding, but it was a little bowed by time—perhaps by care. He had a noble Roman style of countenance; a head that would have pleased a painter; and though some slight furrows on his brow showed that wasting thought had been busy there, yet his eye still beamed with the fire of a poetic soul. There was something in his whole appearance that indicated a being of a different order from the bustling race around him.

I inquired his name, and was informed that it was Roscoe. I drew back with an involuntary feeling of veneration. This, then, was an author of celebrity; this was one of those men whose voices have gone forth to the ends of the earth; with whose minds I have communed even in the solitudes of America. Accustomed, as we are in our country, to know European writers only by their works, we cannot conceive of them, as of other men, engrossed by trivial or sordid pursuits, and jostling with the crowd of common minds in the dusty paths of life. They pass before our imaginations like superior beings, radiant with the emanations of their own genius, and surrounded by a halo of literary glory.

To find, therefore, the elegant historian of the Medici mingling among the busy sons of traffic, at first shocked my poetical ideas; but it is from the very circumstances and situation in which he has been placed that Mr. Roscoe derives his highest claims to admiration. It is interesting to notice how some minds seem almost to create themselves; springing up under every disadvantage, and working their solitary but irresistible way through a thousand obstacles. Nature seems to delight in disappointing the assiduities of art, with which it would rear legitimate dullness to maturity; and to glory in the vigor and luxuriance of her chance productions. She scatters the seeds of genius to the winds, and though some may perish among the stony places of the world, and some be choked by the thorns and brambles of early adversity, yet others will now and then strike root even in the clefts of the rock, struggle bravely up into sunshine, and spread over their sterile birthplace all the beauties of vegetation.

Such has been the case with Mr. Roscoe. Born in a place apparently ungenial to the growth of literary talent; in the very market-place of trade; without fortune, family connections, or patronage; self-prompted, self-sustained, and almost self-taught, he has conquered every obstacle, achieved his way to eminence, and, having become one of the ornaments of the nation, has turned the whole force of his talents and influence to advance and embellish his native town.

Indeed, it is this last trait in his character which has given him the greatest interest in my eyes, and induced me particularly to point him out to my countrymen. Eminent as are his literary merits, he is but one among the many distinguished authors of this intellectual nation. They, however, in general, live but for their own fame, or their own pleasures. Their private history presents no lesson to the world, or, perhaps, a humiliating one of human frailty and inconsistency. At best, they are prone to steal away from the bustle and commonplace of busy existence; to indulge in the selfishness of lettered ease; and to revel in scenes of mental, but exclusive enjoyment.

Mr. Roscoe, on the contrary, has claimed none of the accorded privileges of talent. He has shut himself up in no garden of thought, nor elysium of fancy; but has gone forth into the highways and thoroughfares of life, he has planted bowers by the wayside, for the refreshment of the pilgrim and the sojourner, and has opened pure fountains, where the laboring man may turn aside from the dust and heat of the day, and drink of the living streams of knowledge. There is a "daily beauty in his life," on which mankind may meditate, and grow better. It exhibits no lofty and almost useless, because inimitable, example of excellence; but presents a picture of active, yet simple and imitable virtues, which are within every man's reach, but which, unfortunately, are not exercised by many, or this world would be a paradise.

But his private life is peculiarly worthy the attention of the citizens of our young and busy country, where literature and the elegant arts must grow up side by side with the coarser plants of daily necessity; and must depend for their culture, not on the exclusive devotion of time and wealth, nor the quickening rays of titled patronage, but on hours and seasons snatched from the pursuit of worldly interests by intelligent and public-spirited individuals.

He has shown how much may be done for a place in hours of leisure by one master spirit, and how completely it can give its own impress to surrounding objects. Like his own Lorenzo de Medici, on whom he seems to have fixed his eye, as on a pure model of antiquity, he has interwoven the history of his life with the history of his native town, and has made the foundations of its fame the monuments of his virtues. Wherever you go, in Liverpool, you perceive traces of his footsteps in all that is elegant and liberal. He found the tide of wealth flowing merely in the channels of traffic; he has diverted from it invigorating rills to refresh the gardens of literature. By his own example and constant exertions he has effected that union of commerce and the intellectual pursuits, so eloquently recommended in one of his latest writings;* and has practically proved how beautifully they may be brought to harmonize, and to benefit each other. The noble institutions for literary and scientific purposes, which reflect such credit on Liverpool, and are giving such an impulse to the public mind, have most been originated, and have all been effectively promoted, by Mr. Roscoe: and when we consider the rapidly increasing opulence and magnitude of that town, which promises to vie in commercial importance with the metropolis, it will be perceived that in awakening an ambition of mental improvement among its inhabitants he has effected a great benefit to the cause of British literature.

In America, we know Mr. Roscoe only as the author—in

---

* Address on the opening of the Liverpool Institution.

Liverpool, he is spoken of as the banker; and I was told of
his having been unfortunate in business. I could not pity
him, as I heard some rich men do. I considered him far
above the reach of my pity. Those who live only for the
world, and in the world, may be cast down by the frowns of
adversity; but a man like Roscoe is not to be overcome by
the reverses of fortune. They do but drive him in upon the
resources of his own mind; to the superior society of his own
thoughts; which the best of men are apt sometimes to neglect, and to roam abroad in search of less worthy associates.
He is independent of the world around him. He lives with
antiquity, and with posterity: with antiquity, in the sweet
communion of studious retirement; and with posterity, in
the generous aspirings after future renown. The solitude of
such a mind is its state of highest enjoyment. It is then
visited by those elevated meditations which are the proper
aliment of noble souls, and are, like manna, sent from heaven,
in the wilderness of this world.

While my feelings were yet alive on the subject, it was
my fortune to light on further traces of Mr. Roscoe. I was
riding out with a gentleman, to view the environs of Liverpool, when he turned off, through a gate, into some ornamented grounds. After riding a short distance, we came to
a spacious mansion of freestone, built in the Grecian style.
It was not in the purest taste, yet it had an air of elegance,
and the situation was delightful. A fine lawn sloped away
from it, studded with clumps of trees, so disposed as to break
a soft fertile country into a variety of landscapes. The Mersey was seen winding a broad quiet sheet of water through
an expanse of green meadow land; while the Welsh mountains, blending with clouds, and melting into distance, bordered the horizon.

This was Roscoe's favorite residence during the days of
his prosperity. It had been the seat of elegant hospitality
and literary refinement. The house was now silent and deserted. I saw the windows of the study, which looked out
upon the soft scenery I have mentioned. The windows were

closed—the library was gone. Two or three ill-favored beings
were loitering about the place, whom my fancy pictured into
retainers of the law. It was like visiting some classic fountain that had once welled its pure waters in a sacred shade,
but finding it dry and dusty with the lizard and the toad
brooding over the shattered marbles.

I inquired after the fate of Mr. Roscoe's library, which
had consisted of scarce and foreign books, from many of
which he had drawn the materials for his Italian histories.
It had passed under the hammer of the auctioneer, and was
dispersed about the country.

The good people of the vicinity thronged like wreckers to
get some part of the noble vessel that had been driven on
shore. Did such a scene admit of ludicrous associations, we
might imagine something whimsical in this strange irruption
into the regions of learning. Pigmies rummaging the armory
of a giant, and contending for the possession of weapons
which they could not wield. We might picture to ourselves
some knot of speculators debating with calculating brow over
the quaint binding and illuminated margin of an obsolete
author; or the air of intense, but baffled sagacity, with
which some successful purchaser attempted to dive into the
black-letter bargain he had secured.

It is a beautiful incident in the story of Mr. Roscoe's misfortunes, and one which cannot fail to interest the studious
mind, that the parting with his books seems to have touched
upon his tenderest feelings, and to have been the only circumstance that could provoke the notice of his muse. The
scholar only knows how dear these silent, yet eloquent, companions of pure thoughts and innocent hours become in the
season of adversity. When all that is worldly turns to dross
around us, these only retain their steady value. When
friends grow cold, and the converse of intimates languishes
into vapid civility and commonplace, these only continue the
unaltered countenance of happier days, and cheer us with
that true friendship which never deceived hope, nor deserted
sorrow.

I do not wish to censure; but, surely, if the people of Liverpool had been properly sensible of what was due to Mr. Roscoe and to themselves, his library would never have been sold.

Good worldly reasons may, doubtless, be given for the circumstance, which it would be difficult to combat with others that might seem merely fanciful; but it certainly appears to me such an opportunity as seldom occurs, of cheering a noble mind struggling under misfortunes by one of the most delicate, but most expressive tokens of public sympathy. It is difficult, however, to estimate a man of genius properly who is daily before our eyes. He becomes mingled and confounded with other men. His great qualities lose their novelty, and we become too familiar with the common materials which form the basis even of the loftiest character. Some of Mr. Roscoe's townsmen may regard him merely as a man of business; others as a politician; all find him engaged like themselves in ordinary occupations, and surpassed, perhaps, by themselves on some points of worldly wisdom. Even that amiable and unostentatious simplicity of character, which gives the name less grace to real excellence, may cause him to be undervalued by some coarse minds, who do not know that true worth is always void of glare and pretension. But the man of letters who speaks of Liverpool, speaks of it as the residence of Roscoe.—The intelligent traveler who visits it, inquires where Roscoe is to be seen.—He is the literary landmark of the place, indicating its existence to the distant scholar.—He is like Pompey's column at Alexandria, towering alone in classic dignity.

The following sonnet, addressed by Mr. Roscoe to his books on parting with them, is alluded to in the preceding article. If anything can add effect to the pure feeling and elevated thought here displayed, it is the conviction that the whole is no effusion of fancy, but a faithful transcript from the writer's heart:

TO MY BOOKS.

"As one, who, destined from his friends to part,
    Regrets his loss, but hopes again erewhile
    To share their converse, and enjoy their smile,
And tempers, as he may, affliction's dart;

"Thus, loved associates, chiefs of elder art,
    Teachers of wisdom, who could once beguile
    My tedious hours, and lighten every toil,
I now resign you; nor with fainting heart;

"For pass a few short years, or days, or hours,
    And happier seasons may their dawn unfold,
And all your sacred fellowship restore;
When freed from earth, unlimited its powers,
    Mind shall with mind direct communion hold,
And kindred spirits meet to part no more."

THE WIFE

"The treasures of the deep are not so precious
As are the concealed comforts of a man
Lock'd up in woman's love. I scent the air
Of blessings, when I come but near the house.
What a delicious breath marriage sends forth—
The violet bed 's not sweeter!"—MIDDLETON

I HAVE often had occasion to remark the fortitude with which women sustain the most overwhelming reverses of fortune. Those disasters which break down the spirit of a man, and prostrate him in the dust, seem to call forth all the energies of the softer sex, and give such intrepidity and elevation to their character that at times it approaches to sublimity. Nothing can be more touching than to behold a soft and tender female, who had been all weakness and dependence, and alive to every trivial roughness, while threading the prosperous paths of life, suddenly rising in mental force to be the comforter and supporter of her husband under misfortune, and abiding, with unshrinking firmness, the bitterest blasts of adversity.

As the vine, which has long twined its graceful foliage about the oak, and been lifted by it into sunshine, will, when the hardy plant is rifted by the thunderbolt, cling round it with its caressing tendrils, and bind up its shattered boughs; so is it beautifully ordered by Providence that woman, who is the mere dependent and ornament of man in his happier hours, should be his stay and solace when smitten with sudden calamity; winding herself into the rugged recesses of his nature, tenderly supporting the drooping head, and binding up the broken heart.

I was once congratulating a friend, who had around him a blooming family, knit together in the strongest affection. "I can wish you no better lot," said he, with enthusiasm, "than to have a wife and children. If you are prosperous, there they are to share your prosperity; if otherwise, there they are to comfort you." And, indeed, I have observed that a married man falling into misfortune is more apt to retrieve his situation in the world than a single one; partly, because he is more stimulated to exertion by the necessities of the helpless and beloved beings who depend upon him for subsistence; but chiefly, because his spirits are soothed and relieved by domestic endearments, and his self-respect kept alive by finding that though all abroad is darkness and humiliation, yet there is still a little world of love at home, of which he is the monarch. Whereas, a single man is apt to run to waste and self-neglect; to fancy himself lonely and abandoned, and his heart to fall to ruin, like some deserted mansion, for want of an inhabitant.

These observations call to mind a little domestic story of which I was once a witness. My intimate friend, Leslie, had married a beautiful and accomplished girl who had been brought up in the midst of fashionable life. She had, it is true, no fortune, but that of my friend was ample; and he delighted in the anticipation of indulging her in every elegant pursuit, and administering to those delicate tastes and fancies that spread a kind of witchery about the sex.—"Her life," said he, "shall be like a fairy tale."

The very difference in their characters produced a harmonious combination; he was of a romantic and somewhat serious cast; she was all life and gladness. I have often noticed the mute rapture with which he would gaze upon her in company, of which her sprightly powers made her the delight; and how, in the midst of applause, her eye would still turn to him, as if there alone she sought favor and acceptance. When leaning on his arm, her slender form contrasted finely with his tall, manly person. The fond confiding air with which she looked up to him seemed to call forth a flush of triumphant pride and cherishing tenderness, as if he doted on his lovely burden for its very helplessness. Never did a couple set forward on the flowery path of early and well-suited marriage with a fairer prospect of felicity.

It was the misfortune of my friend, however, to have embarked his property in large speculations; and he had not been married many months, when, by a succession of sudden disasters it was swept from him, and he found himself reduced to almost penury. For a time he kept his situation to himself, and went about with a haggard countenance and a breaking heart. His life was but a protracted agony; and what rendered it more insupportable was the necessity of keeping up a smile in the presence of his wife; for he could not bring himself to overwhelm her with the news. She saw, however, with the quick eyes of affection, that all was not well with him. She marked his altered looks and stifled sighs, and was not to be deceived by his sickly and vapid attempts at cheerfulness. She tasked all her sprightly powers and tender blandishments to win him back to happiness; but she only drove the arrow deeper into his soul. The more he saw cause to love her, the more torturing was the thought that he was soon to make her wretched. A little while, thought he, and the smile will vanish from that cheek—the song will die away from those lips—the luster of those eyes will be quenched with sorrow—and the happy heart which now beats lightly in that bosom will be weighed down, like mine, by the cares and miseries of the world.

At length he came to me one day, and related his whole situation in a tone of the deepest despair. When I had heard him through, I inquired, "Does your wife know all this?" At the question he burst into an agony of tears. "For God's sake!" cried he, "if you have any pity on me, don't mention my wife; it is the thought of her that drives me almost to madness!"

"And why not?" said I. "She must know it sooner or later; you cannot keep it long from her, and the intelligence may break upon her in a more startling manner than if imparted by yourself; for the accents of those we love soften the harshest tidings. Besides, you are depriving yourself of the comforts of her sympathy; and not merely that, but also endangering the only bond that can keep hearts together—an unreserved community of thought and feeling. She will soon perceive that something is secretly preying upon your mind; and true love will not brook reserve: it feels undervalued and outraged, when even the sorrows of those it loves are concealed from it."

"Oh, but my friend! to think what a blow I am to give to all her future prospects—how I am to strike her very soul to the earth, by telling her that her husband is a beggar!—that she is to forego all the elegancies of life—all the pleasures of society—to shrink with me into indigence and obscurity! To tell her that I have dragged her down from the sphere in which she might have continued to move in constant brightness—the light of every eye—the admiration of every heart!—How can she bear poverty? She has been brought up in all the refinements of opulence. How can she bear neglect? She has been the idol of society. Oh, it will break her heart—it will break her heart!"

I saw his grief was eloquent, and I let it have its flow; for sorrow relieves itself by words. When his paroxysm had subsided, and he had relapsed into moody silence, I resumed the subject gently, and urged him to break his situation at once to his wife. He shook his head mournfully, but positively.

"But how are you to keep it from her? It is necessary she should know it, that you may take the steps proper to the alteration of your circumstances. You must change your style of living—nay," observing a pang to pass across his countenance, "don't let that afflict you. I am sure you have never placed your happiness in outward show—you have yet friends, warm friends, who will not think the worse of you for being less splendidly lodged; and surely it does not require a palace to be happy with Mary—"—"I could be happy with her," cried he, convulsively, "in a hovel!—I could go down with her into poverty and the dust!—I could—I could —God bless her!—God bless her!" cried he, bursting into a transport of grief and tenderness.

"And believe me, my friend," said I, stepping up, and grasping him warmly by the hand, "believe me, she can be the same with you. Ay, more; it will be a source of pride and triumph to her—it will call forth all the latent energies and fervent sympathies of her nature; for she will rejoice to prove that she loves you for yourself. There is in every true woman's heart a spark of heavenly fire, which lies dormant in the broad daylight of prosperity; but which kindles up, and beams and blazes in the dark hour of adversity. No man knows what the wife of his bosom is—no man knows what a ministering angel she is—until he has gone with her through the fiery trials of this world."

There was something in the earnestness of my manner, and the figurative style of my language, that caught the excited imagination of Leslie. I knew the auditor I had to deal with; and following up the impression I had made, I finished by persuading him to go home and unburden his sad heart to his wife.

I must confess, notwithstanding all I had said, I felt some little solicitude for the result. Who can calculate on the fortitude of one whose whole life has been a round of pleasures? Her gay spirits might revolt at the dark, downward

path of low humility, suddenly pointed out before her, and
might cling to the sunny regions in which they had hitherto
reveled.   Besides, ruin in fashionable life is accompanied by
so many galling mortifications, to which, in other ranks, it is
a stranger.—In short, I could not meet Leslie, the next morning, without trepidation.   He had made the disclosure.

"And how did she bear it?"

"Like an angel!   It seemed rather to be a relief to her
mind, for she threw her arms round my neck, and asked if
this was all that had lately made me unhappy.—But, poor
girl," added he, "she cannot realize the change we must undergo.   She has no idea of poverty but in the abstract: she
has only read of it in poetry, where it is allied to love.   She
feels as yet no privation: she suffers no loss of accustomed
conveniences nor elegancies.   When we come practically to
experience its sordid cares, its paltry wants, its petty humilia-
tions—then will be the real trial."

"But," said I, "now that you have got over the severest
task, that of breaking it to her, the sooner you let the world
into the secret the better.   The disclosure may be mortify-
ing; but then it is a single misery, and soon over; whereas
you otherwise suffer it, in anticipation, every hour in the
day.   It is not poverty, so much as pretense, that harasses a
ruined man—the struggle between a proud mind and an empty
purse—the keeping up a hollow show that must soon come to
an end.   Have the courage to appear poor, and you disarm
poverty of its sharpest sting."   On this point I found Leslie
perfectly prepared.   He had no false pride himself, and as to
his wife, she was only anxious to conform to their altered
fortunes.

Some days afterward, he called upon me in the evening.
He had disposed of his dwelling-house, and taken a small
cottage in the country, a few miles from town.   He had
been busied all day in sending out furniture.   The new establishment required few articles, and those of the simplest kind.
All the splendid furniture of his late residence had been sold,
excepting his wife's harp.   That, he said, was too closely as-

sociated with the idea of herself; it belonged to the little story of their loves; for some of the sweetest moments of their courtship were those when he had leaned over that instrument, and listened to the melting tones of her voice. I could not but smile at this instance of romantic gallantry in a doting husband.

He was now going out to the cottage, where his wife had been all day, superintending its arrangement. My feelings had become strongly interested in the progress of this family story, and as it was a fine evening, I offered to accompany him.

He was wearied with the fatigues of the day, and as we walked out, fell into a fit of gloomy musing.

"Poor Mary!" at length broke, with a heavy sigh, from his lips.

"And what of her," asked I, "has anything happened to her?"

"What," said he, darting an impatient glance, "is it nothing to be reduced to this paltry situation—to be caged in a miserable cottage—to be obliged to toil almost in the menial concerns of her wretched habitation?"

"Has she then repined at the change?"

"Repined! She has been nothing but sweetness and good humor. Indeed, she seems in better spirits than I have ever known her; she has been to me all love, and tenderness, and comfort!"

"Admirable girl!" exclaimed I. "You call yourself poor, my friend; you never were so rich—you never knew the boundless treasures of excellence you possessed in that woman."

"Oh! but, my friend, if this first meeting at the cottage were over, I think I could then be comfortable. But this is her first day of real experience; she has been introduced into an humble dwelling—she has been employed all day in arranging its miserable equipments—she has for the first time known the fatigues of domestic employment—she has for the first time looked around her on a home destitute of everything elegant—almost of everything convenient; and may now be sitting down, exhausted and spiritless, brooding over a prospect of future poverty."

There was a degree of probability in this picture that I could not gainsay, so we walked on in silence.

After turning from the main road up a narrow lane, so thickly shaded by forest trees as to give it a complete air of seclusion, we came in sight of the cottage. It was humble enough in its appearance for the most pastoral poet; and yet it had a pleasing rural look. A wild vine had overrun one end with a profusion of foliage; a few trees threw their branches gracefully over it; and I observed several pots of flowers tastefully disposed about the door, and on the grass-plot in front. A small wicket-gate opened upon a footpath that wound through some shrubbery to the door. Just as we approached we heard the sound of music—Leslie grasped my arm; we paused and listened. It was Mary's voice, singing, in a style of the most touching simplicity, a little air of which her husband was peculiarly fond.

I felt Leslie's hand tremble on my arm. He stepped forward to hear more distinctly. His step made a noise on the gravel-walk. A bright, beautiful face glanced out at the window, and vanished—a light footstep was heard—and Mary came tripping forth to meet us. She was in a pretty rural dress of white; a few wild flowers were twisted in her fine hair; a fresh bloom was on her cheek; her whole countenance beamed with smiles—I had never seen her look so lovely.

"My dear George," cried she, "I am so glad you are come; I have been watching and watching for you; and running down the lane, and looking out for you. I've set out a table under a beautiful tree behind the cottage; and I've been gathering some of the most delicious strawberries, for I know you are fond of them—and we have such excellent cream—and everything is so sweet and still here.—Oh!" said she, putting her arm within his, and looking up brightly in his face, "oh, we shall be so happy!"

Poor Leslie was overcome.—He caught her to his bosom
—he folded his arms round her—he kissed her again and
again—he could not speak, but the tears gushed into his
eyes; and he has often assured me that though the world
has since gone prosperously with him, and his life has indeed
been a happy one, yet never has he experienced a moment of
more exquisite felicity.

[The following Tale was found among the papers of the
late Diedrich Knickerbocker, an old gentleman of New York,
who was very curious, in the Dutch History of the province,
and the manners of the descendants from its primitive settlers. His historical researches, however, did not lie so much
among books as among men; for the former are lamentably
scanty on his favorite topics; whereas he found the old
burghers, and still more, their wives, rich in that legendary
lore, so invaluable to true history. Whenever, therefore, he
happened upon a genuine Dutch family, snugly shut up in
its low-roofed farmhouse under a spreading sycamore, he
looked upon it as a little clasped volume of black-letter, and
studied it with the zeal of a bookworm.

The result of all these researches was a history of the
province during the reign of the Dutch governors, which he
published some years since. There have been various opinions as to the literary character of his work, and, to tell the
truth, it is not a whit better than it should be. Its chief
merit is its scrupulous accuracy, which, indeed, was a little
questioned on its first appearance, but has since been completely established; and it is now admitted into all historical
collections as a book of unquestionable authority.

The old gentleman died shortly after the publication of
his work, and, now that he is dead and gone, it cannot do
much harm to his memory to say that his time might have
been much better employed in weightier labors. He, however, was apt to ride his hobby his own way; and though it
did now and then kick up the dust a little in the eyes of his
neighbors, and grieve the spirit of some friends for whom
he felt the truest deference and affection, yet his errors and
follies are remembered "more in sorrow than in anger,"*

---

* Vide the excellent discourse of G. C. Verplanck, Esq., before the
New York Historical Society.

and it begins to be suspected that he never intended to injure
or offend. But however his memory may be appreciated by
critics, it is still held dear among many folk, whose good
opinion is well worth having; particularly by certain biscuit
bakers, who have gone so far as to imprint his likeness on
their new year cakes, and have thus given him a chance for
immortality almost equal to the being stamped on a Waterloo
medal, or a Queen Anne's farthing.]

RIP VAN WINKLE

A POSTHUMOUS WRITING OF DIEDRICH KNICKERBOCKER

> "By Woden, God of Saxons,
> From whence comes Wensday, that is Wodensday,
> Truth is a thing that ever I will keep
> Until thylke day in which I creep into
> My sepulchre—"   —CARTWRIGHT

WHOEVER has made a voyage up the Hudson must remember the Kaatskill mountains. They are a dismembered
branch of the great Appalachian family, and are seen away
to the west of the river, swelling up to a noble height, and
lording it over the surrounding country. Every change of
season, every change of weather, indeed every hour of the
day, produces some change in the magical hues and shapes
of these mountains; and they are regarded by all the good
wives, far and near, as perfect barometers. When the
weather is fair and settled they are clothed in blue and
purple, and print their bold outlines on the clear evening
sky; but sometimes, when the rest of the landscape is cloudless, they will gather a hood of gray vapors about their summits, which, in the last rays of the setting sun, will glow
and light up like a crown of glory.

At the foot of these fairy mountains the voyager may
have descried the light smoke curling up from a village,
whose shingle roofs gleam among the trees just where the

blue tints of the upland melt away into the fresh green of the nearer landscape. It is a little village of great antiquity, having been founded by some of the Dutch colonists, in the early times of the province, just about the beginning of the government of the good Peter Stuyvesant (may he rest in peace!), and there were some of the houses of the original settlers standing within a few years, built of small yellow bricks brought from Holland, having latticed windows and gable fronts, surmounted with weathercocks.

In that same village, and in one of these very houses (which, to tell the precise truth, was sadly time-worn and weather-beaten), there lived many years since, while the country was yet a province of Great Britain, a simple, good-natured fellow, of the name of Rip Van Winkle. He was a descendant of the Van Winkles who figured so gallantly in the chivalrous days of Peter Stuyvesant, and accompanied him to the siege of Fort Christina. He inherited, however, but little of the martial character of his ancestors. I have observed that he was a simple, good-natured man; he was moreover a kind neighbor, and an obedient henpecked husband. Indeed, to the latter circumstance might be owing that meekness of spirit which gained him such universal popularity; for those men are most apt to be obsequious and conciliating abroad who are under the discipline of shrews at home. Their tempers, doubtless, are rendered pliant and malleable in the fiery furnace of domestic tribulation, and a curtain lecture is worth all the sermons in the world for teaching the virtues of patience and long-suffering. A termagant wife may, therefore, in some respects, be considered a tolerable blessing; and, if so, Rip Van Winkle was thrice blessed.

Certain it is that he was a great favorite among all the good wives of the village, who, as usual with the amiable sex, took his part in all family squabbles, and never failed, whenever they talked those matters over in their evening gossipings, to lay all the blame on Dame Van Winkle. The children of the village, too, would shout with joy whenever he approached. He assisted at their sports, made their play-things, taught them to fly kites and shoot marbles, and told them long stories of ghosts, witches, and Indians. When-ever he went dodging about the village, he was surrounded by a troop of them hanging on his skirts, clambering on his back, and playing a thousand tricks on him with impunity; and not a dog would bark at him throughout the neighbor-hood.

The great error in Rip's composition was an insuperable aversion to all kinds of profitable labor. It could not be from the want of assiduity or perseverance; for he would sit on a wet rock, with a rod as long and heavy as a Tartar's lance, and fish all day without a murmur, even though he should not be encouraged by a single nibble. He would carry a fowling-piece on his shoulder, for hours together, trudging through woods and swamps, and up hill and down dale, to shoot a few squirrels or wild pigeons. He would never refuse to assist a neighbor even in the roughest toil, and was a foremost man at all country frolics for husking Indian corn, or building stone fences. The women of the village, too, used to employ him to run their errands, and to do such little odd jobs as their less obliging husbands would not do for them—in a word, Rip was ready to attend to any-body's business but his own; but as to doing family duty, and keeping his farm in order, he found it impossible.

In fact, he declared it was of no use to work on his farm; it was the most pestilent little piece of ground in the whole country; everything about it went wrong, and would go wrong in spite of him. His fences were continually falling to pieces; his cow would either go astray, or get among the cabbages; weeds were sure to grow quicker in his fields than anywhere else; the rain always made a point of setting in just as he had some outdoor work to do; so that, though his patrimonial estate had dwindled away under his manage-ment, acre by acre, until there was little more left than a mere patch of Indian corn and potatoes, yet it was the worst conditioned farm in the neighborhood.

His children, too, were as ragged and wild as if they belonged to nobody. His son Rip, an urchin begotten in his own likeness, promised to inherit the habits, with the old clothes of his father. He was generally seen trooping like a colt at his mother's heels, equipped in a pair of his father's cast-off galligaskins, which he had much ado to hold up with one hand, as a fine lady does her train in bad weather.

Rip Van Winkle, however, was one of those happy mortals, of foolish, well-oiled dispositions, who take the world easy, eat white bread or brown, whichever can be got with least thought or trouble, and would rather starve on a penny than work for a pound. If left to himself, he would have whistled life away, in perfect contentment; but his wife kept continually dinning in his ears about his idleness, his carelessness, and the ruin he was bringing on his family.

Morning, noon, and night, her tongue was incessantly going, and everything he said or did was sure to produce a torrent of household eloquence. Rip had but one way of replying to all lectures of the kind, and that, by frequent use, had grown into a habit. He shrugged his shoulders, shook his head, cast up his eyes, but said nothing. This, however, always provoked a fresh volley from his wife, so that he was fain to draw off his forces, and take to the outside of the house—the only side which, in truth, belongs to a henpecked husband.

Rip's sole domestic adherent was his dog Wolf, who was as much henpecked as his master; for Dame Van Winkle regarded them as companions in idleness, and even looked upon Wolf with an evil eye, as the cause of his master's going so often astray. True it is, in all points of spirit befitting an honorable dog, he was as courageous an animal as ever scoured the woods—but what courage can withstand the ever-during and all-besetting terrors of a woman's tongue? The moment Wolf entered the house, his crest fell, his tail drooped to the ground, or curled between his legs, he sneaked about with a gallows air, casting many a sidelong glance at Dame Van Winkle, and at the least flourish of a broomstick or ladle he would fly to the door with yelping precipitation.

Times grew worse and worse with Rip Van Winkle, as years of matrimony rolled on: a tart temper never mellows with age, and a sharp tongue is the only edge tool that grows keener with constant use. For a long while he used to console himself, when driven from home, by frequenting a kind of perpetual club of the sages, philosophers, and other idle personages of the village, which held its sessions on a bench before a small inn, designated by a rubicund portrait of his Majesty George the Third. Here they used to sit in the shade, of a long lazy summer's day, talking listlessly over village gossip, or telling endless sleepy stories about nothing. But it would have been worth any statesman's money to have heard the profound discussions which sometimes took place, when by chance an old newspaper fell into their hands from some passing traveler. How solemnly they would listen to the contents, as drawled out by Derrick Van Bummel, the schoolmaster, a dapper learned little man, who was not to be daunted by the most gigantic word in the dictionary; and how sagely they would deliberate upon public events some months after they had taken place.

The opinions of this junto were completely controlled by Nicholas Vedder, a patriarch of the village, and landlord of the inn, at the door of which he took his seat from morning till night, just moving sufficiently to avoid the sun, and keep in the shade of a large tree; so that the neighbors could tell the hour by his movements as accurately as by a sun-dial. It is true, he was rarely heard to speak, but smoked his pipe incessantly. His adherents, however (for every great man has his adherents), perfectly understood him, and knew how to gather his opinions. When anything that was read or related displeased him, he was observed to smoke his pipe vehemently, and to send forth short, frequent, and angry puffs; but when pleased, he would inhale the smoke slowly and tranquilly, and emit it in light and placid clouds, and sometimes taking the pipe from his mouth, and letting the fragrant vapor curl about his nose, would gravely nod his head in token of perfect approbation.

From even this stronghold the unlucky Rip was at length routed by his termagant wife, who would suddenly break in upon the tranquillity of the assemblage, and call the members all to naught; nor was that august personage, Nicholas Vedder himself, sacred from the daring tongue of this terrible virago, who charged him outright with encouraging her husband in habits of idleness.

Poor Rip was at last reduced almost to despair, and his only alternative to escape from the labor of the farm and the clamor of his wife was to take gun in hand and stroll away into the woods. Here he would sometimes seat himself at the foot of a tree, and share the contents of his wallet with Wolf, with whom he sympathized as a fellow-sufferer in persecution. "Poor Wolf," he would say, "thy mistress leads thee a dog's life of it; but never mind, my lad, while I live thou shalt never want a friend to stand by thee!" Wolf would wag his tail, look wistfully in his master's face, and if dogs can feel pity, I verily believe he reciprocated the sentiment with all his heart.

In a long ramble of the kind, on a fine autumnal day, Rip had unconsciously scrambled to one of the highest parts of the Kaatskill mountains. He was after his favorite sport of squirrel-shooting, and the still solitudes had echoed and re-echoed with the reports of his gun. Panting and fatigued, he threw himself, late in the afternoon, on a green knoll covered with mountain herbage that crowned the brow of a precipice. From an opening between the trees, he could overlook all the lower country for many a mile of rich woodland. He saw at a distance the lordly Hudson, far, far below him, moving on its silent but majestic course, with the reflection of a purple cloud, or the sail of a lagging bark, here and there sleeping on its glassy bosom, and at last losing itself in the blue highlands.

On the other side he looked down into a deep mountain glen, wild, lonely, and shagged, the bottom filled with fragments from the impending cliffs, and scarcely lighted by the reflected rays of the setting sun. For some time Rip lay musing on this scene; evening was gradually advancing; the mountains began to throw their long blue shadows over the valleys; he saw that it would be dark long before he could reach the village; and he heaved a heavy sigh when he thought of encountering the terrors of Dame Van Winkle.

As he was about to descend he heard a voice from a distance hallooing, "Rip Van Winkle! Rip Van Winkle!" He looked around, but could see nothing but a crow winging its solitary flight across the mountain. He thought his fancy must have deceived him, and turned again to descend, when he heard the same cry ring through the still evening air, "Rip Van Winkle! Rip Van Winkle!"—at the same time Wolf bristled up his back, and giving a low growl, skulked to his master's side, looking fearfully down into the glen. Rip now felt a vague apprehension stealing over him: he looked anxiously in the same direction, and perceived a strange figure slowly toiling up the rocks, and bending under the weight of something he carried on his back. He was surprised to see any human being in this lonely and unfrequented place, but supposing it to be some one of the neighborhood in need of his assistance, he hastened down to yield it.

On nearer approach, he was still more surprised at the singularity of the stranger's appearance. He was a short square built old fellow, with thick bushy hair, and a grizzled beard. His dress was of the antique Dutch fashion—a cloth jerkin strapped round the waist—several pair of breeches, the outer one of ample volume, decorated with rows of buttons down the sides, and bunches at the knees. He bore on his shoulders a stout keg, that seemed full of liquor, and made signs for Rip to approach and assist him with the load. Though rather shy and distrustful of this new acquaintance, Rip complied with his usual alacrity, and, mutually relieving each other, they clambered up a narrow gully, apparently the dry bed of a mountain torrent. As they ascended, Rip

every now and then heard long rolling peals, like distant
thunder, that seemed to issue out of a deep ravine, or rather
cleft, between lofty rocks, toward which their rugged path
conducted.　He paused for an instant, but supposing it to be
the muttering of one of those transient thunder-showers which
often take place in mountain heights, he proceeded.　Passing through the ravine, they came to a hollow, like a small
amphitheater, surrounded by perpendicular precipices, over
the brinks of which impending trees shot their branches, so
that you only caught glimpses of the azure sky, and the
bright evening cloud.　During the whole time, Rip and his
companion had labored on in silence; for though the former
marveled greatly what could be the object of carrying a keg
of liquor up this wild mountain, yet there was something
strange and incomprehensible about the unknown that inspired awe, and checked familiarity.

On entering the amphitheater, new objects of wonder presented themselves.　On a level spot in the center was a company of odd-looking personages playing at nine-pins.　They
were dressed in a quaint outlandish fashion: some wore short
doublets, others jerkins, with long knives in their belts, and
most of them had enormous breeches, of similar style with
that of the guide's.　Their visages, too, were peculiar: one
had a large head, broad face, and small piggish eyes; the
face of another seemed to consist entirely of nose, and was
surmounted by a white sugar-loaf hat, set off with a little
red cock's tail.　They all had beards, of various shapes and
colors.　There was one who seemed to be the commander.
He was a stout old gentleman, with a weather-beaten countenance; he wore a laced doublet, broad belt and hanger, high-
crowned hat and feather, red stockings, and high-heeled
shoes, with roses in them.　The whole group reminded Rip
of the figures in an old Flemish painting, in the parlor of
Dominie Van Schaick, the village parson, and which had
been brought over from Holland at the time of the settlement.

What seemed particularly odd to Rip, was, that though

these folks were evidently amusing themselves, yet they maintained the gravest faces, the most mysterious silence, and were, withal, the most melancholy party of pleasure he had ever witnessed. Nothing interrupted the stillness of the scene but the noise of the balls, which, whenever they rolled, echoed along the mountains like rumbling peals of thunder.

As Rip and his companion approached them, they suddenly desisted from their play, and stared at him with such a fixed statue-like gaze, and such strange, uncouth, lackluster countenances, that his heart turned within him, and his knees smote together. His companion now emptied the contents of the keg into large flagons, and made signs to him to wait upon the company. He obeyed with fear and trembling; they quaffed the liquor in profound silence, and then returned to their game.

By degrees Rip's awe and apprehension subsided. He even ventured, when no eye was fixed upon him, to taste the beverage, which he found had much of the flavor of excellent Hollands. He was naturally a thirsty soul, and was soon tempted to repeat the draught. One taste provoked another, and he reiterated his visits to the flagon so often that at length his senses were overpowered, his eyes swam in his head, his head gradually declined, and he fell into a deep sleep.

On waking, he found himself on the green knoll from whence he had first seen the old man of the glen. He rubbed his eyes—it was a bright sunny morning. The birds were hopping and twittering among the bushes, and the eagle was wheeling aloft, and breasting the pure mountain breeze. "Surely," thought Rip, "I have not slept here all night." He recalled the occurrences before he fell asleep. The strange man with the keg of liquor—the mountain ravine—the wild retreat among the rocks—the woe-begone party at nine-pins—the flagon—"Oh! that wicked flagon!" thought Rip—"what excuse shall I make to Dame Van Winkle?"

He looked round for his gun, but in place of the clean,

well-oiled fowling-piece, he found an old firelock lying by him, the barrel incrusted with rust, the lock falling off, and the stock worm-eaten. He now suspected that the grave roisterers of the mountain had put a trick upon him, and having dosed him with liquor, had robbed him of his gun. Wolf, too, had disappeared, but he might have strayed away after a squirrel or partridge. He whistled after him, and shouted his name, but all in vain; the echoes repeated his whistle and shout, but no dog was to be seen.

He determined to revisit the scene of the last evening's gambol, and if he met with any of the party, to demand his dog and gun. As he rose to walk, he found himself stiff in the joints, and wanting in his usual activity. "These mountain beds do not agree with me," thought Rip, "and if this frolic should lay me up with a fit of the rheumatism, I shall have a blessed time with Dame Van Winkle." With some difficulty he got down into the glen; he found the gully up which he and his companion had ascended the preceding evening; but to his astonishment a mountain stream was now foaming down it, leaping from rock to rock, and filling the glen with babbling murmurs. He, however, made shift to scramble up its sides, working his toilsome way through thickets of birch, sassafras, and witch-hazel; and sometimes tripped up or entangled by the wild grape-vines that twisted their coils and tendrils from tree to tree, and spread a kind of network in his path.

At length he reached to where the ravine had opened through the cliffs to the amphitheater; but no traces of such opening remained. The rocks presented a high impenetrable wall, over which the torrent came tumbling in a sheet of feathery foam, and fell into a broad deep basin, black from the shadows of the surrounding forest. Here, then, poor Rip was brought to a stand. He again called and whistled after his dog; he was only answered by the cawing of a flock of idle crows, sporting high in air about a dry tree that overhung a sunny precipice; and who, secure in their elevation, seemed to look down and scoff at the poor man's perplexities.

What was to be done? The morning was passing away, and Rip felt famished for want of his breakfast. He grieved to give up his dog and gun; he dreaded to meet his wife; but it would not do to starve among the mountains. He shook his head, shouldered the rusty firelock, and, with a heart full of trouble and anxiety, turned his steps homeward.

As he approached the village, he met a number of people, but none whom he knew, which somewhat surprised him, for he had thought himself acquainted with every one in the country round. Their dress, too, was of a different fashion from that to which he was accustomed. They all stared at him with equal marks of surprise, and whenever they cast eyes upon him, invariably stroked their chins. The constant recurrence of this gesture induced Rip, involuntarily, to do the same, when, to his astonishment, he found his beard had grown a foot long.

He had now entered the skirts of the village. A troop of strange children ran at his heels, hooting after him, and pointing at his gray beard. The dogs, too, not one of which he recognized for an old acquaintance, barked at him as he passed. The very village was altered: it was larger and more populous. There were rows of houses which he had never seen before, and those which had been his familiar haunts had disappeared. Strange names were over the doors — strange faces at the windows — everything was strange. His mind now misgave him; he began to doubt whether both he and the world around him were not bewitched. Surely this was his native village, which he had left but a day before. There stood the Kaatskill mountains —there ran the silver Hudson at a distance—there was every hill and dale precisely as it had always been—Rip was sorely perplexed—"That flagon last night," thought he, "has addled my poor head sadly!"

It was with some difficulty that he found the way to his own house, which he approached with silent awe, expecting every moment to hear the shrill voice of Dame Van Winkle. He found the house gone to decay—the roof fallen in, the windows shattered, and the doors off the hinges. A half-starved dog, that looked like Wolf, was skulking about it. Rip called him by name, but the cur snarled, showed his teeth, and passed on. This was an unkind cut indeed.— "My very dog," sighed poor Rip, "has forgotten me!"

He entered the house, which, to tell the truth, Dame Van Winkle had always kept in neat order. It was empty, forlorn, and apparently abandoned. This desolateness overcame all his connubial fears—he called loudly for his wife and children—the lonely chambers rang for a moment with his voice, and then all again was silence.

He now hurried forth, and hastened to his old resort, the village inn—but it too was gone. A large rickety wooden building stood in its place, with great gaping windows, some of them broken, and mended with old hats and petticoats, and over the door was painted, "The Union Hotel, by Jonathan Doolittle." Instead of the great tree that used to shelter the quiet little Dutch inn of yore, there now was reared a tall naked pole, with something on the top that looked like a red night-cap, and from it was fluttering a flag, on which was a singular assemblage of stars and stripes— all this was strange and incomprehensible. He recognized on the sign, however, the ruby face of King George, under which he had smoked so many a peaceful pipe, but even this was singularly metamorphosed. The red coat was changed for one of blue and buff, a sword was held in the hand instead of a scepter, the head was decorated with a cocked hat, and underneath was painted in large characters, GENERAL WASHINGTON.

There was, as usual, a crowd of folk about the door, but none that Rip recollected. The very character of the people seemed changed. There was a busy, bustling, disputatious tone about it, instead of the accustomed phlegm and drowsy tranquillity. He looked in vain for the sage Nicholas Vedder, with his broad face, double chin, and fair long pipe, uttering clouds of tobacco smoke, instead of idle speeches; or Van Bummel, the schoolmaster, doling forth the contents of

an ancient newspaper. In place of these, a lean, bilious-looking fellow, with his pockets full of handbills, was harangu-
ing vehemently about rights of citizens—election—members
of Congress—liberty—Bunker's hill—heroes of seventy-six
—and other words, that were a perfect Babylonish jargon
to the bewildered Van Winkle.

The appearance of Rip, with his long, grizzled beard, his
rusty fowling-piece, his uncouth dress, and the army of
women and children that had gathered at his heels, soon
attracted the attention of the tavern politicians. They
crowded round him, eying him from head to foot, with
great curiosity. The orator bustled up to him, and drawing
him partly aside, inquired, "on which side he voted?" Rip
stared in vacant stupidity. Another short but busy little
fellow pulled him by the arm, and rising on tiptoe, inquired
in his ear, "whether he was Federal or Democrat." Rip
was equally at a loss to comprehend the question; when a
knowing, self-important old gentleman, in a sharp cocked
hat, made his way through the crowd, putting them to the
right and left with his elbows as he passed, and planting
himself before Van Winkle, with one arm akimbo, the other
resting on his cane, his keen eyes and sharp hat penetrating,
as it were, into his very soul, demanded in an austere tone,
"what brought him to the election with a gun on his shoulder, and a mob at his heels, and whether he meant to breed
a riot in the village?"

"Alas! gentlemen," cried Rip, somewhat dismayed, "I
am a poor, quiet man, a native of the place, and a loyal subject of the King, God bless him!"

Here a general shout burst from the bystanders—"a
Tory! a Tory! a spy! a refugee! hustle him! away with
him!"

It was with great difficulty that the self-important man
in the cocked hat restored order; and having assumed a tenfold austerity of brow, demanded again of the unknown culprit, what he came there for, and whom he was seeking.
The poor man humbly assured him that he meant no harm,

but merely came there in search of some of his neighbors, who used to keep about the tavern.

"Well—who are they?—name them."

Rip bethought himself a moment, and inquired, "Where's Nicholas Vedder?"

There was a silence for a little while, when an old man replied, in a thin, piping voice, "Nicholas Vedder? why, he is dead and gone these eighteen years! There was a wooden tombstone in the churchyard that used to tell all about him, but that's rotten and gone too."

"Where's Brom Dutcher?"

"Oh, he went off to the army in the beginning of the war; some say he was killed at the storming of Stony-Point—others say he was drowned in the squall, at the foot of Anthony's Nose. I don't know—he never came back again."

"Where's Van Bummel, the schoolmaster?"

"He went off to the wars, too; was a great militia general, and is now in Congress."

Rip's heart died away at hearing of these sad changes in his home and friends, and finding himself thus alone in the world. Every answer puzzled him, too, by treating of such enormous lapses of time, and of matters which he could not understand: war—Congress—Stony-Point!—he had no courage to ask after any more friends, but cried out in despair, "Does nobody here know Rip Van Winkle?"

"Oh, Rip Van Winkle!" exclaimed two or three. "Oh, to be sure! that's Rip Van Winkle yonder, leaning against the tree."

Rip looked, and beheld a precise counterpart of himself as he went up the mountain; apparently as lazy, and certainly as ragged. The poor fellow was now completely confounded. He doubted his own identity, and whether he was himself or another man. In the midst of his bewilderment, the man in the cocked hat demanded who he was, and what was his name?

"God knows," exclaimed he, at his wit's end; "I'm not myself—I'm somebody else—that's me yonder—no—that's somebody else, got into my shoes—I was myself last night, but I fell asleep on the mountain, and they've changed my gun, and everything's changed, and I'm changed, and I can't tell what's my name, or who I am!"

The bystanders began now to look at each other, nod, wink significantly, and tap their fingers against their foreheads. There was a whisper, also, about securing the gun, and keeping the old fellow from doing mischief; at the very suggestion of which, the self-important man with the cocked hat retired with some precipitation. At this critical moment a fresh comely woman passed through the throng to get a peep at the gray-bearded man. She had a chubby child in her arms, which, frightened at his looks, began to cry. "Hush, Rip," cried she, "hush, you little fool; the old man won't hurt you." The name of the child, the air of the mother, the tone of her voice, all awakened a train of recollections in his mind.

"What is your name, my good woman?" asked he.

"Judith Gardenier."

"And your father's name?"

"Ah, poor man, his name was Rip Van Winkle; it's twenty years since he went away from home with his gun, and never has been heard of since—his dog came home without him; but whether he shot himself, or was carried away by the Indians, nobody can tell. I was then but a little girl."

Rip had but one question more to ask; but he put it with a faltering voice:

"Where's your mother?"

Oh, she too had died but a short time since: she broke a blood-vessel in a fit of passion at a New England peddler.

There was a drop of comfort, at least, in this intelligence. The honest man could contain himself no longer. He caught his daughter and her child in his arms. "I am your father!" cried he—"young Rip Van Winkle once—old Rip Van Winkle now!—Does nobody know poor Rip Van Winkle!"

All stood amazed, until an old woman, tottering out from

among the crowd, put her hand to her brow, and peering under it in his face for a moment, exclaimed, "Sure enough! it is Rip Van Winkle—it is himself. Welcome home again, old neighbor. Why, where have you been these twenty long years?"

Rip's story was soon told, for the whole twenty years had been to him but as one night. The neighbors stared when they heard it; some were seen to wink at each other, and put their tongues in their cheeks; and the self-important man in the cocked hat, who, when the alarm was over, had returned to the field, screwed down the corners of his mouth, and shook his head—upon which there was a general shaking of the head throughout the assemblage.

It was determined, however, to take the opinion of old Peter Vanderdonk, who was seen slowly advancing up the road. He was a descendant of the historian of that name, who wrote one of the earliest accounts of the province. Peter was the most ancient inhabitant of the village, and well versed in all the wonderful events and traditions of the neighborhood. He recollected Rip at once, and corroborated his story in the most satisfactory manner. He assured the company that it was a fact, handed down from his ancestor the historian, that the Kaatskill mountains had always been haunted by strange beings. That it was affirmed that the great Hendrick Hudson, the first discoverer of the river and country, kept a kind of vigil there every twenty years, with his crew of the "Half Moon," being permitted in this way to revisit the scenes of his enterprise, and keep a guardian eye upon the river and the great city called by his name. That his father had once seen them in their old Dutch dresses playing at nine-pins in a hollow of the mountain; and that he himself had heard, one summer afternoon, the sound of their balls, like distant peals of thunder.

To make a long story short, the company broke up, and returned to the more important concerns of the election. Rip's daughter took him home to live with her; she had a snug, well-furnished house, and a stout cheery farmer for a husband, whom Rip recollected for one of the urchins that used to climb upon his back. As to Rip's son and heir, who was the ditto of himself, seen leaning against the tree, he was employed to work on the farm; but evinced a hereditary disposition to attend to anything else but his business.

Rip now resumed his old walks and habits; he soon found many of his former cronies, though all rather the worse for the wear and tear of time; and preferred making friends among the rising generation, with whom he soon grew into great favor.

Having nothing to do at home, and being arrived at that happy age when a man can do nothing with impunity, he took his place once more on the bench, at the inn door, and was reverenced as one of the patriarchs of the village, and a chronicle of the old times "before the war." It was some time before he could get into the regular track of gossip, or could be made to comprehend the strange events that had taken place during his torpor. How that there had been a revolutionary war—that the country had thrown off the yoke of old England—and that, instead of being a subject of his Majesty George the Third, he was now a free citizen of the United States. Rip, in fact, was no politician; the changes of states and empires made but little impression on him; but there was one species of despotism under which he had long groaned, and that was—petticoat government. Happily that was at an end; he had got his neck out of the yoke of matrimony, and could go in and out whenever he pleased, without dreading the tyranny of Dame Van Winkle. Whenever her name was mentioned, however, he shook his head, shrugged his shoulders, and cast up his eyes; which might pass either for an expression of resignation to his fate, or joy at his deliverance.

He used to tell his story to every stranger that arrived at Mr. Doolittle's hotel. He was observed, at first, to vary on some points every time he told it, which was doubtless owing to his having so recently awaked. It at last settled down precisely to the tale I have related, and not a man, woman, or child in the neighborhood but knew it by heart. Some always pretended to doubt the reality of it, and insisted that Rip had been out of his head, and that this was one point on which he always remained flighty. The old Dutch inhabitants, however, almost universally gave it full credit. Even to this day, they never hear a thunderstorm of a summer afternoon about the Kaatskill, but they say Hendrick Hudson and his crew are at their game of nine-pins; and it is a common wish of all henpecked husbands in the neighborhood, when life hangs heavy on their hands, that they might have a quieting draught out of Rip Van Winkle's flagon.

NOTE.—The foregoing tale, one would suspect, had been suggested to Mr. Knickerbocker by a little German superstition about the Emperor Frederick *der Rothbart* and the Kypphauser mountain; the subjoined note, however, which he had appended to the tale, shows that it is an absolute fact, narrated with his usual fidelity.

"The story of Rip Van Winkle may seem incredible to many, but nevertheless I give it my full belief, for I know the vicinity of our old Dutch settlements to have been very subject to marvelous events and appearances. Indeed, I have heard many stranger stories than this, in the villages along the Hudson, all of which were too well authenticated to admit of a doubt. I have even talked with Rip Van Winkle myself, who, when last I saw him, was a very venerable old man, and so perfectly rational and consistent on every other point that I think no conscientious person could refuse to take this into the bargain; nay, I have seen a certificate on the subject taken before a country justice, and signed with a cross, in the justice's own handwriting. The story, therefore, is beyond the possibility of doubt."

ENGLISH WRITERS ON AMERICA

"Methinks I see in my mind a noble puissant nation, rousing herself like a strong man after sleep, and shaking her invincible locks; methinks I see her as an eagle, mewing her mighty youth, and kindling her endazzled eyes at the full midday beam."

—MILTON ON THE LIBERTY OF THE PRESS

IT is with feelings of deep regret that I observe the literary animosity daily growing up between England and America. Great curiosity has been awakened of late with respect to the United States, and the London press has teemed with volumes of travels through the Republic; but they seem intended to diffuse error rather than knowledge; and so successful have they been that, notwithstanding the constant intercourse between the nations, there is no people concerning whom the great mass of the British public have less pure information, or entertain more numerous prejudices.

English travelers are the best and the worst in the world. Where no motives of pride or interest intervene, none can equal them for profound and philosophical views of society, or faithful and graphical descriptions of external objects; but when either the interest or reputation of their own country comes in collision with that of another, they go to the opposite extreme, and forget their usual probity and candor, in the indulgence of splenetic remark, and an illiberal spirit of ridicule.

Hence, their travels are more honest and accurate the more remote the country described. I would place implicit confidence in an Englishman's description of the regions beyond the cataracts of the Nile; of unknown islands in the Yellow Sea; of the interior of India; or of any other tract

which other travelers might be apt to picture out with the
illusions of their fancies.   But I would cautiously receive his
account of his immediate neighbors, and of those nations with
which he is in habits of most frequent intercourse.   However
I might be disposed to trust his probity, I dare not trust his
prejudices.

It has also been the peculiar lot of our country to be
visited by the worst kind of English travelers.   While men
of philosophical spirit and cultivated minds have been sent
from England to ransack the poles, to penetrate the deserts,
and to study the manners and customs of barbarous nations,
with which she can have no permanent intercourse of profit
or pleasure; it has been left to the broken-down tradesman,
the scheming adventurer, the wandering mechanic, the Manchester and Birmingham agent, to be her oracles respecting
America.   From such sources she is content to receive her
information respecting a country in a singular state of moral
and physical development; a country in which one of the
greatest political experiments in the history of the world is
now performing, and which presents the most profound and
momentous studies to the statesman and the philosopher.

That such men should give prejudiced accounts of America
is not a matter of surprise.   The themes it offers for contemplation are too vast and elevated for their capacities.   The
national character is yet in a state of fermentation: it may
have its frothiness and sediment, but its ingredients are sound
and wholesome: it has already given proofs of powerful and
generous qualities; and the whole promises to settle down
into something substantially excellent.   But the causes which
are operating to strengthen and ennoble it, and its daily indications of admirable properties, are all lost upon these pur-
blind observers; who are only affected by the little asperities
incident to its present situation.   They are capable of judging only of the surface of things; of those matters which
come in contact with their private interests and personal
gratifications.   They miss some of the snug conveniences
and petty comforts which belong to an old, highly-finished,

and over-populous state of society; where the ranks of useful labor are crowded, and many earn a painful and servile subsistence, by studying the very caprices of appetite and self-indulgence. These minor comforts, however, are all-important in the estimation of narrow minds; which either do not perceive, or will not acknowledge, that they are more than counterbalanced among us, by great and generally diffused blessings.

They may, perhaps, have been disappointed in some unreasonable expectation of sudden gain. They may have pictured America to themselves an El Dorado, where gold and silver abounded, and the natives were lacking in sagacity; and where they were to become strangely and suddenly rich in some unforeseen but easy manner. The same weakness of mind that indulges absurd expectations produces petulance in disappointment. Such persons become imbittered against the country on finding that there, as everywhere else, a man must sow before he can reap; must win wealth by industry and talent; and must contend with the common difficulties of nature, and the shrewdness of an intelligent and enterprising people.

Perhaps, through mistaken or ill-directed hospitality, or from the prompt disposition to cheer and countenance the stranger, prevalent among my countrymen, they have been treated with unwonted respect in America; and, having been accustomed all their lives to consider themselves below the surface of good society, and brought up in a servile feeling of inferiority, they become arrogant on the common boon of civility; they attribute to the lowliness of others their own elevation; and underrate a society where there are no artificial distinctions, and where by any chance such individuals as themselves can rise to consequence.

One would suppose, however, that information coming from such sources, on a subject where the truth is so desirable, would be received with caution by the censors of the press; that the motives of these men, their veracity, their opportunities of inquiry and observation, and their capacities

for judging correctly, would be rigorously scrutinized, before
their evidence was admitted, in such sweeping extent, against
a kindred nation. The very reverse, however, is the case,
and it furnishes a striking instance of human inconsistency.
Nothing can surpass the vigilance with which English critics
will examine the credibility of the traveler who publishes an
account of some distant, and comparatively unimportant,
country. How warily will they compare the measurements
of a pyramid, or the description of a ruin; and how sternly
will they censure any inaccuracy in these contributions of
merely curious knowledge; while they will receive, with
eagerness and unhesitating faith the gross misrepresentations
of coarse and obscure writers, concerning a country with
which their own is placed in the most important and delicate
relations. Nay, they will even make these apocryphal volumes text-books, on which to enlarge, with zeal and an ability
worthy of a more generous cause.

I shall not, however, dwell on this irksome and hackneyed
topic; nor should I have adverted to it but for the undue interest apparently taken in it by my countrymen, and certain
injurious effects which I apprehend it might produce upon
the national feeling. We attach too much consequence to
these attacks. They cannot do us any essential injury. The
tissue of misrepresentations attempted to be woven round
us, are like cobwebs woven round the limbs of an infant
giant. Our country continually outgrows them. One false-
hood after another falls off of itself. We have but to live
on, and every day we live a whole volume of refutation.
All the writers of England united, if we could for a moment
suppose their great minds stooping to so unworthy a combination, could not conceal our rapidly growing importance
and matchless prosperity. They could not conceal that these
are owing, not merely to physical and local, but also to moral
causes; — to the political liberty, the general diffusion of
knowledge, the prevalence of sound, moral, and religious
principles, which give force and sustained energy to the
character of a people; and which, in fact, have been the

acknowledged and wonderful supporters of their own national power and glory.

But why are we so exquisitely alive to the aspersions of England? Why do we suffer ourselves to be so affected by the contumely she has endeavored to cast upon us? It is not in the opinion of England alone that honor lives, and reputation has its being. The world at large is the arbiter of a nation's fame: with its thousand eyes it witnesses a nation's deeds, and from their collective testimony is national glory or national disgrace established.

For ourselves, therefore, it is comparatively of but little importance whether England does us justice or not; it is, perhaps, of far more importance to herself. She is instilling anger and resentment into the bosom of a youthful nation, to grow with its growth, and strengthen with its strength. If in America, as some of her writers are laboring to convince her, she is hereafter to find an invidious rival, and a gigantic foe, she may thank those very writers for having provoked rivalship, and irritated hostility. Every one knows the all-pervading influence of literature at the present day, and how much the opinions and passions of mankind are under its control. The mere contests of the sword are temporary; their wounds are but in the flesh, and it is the pride of the generous to forgive and forget them; but the slanders of the pen pierce to the heart; they rankle longest in the noblest spirits; they dwell ever present in the mind, and render it morbidly sensitive to the most trifling collision. It is but seldom that any one overt act produces hostilities between two nations; there exists, most commonly, a previous jealousy and ill-will, a predisposition to take offense. Trace these to their cause, and how often will they be found to originate in the mischievous effusions of mercenary writers; who, secure in their closets, and for ignominious bread, concoct and circulate the venom that is to inflame the generous and the brave.

I am not laying too much stress upon this point; for it applies most emphatically to our particular case. Over no nation does the press hold a more absolute control than over the people of America; for the universal education of the poorest classes makes every individual a reader. There is nothing published in England on the subject of our country that does not circulate through every part of it. There is not a calumny dropped from an English pen, nor an unworthy sarcasm uttered by an English statesman, that does not go to blight good-will, and add to the mass of latent resentment. Possessing, then, as England does, the fountain head from whence the literature of the language flows, how completely is it in her power, and how truly is it her duty, to make it the medium of amiable and magnanimous feeling—a stream where the two nations might meet together, and drink in peace and kindness. Should she, however, persist in turning it to waters of bitterness, the time may come when she may repent her folly. The present friendship of America may be of but little moment to her; but the future destinies of that country do not admit of a doubt: over those of England there lower some shadows of uncertainty. Should, then, a day of gloom arrive—should those reverses overtake her, from which the proudest empires have not been exempt—she may look back with regret at her infatuation, in repulsing from her side a nation she might have grappled to her bosom, and thus destroying her only chance for real friendship beyond the boundaries of her own dominions.

There is a general impression in England that the people of the United States are inimical to the parent country. It is one of the errors which has been diligently propagated by designing writers. There is, doubtless, considerable political hostility, and a general soreness at the illiberality of the English press; but, collectively speaking, the prepossessions of the people are strongly in favor of England. Indeed, at one time they amounted, in many parts of the Union, to an absurd degree of bigotry. The bare name of Englishman was a passport to the confidence and hospitality of every family, and too often gave a transient currency to the worthless and the ungrateful. Throughout the country, there was something of enthusiasm connected with the idea of England. We looked to it with a hallowed feeling of tenderness and veneration as the land of our forefathers—the august repository of the monuments and antiquities of our race—the birthplace and mausoleum of the sages and heroes of our paternal history. After our own country, there was none in whose glory we more delighted—none whose good opinion we were more anxious to possess—none toward which our hearts yearned with such throbbings of warm consanguinity. Even during the late war, whenever there was the least opportunity for kind feelings to spring forth, it was the delight of the generous spirits of our country to show that in the midst of hostilities they still kept alive the sparks of future friendship.

Is all this to be at an end? Is this golden band of kindred sympathies, so rare between nations, to be broken forever?—Perhaps it is for the best—it may dispel an allusion which might have kept us in mental vassalage; which might have interfered occasionally with our true interests, and prevented the growth of proper national pride. But it is hard to give up the kindred tie!—and there are feelings dearer than interest—closer to the heart than pride—that will still make us cast back a look of regret as we wander further and further from the paternal roof, and lament the waywardness of the parent that would repel the affections of the child.

Short-sighted and injudicious, however, as the conduct of England may be in this system of aspersion, recrimination on our part would be equally ill-judged. I speak not of a prompt and spirited vindication of our country, or the keenest castigation of her slanderers, but I allude to a disposition to retaliate in kind, to retort sarcasm and inspire prejudice, which seems to be spreading widely among our writers. Let us guard particularly against such a temper; for it would double the evil, instead of redressing the wrong. Nothing is so easy and inviting as the retort of abuse and sarcasm; but it is a paltry and unprofitable contest. It is the alternative of a morbid mind, fretted into petulance, rather than warmed into indignation. If England is willing to permit the mean jealousies of trade, or the rancorous animosities of politics, to deprave the integrity of her press, and poison the fountain of public opinion, let us beware of her example. She may deem it her interest to diffuse error, and engender antipathy, for the purpose of checking emigration; we have no purpose of the kind to serve. Neither have we any spirit of national jealousy to gratify; for as yet, in all our rivalships with England, we are the rising and the gaining party. There can be no end to answer, therefore, but the gratification of resentment—a mere spirit of retaliation; and even that is impotent. Our retorts are never republished in England; they fall short, therefore, of their aim; but they foster a querulous and peevish temper among our writers; they sour the sweet flow of our early literature, and sow thorns and brambles among its blossoms. What is still worse, they circulate through our own country, and, as far as they have effect, excite virulent national prejudices. This last is the evil most especially to be deprecated. Governed, as we are, entirely by public opinion, the utmost care should be taken to preserve the purity of the public mind. Knowledge is power, and truth is knowledge; whoever, therefore, knowingly propagates a prejudice, willfully saps the foundation of his country's strength.

The members of a republic, above all other men, should be candid and dispassionate. They are, individually, portions of the sovereign mind and sovereign will, and should be enabled to come to all questions of national concern with calm and unbiased judgments. From the peculiar nature of our relations with England, we must have more frequent questions of a difficult and delicate character with her than with any other nation; questions that affect the most acute and excitable feelings: and as, in the adjusting of these, our national measures must ultimately be determined by popular sentiment, we cannot be too anxiously attentive to purify it from all latent passion or prepossession.

Opening too, as we do, an asylum for strangers from every portion of the earth, we should receive all with impartiality. It should be our pride to exhibit an example of one nation, at least, destitute of national antipathies, and exercising, not merely the overt acts of hospitality, but those more rare and noble courtesies which spring from liberality of opinion.

What have we to do with national prejudices? They are the inveterate diseases of old countries, contracted in rude and ignorant ages, when nations knew but little of each other, and looked beyond their own boundaries with distrust and hostility. We, on the contrary, have sprung into national existence in an enlightened and philosophic age, when the different parts of the habitable world, and the various branches of the human family, have been indefatigably studied and made known to each other; and we forego the advantages of our birth, if we do not shake off the national prejudices, as we would the local superstitions, of the old world.

But, above all, let us not be influenced by any angry feelings, so far as to shut our eyes to the perception of what is really excellent and amiable in the English character. We are a young people, necessarily an imitative one, and must take our examples and models, in a great degree, from the existing nations of Europe. There is no country more worthy of our study than England. The spirit of her constitution is most analogous to ours. The manners of her people—their intellectual activity—their freedom of opinion—their habits of thinking on those subjects which concern the dearest interests and most sacred charities of private life, are all congenial to the American character; and, in fact, are all intrinsically excellent; for it is in the moral feeling of the people that the deep foundations of British prosperity are laid; and however the superstructure may be time-worn, or overrun by abuses, there must be something solid in the basis, admirable in the materials, and stable in the structure of an edifice that so long has towered unshaken amid the tempests of the world.

Let it be the pride of our writers, therefore, discarding all feelings of irritation, and disdaining to retaliate the illiberality of British authors, to speak of the English nation without prejudice and with determined candor. While they rebuke the indiscriminating bigotry with which some of our countrymen admire and imitate everything English merely because it is English, let them frankly point out what is really worthy of approbation. We may thus place England before us as a perpetual volume of reference, wherein are recorded sound deductions from ages of experience; and while we avoid the errors and absurdities which may have crept into the page, we may draw thence golden maxims of practical wisdom, wherewith to strengthen and to embellish our national character.

RURAL LIFE IN ENGLAND

"Oh! friendly to the best pursuits of man,
　Friendly to thought, to virtue, and to peace,
　Domestic life in rural pleasures past!"
　　　　　　　—COWPER

THE stranger who would form a correct opinion of the English character must not confine his observations to the metropolis. He must go forth into the country; he must sojourn in villages and hamlets; he must visit castles, villas, farmhouses, cottages; he must wander through parks and gardens; along hedges and green lanes; he must loiter about country churches; attend wakes and fairs, and other rural festivals; and cope with the people in all their conditions, and all their habits and humors.

In some countries, the large cities absorb the wealth and fashion of the nation; they are the only fixed abodes of elegant and intelligent society, and the country is inhabited almost entirely by boorish peasantry. In England, on the contrary, the metropolis is a mere gathering-place, or general rendezvous, of the polite classes, where they devote a small portion of the year to a hurry of gayety and dissipation, and, having indulged this kind of carnival, return again to the apparently more congenial habits of rural life. The various orders of society are therefore diffused over the whole surface of the kingdom, and the most retired neighborhoods afford specimens of the different ranks.

The English, in fact, are strongly gifted with the rural feeling. They possess a quick sensibility to the beauties of nature, and a keen relish for the pleasures and employments of the country. This passion seems inherent in them. Even the inhabitants of cities, born and brought up among brick walls and bustling streets, enter with facility into rural habits, and evince a tact for rural occupation. The merchant has his snug retreat in the vicinity of the metropolis, where he often displays as much pride and zeal in the cultivation of his flower-garden, and the maturing of his fruits, as he does in the conduct of his business and the success of a commercial enterprise. Even those less fortunate individuals, who are doomed to pass their lives in the midst of din and traffic, contrive to have something that shall remind them of the green aspect of nature. In the most dark and dingy quarters of the city the drawing-room window resembles frequently a bank of flowers; every spot capable of vegetation has its grass-plot and flower-bed; and every square its mimic park, laid out with picturesque taste, and gleaming with refreshing verdure.

Those who see the Englishman only in town are apt to form an unfavorable opinion of his social character. He is either absorbed in business, or distracted by the thousand engagements that dissipate time, thought, and feeling, in this huge metropolis. He has, therefore, too commonly, a look of hurry and abstraction. Wherever he happens to be, he is on the point of going somewhere else; at the moment he is talking on one subject his mind is wandering to another; and while paying a friendly visit he is calculating how he shall economize time so as to pay the other visits allotted to the morning. An immense metropolis, like London, is calculated to make men selfish and uninteresting. In their casual and transient meetings they can but deal briefly in commonplaces. They present but the cold superficies of character—its rich and genial qualities have no time to be warmed into a flow.

It is in the country that the Englishman gives scope to his natural feelings. He breaks loose gladly from the cold formalities and negative civilities of town; throws off his habits of shy reserve, and becomes joyous and free-hearted. He manages to collect round him all the conveniencies and elegancies of polite life, and to banish its restraints. His country-seat abounds with every requisite, either for studious retirement, tasteful gratification, or rural exercise. Books, paintings, music, horses, dogs, and sporting implements of all kinds, are at hand. He puts no constraint, either upon his guests or himself, but, in the true spirit of hospitality, provides the means of enjoyment, and leaves every one to partake according to his inclination.

The taste of the English in the cultivation of land, and in what is called landscape gardening, is unrivaled. They have studied Nature intently, and discovered an exquisite sense of her beautiful forms and harmonious combinations. Those charms which, in other countries, she lavishes in wild solitudes, are here assembled round the haunts of domestic life. They seem to have caught her coy and furtive graces, and spread them, like witchery, about their rural abodes.

Nothing can be more imposing than the magnificence of English park scenery. Vast lawns that extend like sheets of vivid green, with here and there clumps of gigantic trees, heaping up rich piles of foliage. The solemn pomp of groves and woodland glades, with the deer trooping in silent herds across them; the hare, bounding away to the covert; or the pheasant, suddenly bursting upon the wing. The brook, taught to wind in natural meanderings, or expand into a glassy lake—the sequestered pool, reflecting the quivering trees, with the yellow leaf sleeping on its bosom, and the trout roaming fearlessly about its limpid waters; while some rustic temple, or sylvan statue, grown green and dank with age, gives an air of classic sanctity to the seclusion.

These are but a few of the features of park scenery; but what most delights me is the creative talent with which the English decorate the unostentatious abodes of middle life. The rudest habitation, the most unpromising and scanty portion of land, in the hands of an Englishman of taste, becomes a little paradise. With a nicely discriminating eye, he seizes at once upon its capabilities, and pictures in his mind the future landscape. The sterile spot grows into loveliness under his hand; and yet the operations of art which produce the effect are scarcely to be perceived. The cherishing and training of some trees; the cautious pruning of others; the nice distribution of flowers and plants of tender and graceful foliage; the introduction of a green slope of velvet turf; the partial opening to a peep of blue distance, or silver gleam of water—all these are managed with a delicate tact, a pervading yet quiet assiduity, like the magic touchings with which a painter finishes up a favorite picture.

The residence of people of fortune and refinement in the country has diffused a degree of taste and elegance in rural economy that descends to the lowest class. The very laborer, with his thatched cottage and narrow slip of ground, attends to their embellishment. The trim hedge, the grass-plot before the door, the little flower-bed bordered with snug box, the woodbine trained up against the wall, and hanging its blossoms about the lattice; the pot of flowers in the window; the holly, providently planted about the house, to cheat winter of its dreariness, and to throw in a semblance of green summer to cheer the fireside:—all these bespeak the influence of taste, flowing down from high sources, and pervading the lowest levels of the public mind. If ever Love, as poets sing, delights to visit a cottage, it must be the cottage of an English peasant.

The fondness for rural life among the higher classes of the English has had a great and salutary effect upon the

national character. I do not know a finer race of men than
the English gentlemen. Instead of the softness and effeminacy which characterize the men of rank in most countries,
they exhibit a union of elegance and strength, a robustness
of frame and freshness of complexion, which I am inclined to
attribute to their living so much in the open air, and pursuing so eagerly the invigorating recreations of the country.
The hardy exercises produce also a healthful tone of mind
and spirits, and a manliness and simplicity of manners, which
even the follies and dissipations of the town cannot easily
pervert, and can never entirely destroy. In the country,
too, the different orders of society seem to approach more
freely, to be more disposed to blend and operate favorably
upon each other. The distinctions between them do not appear to be so marked and impassable as in the cities. The
manner in which property has been distributed into small
estates and farms has established a regular gradation from
the noblemen, through the classes of gentry, small landed
proprietors, and substantial farmers, down to the laboring
peasantry; and, while it has thus banded the extremes of
society together, has infused into each intermediate rank a
spirit of independence. This, it must be confessed, is not so
universally the case at present as it was formerly; the larger
estates having, in late years of distress, absorbed the smaller,
and, in some parts of the country, almost annihilated the
sturdy race of small farmers. These, however, I believe,
are but casual breaks in the general system I have mentioned.

In rural occupation there is nothing mean and debasing.
It leads a man forth among scenes of natural grandeur and
beauty; it leaves him to the workings of his own mind,
operated upon by the purest and most elevating of external
influences. Such a man may be simple and rough, but he
cannot be vulgar. The man of refinement, therefore, finds
nothing revolting in an intercourse with the lower orders in
rural life, as he does when he casually mingles with the
lower orders of cities. He lays aside his distance and re-

serve, and is glad to waive the distinctions of rank, and to
enter into the honest, heartfelt enjoyments of common life.
Indeed, the very amusements of the country bring men more
and more together; and the sound of hound and horn blend
all feelings into harmony.   I believe this is one great reason
why the nobility and gentry are more popular among the
inferior orders in England than they are in any other country; and why the latter have endured so many excessive
pressures and extremities, without repining more generally
at the unequal distribution of fortune and privilege.

To this mingling of cultivated and rustic society may also
be attributed the rural feeling that runs through British literature; the frequent use of illustrations from rural life;
those incomparable descriptions of Nature that abound in the
British poets—that have continued down from "the Flower
and the Leaf" of Chaucer, and have brought into our closets
all the freshness and fragrance of the dewy landscape.   The
pastoral writers of other countries appear as if they had paid
Nature an occasional visit, and become acquainted with her
general charms; but the British poets have lived and reveled
with her—they have wooed her in her most secret haunts—
they have watched her minutest caprices.   A spray could
not tremble in the breeze—a leaf could not rustle to the
ground—a diamond drop could not patter in the stream—a
fragrance could not exhale from the humble violet, nor
a daisy unfold its crimson tints to the morning, but it has
been noticed by these impassioned and delicate observers,
and wrought up into some beautiful morality.

The effect of this devotion of elegant minds to rural occupations has been wonderful on the face of the country.   A
great part of the island is rather level, and would be monoto-
nous were it not for the charms of culture; but it is studded
and gemmed, as it were, with castles and palaces, and em-
broidered with parks and gardens.   It does not abound in
grand and sublime prospects, but rather in little home scenes
of rural repose and sheltered quiet.   Every antique farmhouse and moss-grown cottage is a picture; and as the roads

are continually winding, and the view is shut in by groves and hedges, the eye is delighted by a continual succession of small landscapes of captivating loveliness.

The great charm, however, of English scenery is the moral feeling that seems to pervade it. It is associated in the mind with ideas of order, of quiet, of sober, well-established principles, of hoary usage and reverend custom. Everything seems to be the growth of ages of regular and peaceful existence. The old church, of remote architecture, with its low massive portal; its Gothic tower; its windows, rich with tracery and painted glass, in scrupulous preservation—its stately monuments of warriors and worthies of the olden time, ancestors of the present lords of the soil—its tombstones, recording successive generations of sturdy yeomanry, whose progeny still plow the same fields and kneel at the same altar—the parsonage, a quaint irregular pile, partly antiquated, but repaired and altered in the tastes of various ages and occupants—the stile and footpath leading from the churchyard, across pleasant fields, and along shady hedgerows, according to an immemorable right of way—the neighboring village, with its venerable cottages, its public green, sheltered by trees, under which the forefathers of the present race have sported—the antique family mansion, standing apart in some little rural domain, but looking down with a protecting air on the surrounding scene—all these common features of English landscape evince a calm and settled security, a hereditary transmission of home-bred virtues and local attachments that speak deeply and touchingly for the moral character of the nation.

It is a pleasing sight, of a Sunday morning, when the bell is sending its sober melody across the quiet fields, to behold the peasantry in their best finery, with ruddy faces, and modest cheerfulness, thronging tranquilly along the green lanes to church; but it is still more pleasing to see them in the evenings, gathering about their cottage doors, and appearing to exult in the humble comforts and embellishments which their own hands have spread around them.

It is this sweet home feeling, this settled repose of affection in the domestic scene, that is, after all, the parent of the steadiest virtues and purest enjoyments; and I cannot close these desultory remarks better than by quoting the words of a modern English poet, who has depicted it with remarkable felicity:

> "Through each gradation, from the castled hall,
> The city dome, the villa crown'd with shade,
> But chief from modest mansions numberless,
> In town or hamlet, shelt'ring middle life,
> Down to the cottaged vale, and straw-roof'd shed;
> This western isle hath long been famed for scenes
> Where bliss domestic finds a dwelling-place:
> Domestic bliss, that, like a harmless dove
> (Honor and sweet endearment keeping guard),
> Can center in a little quiet nest
> All that desire would fly for through the earth;
> That can, the world eluding, be itself
> A world enjoy'd; that wants no witnesses
> But its own sharers, and approving Heaven;
> That, like a flower deep hid in rocky cleft,
> Smiles, though 'tis looking only at the sky."*

THE BROKEN HEART

> "I never heard
> Of any true affection, but 'twas nipt
> With care, that, like the caterpillar, eats
> The leaves of the spring's sweetest book, the rose."
> —MIDDLETON

IT is a common practice with those who have outlived the susceptibility of early feeling, or have been brought up in the gay heartlessness of dissipated life, to laugh at all love stories, and to treat the tales of romantic passion as mere fictions of novelists and poets. My observations on human nat-

---

* From a poem on the death of the Princess Charlotte, by the Reverend Rann Kennedy, A.M.

ure have induced me to think otherwise. They have convinced me, that however the surface of the character may be chilled and frozen by the cares of the world, or cultivated into mere smiles by the arts of society, still there are dormant fires lurking in the depths of the coldest bosom, which, when once enkindled, become impetuous, and are sometimes desolating in their effects. Indeed, I am a true believer in the blind deity, and go to the full extent of his doctrines. Shall I confess it?—I believe in broken hearts, and the possibility of dying of disappointed love! I do not, however, consider it a malady often fatal to my own sex; but I firmly believe that it withers down many a lovely woman into an early grave.

Man is the creature of interest and ambition. His nature leads him forth into the struggle and bustle of the world. Love is but the embellishment of his early life, or a song piped in the intervals of the acts. He seeks for fame, for fortune, for space in the world's thought, and dominion over his fellowmen. But a woman's whole life is a history of the affections. The heart is her world; it is there her ambition strives for empire—it is there her avarice seeks for hidden treasures. She sends forth her sympathies on adventure; she embarks her whole soul in the traffic of affection; and if shipwrecked, her case is hopeless—for it is a bankruptcy of the heart.

To a man, the disappointment of love may occasion some bitter pangs: it wounds some feelings of tenderness—it blasts some prospects of felicity; but he is an active being; he may dissipate his thoughts in the whirl of varied occupation, or may plunge into the tide of pleasure; or, if the scene of disappointment be too full of painful associations, he can shift his abode at will, and taking, as it were, the wings of the morning, can "fly to the uttermost parts of the earth, and be at rest."

But woman's is comparatively a fixed, a secluded and a meditative life. She is more the companion of her own thoughts and feelings; and if they are turned to ministers of sorrow, where shall she look for consolation? Her lot is to be wooed and won; and if unhappy in her love, her heart is like some fortress that has been captured, and sacked, and abandoned, and left desolate.

How many bright eyes grow dim—how many soft cheeks grow pale—how many lovely forms fade away into the tomb, and none can tell the cause that blighted their loveliness! As the dove will clasp its wings to its side, and cover and conceal the arrow that is preying on its vitals—so is it the nature of woman to hide from the world the pangs of wounded affection. The love of a delicate female is always shy and silent. Even when fortunate, she scarcely breathes it to herself; but when otherwise, she buries it in the recesses of her bosom, and there lets it cower and brood among the ruins of her peace. With her, the desire of her heart has failed—the great charm of existence is at an end. She neglects all the cheerful exercises which gladden the spirits, quicken the pulses, and send the tide of life in healthful currents through the veins. Her rest is broken—the sweet refreshment of sleep is poisoned by melancholy dreams—"dry sorrow drinks her blood," until her enfeebled frame sinks under the slightest external injury. Look for her, after a little while, and you find friendship weeping over her untimely grave, and wondering that one, who but lately glowed with all the radiance of health and beauty, should so speedily be brought down to "darkness and the worm." You will be told of some wintry chill, some casual indisposition, that laid her low—but no one knows the mental malady that previously sapped her strength and made her so easy a prey to the spoiler.

She is like some tender tree, the pride and beauty of the grove: graceful in its form, bright in its foliage, but with the worm preying at its heart. We find it suddenly withering when it should be most fresh and luxuriant. We see it drooping its branches to the earth, and shedding leaf by leaf; until, wasted and perished away, it falls even in the stillness of the forest; and as we muse over the beautiful ruin we strive in vain to recollect the blast or thunderbolt that could have smitten it with decay.

I have seen many instances of women running to waste and self-neglect, and disappearing gradually from the earth, almost as if they had been exhaled to heaven; and have repeatedly fancied that I could trace their deaths through the various declensions of consumption, cold, debility, languor, melancholy, until I reached the first symptom of disappointed love. But an instance of the kind was lately told to me; the circumstances are well known in the country where they happened, and I shall but give them in the manner in which they were related.

Every one must recollect the tragical story of young E——, the Irish patriot: it was too touching to be soon forgotten. During the troubles in Ireland he was tried, condemned, and executed, on a charge of treason. His fate made a deep impression on public sympathy. He was so young—so intelligent—so generous—so brave—so everything that we are apt to like in a young man. His conduct under trial, too, was so lofty and intrepid. The noble indignation with which he repelled the charge of treason against his country—the eloquent vindication of his name—and his pathetic appeal to posterity, in the hopeless hour of condemnation—all these entered deeply into every generous bosom, and even his enemies lamented the stern policy that dictated his execution.

But there was one heart whose anguish it would be impossible to describe. In happier days and fairer fortunes, he had won the affections of a beautiful and interesting girl, the daughter of a late celebrated Irish barrister. She loved him with the disinterested fervor of a woman's first and early love. When every worldly maxim arrayed itself against him; when blasted in fortune, and disgrace and danger darkened around his name, she loved him the more ardently for his very sufferings. If, then, his fate could awaken the sympathy even of his foes, what must have been the agony of her whose soul was occupied by his image? Let those tell who have had the portals of the tomb suddenly closed between them and the being they most loved on earth—who have sat at its threshold as one shut out in a cold and lonely world, from whence all that was most lovely and loving had departed.

But then the horrors of such a grave!—so frightful, so dishonored! There was nothing for memory to dwell on that could soothe the pang of separation—none of those tender, though melancholy circumstances, that endear the parting scene—nothing to melt sorrow into those blessed tears, sent, like the dews of heaven, to revive the heart in the parting hour of anguish.

To render her widowed situation more desolate, she had incurred her father's displeasure by her unfortunate attachment, and was an exile from the paternal roof. But could the sympathy and kind offices of friends have reached a spirit so shocked and driven in by horror, she would have experienced no want of consolation, for the Irish are a people of quick and generous sensibilities. The most delicate and cherishing attentions were paid her by families of wealth and distinction. She was led into society, and they tried by all kinds of occupation and amusement to dissipate her grief, and wean her from the tragical story of her loves. But it was all in vain. There are some strokes of calamity that scathe and scorch the soul—that penetrate to the vital seat of happiness—and blast it, never again to put forth bud or blossom. She never objected to frequent the haunts of pleasure, but she was as much alone there as in the depths of solitude. She walked about in a sad reverie, apparently unconscious of the world around her. She carried with her an inward woe that mocked at all the blandishments of friendship, and "heeded not the song of the charmer, charm he never so wisely."

The person who told me her story had seen her at a masquerade. There can be no exhibition of far-gone wretchedness more striking and painful than to meet it in such a scene. To find it wandering like a specter, lonely and joyless, where all around is gay—to see it dressed out in the trappings of mirth, and looking so wan and woebegone, as if it had tried in vain to cheat the poor heart into a momentary forgetfulness of sorrow. After strolling through the splendid rooms and giddy crowd with an air of utter abstraction, she sat herself down on the steps of an orchestra, and looking about for some time with a vacant air, that showed her insensibility to the garish scene, she began, with the capriciousness of a sickly heart, to warble a little plaintive air. She had an exquisite voice; but on this occasion it was so simple, so touching—it breathed forth such a soul of wretchedness—that she drew a crowd, mute and silent, around her, and melted every one into tears.

The story of one so true and tender could not but excite great interest in a country remarkable for enthusiasm. It completely won the heart of a brave officer, who paid his addresses to her, and thought that one so true to the dead could not but prove affectionate to the living. She declined his attentions, for her thoughts were irrecoverably engrossed by the memory of her former lover. He, however, persisted in his suit. He solicited not her tenderness, but her esteem. He was assisted by her conviction of his worth, and her sense of her own destitute and dependent situation, for she was existing on the kindness of friends. In a word, he at length succeeded in gaining her hand, though with the solemn assurance that her heart was unalterably another's.

He took her with him to Sicily, hoping that a change of scene might wear out the remembrance of early woes. She was an amiable and exemplary wife, and made an effort to be a happy one; but nothing could cure the silent and devouring melancholy that had entered into her very soul. She wasted away in a slow, but hopeless decline, and at length sunk into the grave, the victim of a broken heart.

It was on her that Moore, the distinguished Irish poet, composed the following lines:

"She is far from the land where her young hero sleeps,
    And lovers around her are sighing;
But coldly she turns from their gaze, and weeps,
    For her heart in his grave is lying.

"She sings the wild song of her dear native plains,
   Every note which he loved awaking—
Ah! little they think, who delight in her strains,
   How the heart of the minstrel is breaking!

"He had lived for his love—for his country he died,
   They were all that to life had entwined him—
Nor soon shall the tears of his country be dried,
   Nor long will his love stay behind him!

"Oh! make her a grave where the sunbeams rest,
   When they promise a glorious morrow;
hey'll shine o'er her sleep, like a smile from the west,
   From her own loved island of sorrow!"

THE ART OF BOOK-MAKING

"If that severe doom of Synesius be true—'it is a greater offense to
steal dead men's labors than their clothes'—what shall become of most
writers?"—BURTON'S *Anatomy of Melancholy*

I HAVE often wondered at the extreme fecundity of the
press, and how it comes to pass that so many heads, on
which Nature seems to have inflicted the curse of barren-
ness, yet teem with voluminous productions. As a man
travels on, however, in the journey of life, his objects of
wonder daily diminish, and he is continually finding out
some very simple cause for some great matter of marvel.
Thus have I chanced, in my peregrinations about this great
metropolis, to blunder upon a scene which unfolded to me
some of the mysteries of the book-making craft, and at once
put an end to my astonishment.

I was one summer's day loitering through the great
saloons of the British Museum, with that listlessness with
which one is apt to saunter about a room in warm weather;
sometimes lolling over the glass cases of minerals, sometimes
studying the hieroglyphics on an Egyptian mummy, and
sometimes trying, with nearly equal success, to comprehend

the allegorical paintings on the lofty ceilings. While I was gazing about in this idle away my attention was attracted to a distant floor, at the end of a suite of apartments. It was closed, but every now and then it would open, and some strange-favored being, generally clothed in black, would steal forth, and glide through the rooms, without noticing any of the surrounding objects. There was an air of mystery about this that piqued my languid curiosity, and I determined to attempt the passage of that strait, and to explore the unknown regions that lay beyond. The door yielded to my hand, with all that facility with which the portals of enchanted castles yield to the adventurous knight-errant. I found myself in a spacious chamber, surrounded with great cases of venerable books. Above the cases, and just under the cornice, were arranged a great number of quaint black-looking portraits of ancient authors. About the room were placed long tables, with stands for reading and writing, at which sat many pale, cadaverous personages, poring intently over dusty volumes, rummaging among mouldy manuscripts, and taking copious notes of their contents. The most hushed stillness reigned through this mysterious apartment, excepting that you might hear the racing of pens over sheets of paper, or, occasionally, the deep sigh of one of these sages, as he shifted his position to turn over the page of an old folio; doubtless arising from that hollowness and flatulency incident to learned research.

Now and then one of these personages would write something on a small slip of paper, and ring a bell, whereupon a familiar would appear, take the paper in profound silence, glide out of the room, and return shortly loaded with ponderous tomes, upon which the other would fall, tooth and nail, with famished voracity. I had no longer a doubt that I had happened upon a body of magi, deeply engaged in the study of occult sciences. The scene reminded me of an old Arabian tale of a philosopher, who was shut up in an enchanted library, in the bosom of a mountain that opened only once a year; where he made the spirits of the place obey his commands, and bring him books of all kinds of dark knowledge, so that at the end of the year, when the magic portal once more swung open on its hinges, he issued forth so versed in forbidden lore as to be able to soar above the heads of the multitude and to control the powers of Nature.

My curiosity being now fully aroused, I whispered to one of the familiars, as he was about to leave the room, and begged an interpretation of the strange scene before me. A few words were sufficient for the purpose: I found that these mysterious personages, whom I had mistaken for magi, were principally authors, and were in the very act of manufacturing books. I was, in fact, in the reading-room of the great British Library, an immense collection of volumes of all ages and languages, many of which are now forgotten, and most of which are seldom read. To these sequestered pools of obsolete literature, therefore, do many modern authors repair, and draw buckets full of classic lore, or "pure English, undefiled," wherewith to swell their own scanty rills of thought.

Being now in possession of the secret, I sat down in a corner, and watched the process of this book manufactory. I noticed one lean, bilious-looking wight, who sought none but the most worm-eaten volumes, printed in black-letter. He was evidently constructing some work of profound erudition that would be purchased by every man who wished to be thought learned, placed upon a conspicuous shelf of his library or laid open upon his table—but never read. I observed him, now and then, draw a large fragment of biscuit out of his pocket, and gnaw; whether it was his dinner, or whether he was endeavoring to keep off that exhaustion of the stomach, produced by much pondering over dry works, I leave to harder students than myself to determine.

There was one dapper little gentleman in bright-colored clothes, with a chirping, gossiping expression of countenance, who had all the appearance of an author on good terms with his bookseller. After considering him attentively, I recognized in him a diligent getter-up of miscellaneous works

which bustled off well with the trade. I was curious to see
how he manufactured his wares. He made more stir and
show of business than any of the others; dipping into various books, fluttering over the leaves of manuscripts, taking
a morsel out of one, a morsel out of another, "line upon line,
precept upon precept, here a little and there a little." The
contents of his book seemed to be as heterogeneous as those
of the witches' caldron in "Macbeth." It was here a finger
and there a thumb, toe of frog and blind worm's sting, with
his own gossip poured in like "baboon's blood," to make the
medley "slab and good."

After all, thought I, may not this pilfering disposition be
implanted in authors for wise purposes? may it not be the
way in which Providence has taken care that the seeds of
knowledge and wisdom shall be preserved from age to age,
in spite of the inevitable decay of the works in which they
were first produced? We see that Nature has wisely, though
whimsically, provided for the conveyance of seeds from clime
to clime, in the maws of certain birds; so that animals, which,
in themselves, are little better than carrion, and apparently
the lawless plunderers of the orchard and the corn-field, are,
in fact, Nature's carriers to disperse and perpetuate her blessings. In like manner, the beauties and fine thoughts of ancient and obsolete writers are caught up by these flights of
predatory authors, and cast forth, again to flourish and bear
fruit in a remote and distant tract of time. Many of their
works, also, undergo a kind of metempsychosis, and spring
up under new forms. What was formerly a ponderous history revives in the shape of a romance—an old legend
changes into a modern play—and a sober, philosophical
treatise furnishes the body for a whole series of bouncing
and sparkling essays. Thus it is in the clearing of our
American woodlands; where we burn down a forest of
stately pines, a progeny of dwarf oaks start up in their
place; and we never see the prostrate trunk of a tree, mouldering into soil, but it gives birth to a whole tribe of fungi.

Let us not, then, lament over the decay and oblivion into

which ancient writers descend; they do but submit to the
great law of Nature, which declares that all sublunary shapes
of matter shall be limited in their duration, but which de-
crees, also, that their elements shall never perish. Generation after generation, both in animal and vegetable life,
passes way, but the vital principle is transmitted to posterity, and the species continue to flourish. Thus, also, do
authors beget authors, and, having produced a numerous
progeny, in a good old age they sleep with their fathers;
that is to say, with the authors who preceded them—and
from whom they had stolen.

While I was indulging in these rambling fancies I had
leaned my head against a pile of reverend folios. Whether
it was owing to the soporific emanations from these works;
or to the profound quiet of the room; or to the lassitude arising from much wandering; or to an unlucky habit of napping
at improper times and places, with which I am grievously
afflicted, so it was that I fell into a doze. Still, however, my
imagination continued busy, and indeed the same scene remained before my mind's eye, only a little changed in some
of the details. I dreamed that the chamber was still decorated with the portraits of ancient authors, but the number
was increased. The long tables had disappeared, and in
place of the sage magi, I beheld a ragged, threadbare throng,
such as may be seen plying about the great repository of cast-
off clothes, Monmouth Street. Whenever they seized upon
a book, by one of those incongruities common to dreams, methought it turned into a garment of foreign or antique fashion, with which they proceeded to equip themselves. I noticed, however, that no one pretended to clothe himself from
any particular suit, but took a sleeve from one, a cape from
another, a skirt from a third, thus decking himself out piecemeal, while some of his original rags would peep out from
among his borrowed finery.

There was a portly, rosy, well-fed parson, whom I observed ogling several mouldy polemical writers through an
eyeglass. He soon contrived to slip on the voluminous

mantle of one of the old fathers, and having purloined the
gray beard of another, endeavored to look exceedingly wise;
but the smirking commonplace of his countenance set at
naught all the trappings of wisdom. One sickly-looking
gentleman was busied embroidering a very flimsy garment
with gold thread drawn out of several old court-dresses of
the reign of Queen Elizabeth. Another had trimmed himself magnificently from an illuminated manuscript, had stuck
a nosegay in his bosom, culled from "The Paradise of Dainty
Devices," and having put Sir Philip Sidney's hat on one side
of his head, strutted off with an exquisite air of vulgar elegance. A third, who was but of puny dimensions, had bol-
stered himself out bravely with the spoils from several obscure tracts of philosophy, so that he had a very imposing
front, but he was lamentably tattered in rear, and I perceived that he had patched his small-clothes with scraps of
parchment from a Latin author.

There were some well-dressed gentlemen, it is true, who
only helped themselves to a gem or so, which sparkled among
their own ornaments, without eclipsing them. Some, too,
seemed to contemplate the costumes of the old writers, merely
to imbibe their principles of taste, and to catch their air and
spirit; but I grieve to say that too many were apt to array
themselves, from top to toe, in the patchwork manner I
have mentioned. I should not omit to speak of one genius,
in drab breeches and gaiters, and an Arcadian hat, who had
a violent propensity to the pastoral, but whose rural wanderings had been confined to the classic haunts of Primrose Hill,
and the solitudes of the Regent's Park. He had decked
himself in wreaths and ribbons from all the old pastoral
poets, and, hanging his head on one side, went about with a
fantastical, lackadaisical air, "babbling about green fields."
But the personage that most struck my attention was a
pragmatical old gentleman, in clerical robes, with a remarkably large and square but bald head. He entered the room
wheezing and puffing, elbowed his way through the throng,
with a look of sturdy self-confidence, and, having laid hands

upon a thick Greek quarto, clapped it upon his head and
swept majestically away in a formidable frizzled wig.

In the height of this literary masquerade a cry suddenly
resounded from every side, of "thieves! thieves!" I looked,
and lo! the portraits about the walls became animated! The
old authors thrust out first a head, then a shoulder, from the
canvas, looked down curiously, for an instant, upon the motley throng, and then descended, with fury in their eyes, to
claim their rifled property. The scene of scampering and
hubbub that ensued baffles all description. The unhappy
culprits endeavored in vain to escape with their plunder.
On one side might be seen half a dozen old monks, stripping
a modern professor; on another, there was sad devastation
carried into the ranks of modern dramatic writers. Beaumont and Fletcher, side by side, raged round the field like
Castor and Pollux, and sturdy Ben Jonson enacted more
wonders than when a volunteer with the army in Flanders.
As to the dapper little compiler of farragos, mentioned some
time since, he had arrayed himself in as many patches and
colors as Harlequin, and there was as fierce a contention of
claimants about him as about the dead body of Patroclus. I
was grieved to see many men, whom I had been accustomed
to look upon with awe and reverence, fain to steal off with
scarce a rag to cover their nakedness. Just then my eye
was caught by the pragmatical old gentleman in the Greek
grizzled wig, who was scrambling away in sore affright with
half a score of authors in full cry after him. They were
close upon his haunches; in a twinkling off went his wig; at
every turn some strip of raiment was peeled away; until in a
few moments, from his domineering pomp, he shrunk into
a little pursy, "chopp'd bald shot," and made his exit with
only a few tags and rags fluttering at his back.

There was something so ludicrous in the catastrophe of
this learned Theban that I burst into an immoderate fit of
laughter, which broke the whole illusion. The tumult and
the scuffle were at an end. The chamber resumed its usual
appearance. The old authors shrunk back into their picture-

frames, and hung in shadowy solemnity along the walls. In short, I found myself wide awake in my corner, with the whole assemblage of bookworms gazing at me with astonishment. Nothing of the dream had been real but my burst of laughter, a sound never before heard in that grave sanctuary, and so abhorrent to the ears of wisdom as to electrify the fraternity.

The librarian now stepped up to me, and demanded whether I had a card of admission. At first I did not comprehend him, but I soon found that the library was a kind of literary "preserve," subject to game laws, and that no one must presume to hunt there without special license and permission. In a word, I stood convicted of being an arrant poacher, and was glad to make a precipitate retreat, lest I should have a whole pack of authors let loose upon me.

A ROYAL POET

"Though your body be confined
And soft love a prisoner bound,
Yet the beauty of your mind
Neither cheek nor chain hath found.
Look out nobly, then, and dare
Even the fetters that you wear."—FLETCHER

ON a soft sunny morning in the genial month of May I made an excursion to Windsor Castle. It is a place full of storied and poetical associations. The very external aspect of the proud old pile is enough to inspire high thought. It rears its irregular walls and massive towers like a mural crown around the brow of a lofty ridge, waves its royal banner in the clouds, and looks down with a lordly air upon the surrounding world.

On this morning, the weather was of this voluptuous vernal kind which calls forth all the latent romance of a man's temperament, filling his mind with music, and disposing him to quote poetry and dream of beauty. In wandering through the magnificent saloons and long echoing galleries of the castle, I passed with indifference by whole rows of portraits of warriors and statesmen, but lingered in the chamber where hang the likenesses of the beauties that graced the gay court of Charles the Second; and as I gazed upon them, depicted with amorous half-disheveled tresses, and the sleepy eye of love, I blessed the pencil of Sir Peter Lely, which had thus enabled me to bask in the reflected rays of beauty. In traversing also the "large green courts," with sunshine beaming on the gray walls and glancing along the velvet turf, my mind was engrossed with the image of the tender, the gallant, but hapless Surrey, and his account of his loiterings about them in his stripling days, when enamored of the Lady Geraldine—

> "With eyes cast up unto the maiden's tower,
> With easie sighs, such as men draw in love."

In this mood of mere poetical susceptibility, I visited the ancient keep of the castle, where James the First of Scotland, the pride and theme of Scottish poets and historians, was for many years of his youth detained a prisoner of state. It is a large gray tower, that has stood the brunt of ages, and is still in good preservation. It stands on a mound which elevates it above the other parts of the castle, and a great flight of steps leads to the interior. In the armory, which is a gothic hall, furnished with weapons of various kinds and ages, I was shown a coat of armor hanging against the wall, which I was told had once belonged to James. From hence I was conducted up a staircase to a suite of apartments of faded magnificence, hung with storied tapestry, which formed his prison, and the scene of that passionate and fanciful amour which has woven into the web of his story the magical hues of poetry and fiction.

The whole history of this amiable but unfortunate prince is highly romantic. At the tender age of eleven he was sent from his home by his father, Robert III., and destined for the French court, to be reared under the eye of the French monarch, secure from the treachery and danger that surrounded the royal house of Scotland. It was his mishap, in the course of his voyage, to fall into the hands of the English, and he was detained a prisoner by Henry IV., notwithstanding that a truce existed between the two countries.

The intelligence of his capture, coming in the train of many sorrows and disasters, proved fatal to his unhappy father.

"The news," we are told, "was brought to him while at supper, and did so overwhelm him with grief that he was almost ready to give up the ghost into the hands of the servants that attended him. But being carried to his bedchamber, he abstained from all food, and in three days died of hunger and grief, at Rothesay." *

James was detained in captivity above eighteen years; but, though deprived of personal liberty, he was treated with the respect due to his rank. Care was taken to instruct him in all the branches of useful knowledge cultivated at that period, and to give him those mental and personal accomplishments deemed proper for a prince. Perhaps in this respect, his imprisonment was an advantage, as it enabled him to apply himself the more exclusively to his improvement, and quietly to imbibe that rich fund of knowledge, and to cherish those elegant tastes, which have given such a luster to his memory. The picture drawn of him in early life, by the Scottish historians, is highly captivating, and seems rather the description of a hero of romance than of a character in real history. He was well learned, we are told, "to fight with the sword, to joust, to tournay, to wrestle, to sing and dance; he was an expert mediciner, right crafty in playing both of lute and harp, and sundry other instruments of music, and was expert in grammar, oratory, and poetry." †

With this combination of manly and delicate accomplishments, fitting him to shine both in active and elegant life,

---

* Buchanan.   † Ballenden's translation of Hector Boyce.

and calculated to give him an intense relish for joyous existence, it must have been a severe trial, in an age of bustle
and chivalry, to pass the springtime of his years in monoto-
nous captivity. It was the good fortune of James, however,
to be gifted with a powerful poetic fancy, and to be visited
in his prison by the choicest inspirations of the muse. Some
minds corrode, and grow inactive, under the loss of personal
liberty; others grow morbid and irritable; but it is the nature of the poet to become tender and imaginative in the
loneliness of confinement. He banquets upon the honey of
his own thoughts, and, like the captive bird, pours forth his
soul in melody.

> "Have you not seen the nightingale
> A pilgrim coop'd into a cage,
> How doth she chant her wonted tale,
> In that her lonely hermitage!
>
> Even there her charming melody doth prove
> That all her boughs are trees, her cage a grove."*

Indeed, it is the divine attribute of the imagination that
it is irrepressible, unconfinable; that when the real world is
shut out it can create a world for itself, and, with necro-
mantic power, can conjure up glorious shapes and forms,
and brilliant visions, to make solitude populous and irradiate
the gloom of the dungeon. Such was the world of pomp
and pageant that lived round Tasso in his dismal cell at Fer-
rara, when he conceived the splendid scenes of his Jerusalem;
and we may conceive the "King's Quair," † composed by
James during his captivity at Windsor, as another of those
beautiful breakings forth of the soul from the restraint and
gloom of the prison-house.

The subject of his poem is his love for the lady Jane
Beaufort, daughter of the Earl of Somerset, and a princess
of the blood-royal of England, of whom he became enamored
in the course of his captivity. What gives it peculiar value
is, that it may be considered a transcript of the royal bard's

---

* Roger L'Estrange.   † Quair, an old term for Book.

true feelings, and the story of his real loves and fortunes. It is not often that sovereigns write poetry, or that poets deal in fact. It is gratifying to the pride of a common man to find a monarch thus suing, as it were, for admission into his closet, and seeking to win his favor by administering to his pleasures. It is a proof of the honest equality of intellectual competition, which strips off all the trappings of factitious dignity, brings the candidate down to a level with his fellowmen, and obliges him to depend on his own native powers for distinction. It is curious, too, to get at the history of a monarch's heart, and to find the simple affections of human nature throbbing under the ermine. But James had learned to be a poet before he was a king; he was schooled in adversity, and reared in the company of his own thoughts. Monarchs have seldom time to parley with their hearts, or to meditate their minds into poetry; and had James been brought up amid the adulation and gayety of a court we should never, in all probability, have had such a poem as the Quair.

I have been particularly interested by those parts of the poem which breathe his immediate thoughts concerning his situation, or which are connected with the apartment in the tower. They have thus a personal and local charm, and are given with such circumstantial truth, as to make the reader present with the captive in his prison and the companion of his meditations.

Such is the account which he gives of his weariness of spirit, and of the incident that first suggested the idea of writing the poem. It was the still mid-watch of a clear moonlight night; the stars, he says, were twinkling as the fire in the high vault of heaven, and "Cynthia rinsing her golden locks in Aquarius"—he lay in bed wakeful and restless, and took a book to beguile the tedious hours. The book he chose was Boetius' "Consolations of Philosophy," a work popular among the writers of that day, and which had been translated by his great prototype Chaucer. From the high eulogium in which he indulges, it is evident this was one of his favorite volumes while in prison; and, indeed, it is an admirable text-book for meditation under adversity. It is the legacy of a noble and enduring spirit, purified by sorrow and suffering, bequeathing to its successors in calamity the maxims of sweet morality, and the trains of eloquent but simple reasoning, by which it was enabled to bear up against the various ills of life. It is a talisman which the unfortunate may treasure up in his bosom, or, like the good King James, lay upon his nightly pillow.

After closing the volume, he turns its contents over in his mind, and gradually falls into a fit of musing on the fickleness of fortune, the vicissitudes of his own life, and the evils that had overtaken him even in his tender youth. Suddenly he hears the bell ringing to matins, but its sound chiming in with his melancholy fancies seems to him like a voice exhorting him to write his story. In the spirit of poetic errantry, he determines to comply with this intimation; he therefore takes pen in hand, makes with it a sign of the cross, to implore a benediction, and sallies forth into the fairyland of poetry. There is something extremely fanciful in all this, and it is interesting as furnishing a striking and beautiful instance of the simple manner in which whole trains of poetical thought are sometimes awakened, and literary enterprises suggested to the mind.

In the course of his poem, he more than once bewails the peculiar hardness of his fate, thus doomed to lonely and inactive life, and shut up from the freedom and pleasure of the world, in which the meanest animal indulges unrestrained. There is a sweetness, however, in his very complaints; they are the lamentations of an amiable and social spirit, at being denied the indulgence of its kind and generous propensities; there is nothing in them harsh or exaggerated; they flow with a natural and touching pathos, and are perhaps rendered more touching by their simple brevity. They contrast finely with those elaborate and iterated repinings which we sometimes meet with in poetry, the effusions of morbid minds, sickening under miseries of their own creating, and venting their bitterness upon an unoffending world. James speaks of his privations with acute sensibility; but having mentioned them, passes on, as if his manly mind disdained to brood over unavoidable calamities. When such a spirit breaks forth into complaint, however brief, we are aware how great must be the suffering that extorts the murmur. We sympathize with James, a romantic, active, and accomplished prince, cut off in the lustihood of youth from all the enterprise, the noble uses and vigorous delights of life, as we do with Milton, alive to all the beauties of nature and glories of art, when he breathes forth brief but deep-toned lamentations over his perpetual blindness.

Had not James evinced a deficiency of poetic artifice, we might almost have suspected that these lowerings of gloomy reflection were meant as preparative to the brightest scene of his story, and to contrast with that effulgence of light and loveliness, that exhilarating accompaniment of bird, and song, and foliage, and flower, and all the revel of the year, with which he ushers in the lady of his heart. It is this scene in particular which throws all the magic of romance about the old castle keep. He had risen, he says, at day-break, according to custom, to escape from the dreary meditations of a sleepless pillow. "Bewailing in his chamber thus alone," despairing of all joy and remedy, "for, tired of thought, and woebegone," he had wandered to the window to indulge the captive's miserable solace of gazing wistfully upon the world from which he is excluded. The window looked forth upon a small garden which lay at the foot of the tower. It was a quiet, sheltered spot, adorned with arbors and green alleys, and protected from the passing gaze by trees and hawthorn hedges.

> "Now was there made fast by the tower's walk
> A garden faire, and in the corners set,
> An arbour green with wandis long and small
> Railed about, and so with leaves beset
> Was all the place, and hawthorn hedges knet,
> That lyf* was none, walkyng there forbye,
> That might within scarce any wight espye.

* *Lyf*, person.

> "So thick the branches and the leves grene,
>   Beshaded all the alleys that there were,
> And midst of every arbour might be seen
>   The sharpe, grene, swete juniper,
> Growing so faire with branches here and there,
>   That as it seemed to a lyf without,
>   The boughs did spread the arbour all about.

> "And on the small green twistis* set
>   The lytel swete nyghtingales, and sung
> So loud and clere, the hymnis consecrate
>   Of lovis use, now soft, now loud among,
> That all the garden and the wallis rung
>   Ryght of their song—"

It was the month of May, when everything was in bloom, and he interprets the song of the nightingale into the language of his enamored feeling.

> "Worship all ye that lovers be this May;
>   For of your bliss the kalends are begun,
> And sing with us, away, winter, away,
>   Come, summer, come, the sweet season and sun."

As he gazes on the scene, and listens to the notes of the birds, he gradually lapses into one of those tender and undefinable reveries which fill the youthful bosom in this delicious season. He wonders what this love may be, of which he has so often read, and which thus seems breathed forth in the quickening breath of May, and melting all nature into ecstasy and song. If it really be so great a felicity, and if it be a boon thus generally dispensed to the most insignificant of beings, why is he alone cut off from its enjoyments?

> "Oft would I think, O Lord, what may this be,
>   That love is of such noble myght and kynde?
> Loving his folk, and such prosperitee,
>   Is it of him, as we in books do find;
> May he oure hertes setten† and unbynd.

---

* *Twistis*, small boughs or twigs.   † *Setten*, incline.
NOTE.—The language of the quotations is generally modernized.

Hath he upon oure hertes such maistrye?
Or is all this but feynit fantasye?
  For giff he be of so grete excellence
    That he of every wight hath care and charge,
  What have I gilt* to him, or done offense,
    That I am thral'd and birdis go at large?"

In the midst of his musing, as he casts his eyes downward, he beholds "the fairest and the freshest young floure"
that ever he had seen. It is the lovely Lady Jane, walking
in the garden to enjoy the beauty of that "fresh May mor-
rowe." Breaking thus suddenly upon his sight in a moment
of loneliness and excited susceptibility, she at once captivates
the fancy of the romantic prince, and becomes the object of
his wandering wishes, the sovereign of his ideal world.

There is in this charming scene an evident resemblance to
the early part of Chaucer's Knight's Tale, where Palamon
and Arcite fall in love with Emilia, whom they see walking
in the garden of their prison. Perhaps the similarity of the
actual fact to the incident which he had read in Chaucer
may have induced James to dwell on it in his poem. His
description of the Lady Jane is given in the picturesque and
minute manner of his master, and being, doubtless, taken
from the life, is a perfect portrait of a beauty of that day.
He dwells with the fondness of a lover on every article of her
apparel, from the net of pearl, splendent with emeralds and
sapphires, that confined her golden hair, even to the "goodly
chaine of small orfeverye" † about her neck, whereby there
hung a ruby in shape of a heart, that seemed, he says, like
a spark of fire burning upon her white bosom. Her dress
of white tissue was looped up, to enable her to walk with
more freedom. She was accompanied by two female attendants, and about her sported a little hound decorated with
bells, probably the small Italian hound, of exquisite symmetry, which was a parlor favorite and pet among the fashionable dames of ancient times. James closes his description
by a burst of general eulogium:

---

* *Gilt*, what injury have I done, etc.   † Wrought gold.

"In her was youth, beauty with humble port,
  Bountee, richesse, and womanly feature,
God better knows than my pen can report,
  Wisdom, largesse,* estate,† and cunning‡ sure.
In every point so guided her measure,
  In word, in deed, in shape, in countenance,
  That nature might no more her child advance."

The departure of the Lady Jane from the garden puts an end to this transient riot of the heart. With her departs the amorous illusion that had shed a temporary charm over the scene of his captivity, and he relapses into loneliness, now rendered tenfold more intolerable by this passing beam of unattainable beauty. Through the long and weary day he repines at his unhappy lot, and when evening approaches and Phœbus, as he beautifully expresses it, had "bade farewell to every leaf and flower," he still lingers at the window, and, laying his head upon the cold stone, gives vent to a mingled flow of love and sorrow, until, gradually lulled by the mute melancholy of the twilight hour, he lapses, "half-sleeping, half-swoon," into a vision, which occupies the remainder of the poem, and in which is allegorically shadowed out the history of his passion.

When he wakes from his trance he rises from his stony pillow, and, pacing his apartment full of dreary reflections, questions his spirit whither it has been wandering; whether, indeed, all that has passed before his dreaming fancy has been conjured up by preceding circumstances, or whether it is a vision intended to comfort and assure him in his despondence. If the latter, he prays that some token may be sent to confirm the promise of happier days, given him in his slumbers.

Suddenly a turtle-dove of the purest whiteness comes flying in at the window, and alights upon his hand, bearing in her bill a branch of red gilliflower, on the leaves of which is written in letters of gold the following sentence:

---

* *Largesse*, bounty.   † *Estate*, dignity.   ‡ *Cunning*, discretion.

> "Awake! awake! I bring, lover, I bring
> The newis glad, that blissful is and sure,
> Of thy comfort; now laugh, and play, and sing,
> For in the heaven decretit is thy cure."

He receives the branch with mingled hope and dread; reads it with rapture, and this he says was the first token of his succeeding happiness. Whether this is a mere poetic fiction, or whether the Lady Jane did actually send him a token of her favor in this romantic way, remains to be determined according to the faith or fancy of the reader. He concludes his poem by intimating that the promise conveyed in the vision, and by the flower, is fulfilled by his being restored to liberty, and made happy in the possession of the sovereign of his heart.

Such is the poetical account given by James of his love adventures in Windsor Castle. How much of it is absolute fact, and how much the embellishment of fancy, it is fruitless to conjecture; do not, however, let us always consider whatever is romantic as incomparable with real life, but let us sometimes take a poet at his word. I have noticed merely such parts of the poem as were immediately connected with the tower, and have passed over a large part which was in the allegorical vein, so much cultivated at that day. The language, of course, is quaint and antiquated, so that the beauty of many of its golden phrases will scarcely be perceived at the present day; but it is impossible not to be charmed with the genuine sentiment, the delightful artlessness and urbanity, which prevail throughout it. The descriptions of nature, too, with which it is embellished, are given with a truth, a discrimination, and a freshness, worthy of the most cultivated period of the arts.

As an amatory poem, it is edifying, in these days of coarser thinking, to notice the nature, refinement, and exquisite delicacy which pervade it, banishing every gross thought, or immodest expression, and presenting female loveliness clothed in all its chivalrous attributes of almost supernatural purity and grace.

James flourished nearly about the time of Chaucer and Gower, and was evidently an admirer and studier of their writings. Indeed, in one of his stanzas he acknowledges them as his masters, and in some parts of his poem we find traces of similarity to their productions, more especially to those of Chaucer. There are always, however, general features of resemblance in the works of contemporary authors, which are not so much borrowed from each other as from the times. Writers, like bees, toll their sweets in the wide world; they incorporate with their own conceptions the anecdotes and thoughts which are current in society, and thus each generation has some features in common characteristic of the age in which it lives. James, in fact, belongs to one of the most brilliant eras of our literary history, and establishes the claims of his country to a participation in its primitive honors. While a small cluster of English writers are constantly cited as the fathers of our verse, the name of their great Scottish compeer is apt to be passed over in silence; but he is evidently worthy of being enrolled in that little constellation of remote, but never-failing luminaries, who shine in the highest firmament of literature, and who, like morning stars, sang together at the bright dawning of British poesy.

Such of my readers as may not be familiar with Scottish history (though the manner in which it has of late been woven with captivating fiction has made it a universal study) may be curious to learn something of the subsequent history of James and the fortunes of his love. His passion for the Lady Jane, as it was the solace of his captivity, so it facilitated his release, it being imagined by the Court that a connection with the blood-royal of England would attach him to its own interests. He was ultimately restored to his liberty and crown, having previously espoused the Lady Jane, who accompanied him to Scotland, and made him a most tender and devoted wife.

He found his kingdom in great confusion, the feudal chieftains having taken advantage of the troubles and irregularities of a long interregnum, to strengthen themselves in their possessions, and place themselves above the power of the laws. James sought to found the basis of his power in the affections of his people. He attached the lower orders to him by the reformation of abuses, the temperate and equable administration of justice, the encouragement of the arts of peace, and the promotion of everything that could diffuse comfort, competency, and innocent enjoyment, through the humblest ranks of society. He mingled occasionally among the common people in disguise; visited their firesides; entered into their cares, their pursuits, and their amusements; informed himself of the mechanical arts, and how they could best be patronized and improved; and was thus an all-pervading spirit, watching with a benevolent eye over the meanest of his subjects. Having in this generous manner made himself strong in the hearts of the common people, he turned himself to curb the power of the factious nobility; to strip them of those dangerous immunities which they had usurped; to punish such as had been guilty of flagrant offenses; and to bring the whole into proper obedience to the crown. For some time they bore this with outward submission, but with secret impatience and brooding resentment. A conspiracy was at length formed against his life, at the head of which was his own uncle, Robert Stewart, Earl of Athol, who, being too old himself for the perpetration of the deed of blood, instigated his grandson, Sir Robert Stewart, together with Sir Robert Graham, and others of less note, to commit the deed. They broke into his bedchamber at the Dominican convent near Perth, where he was residing, and barbarously murdered him by oft-repeated wounds. His faithful queen, rushing to throw her tender body between him and the sword, was twice wounded in the ineffectual attempt to shield him from the assassins; and it was not until she had been forcibly torn from his person that the murder was accomplished.

It was the recollection of this romantic tale of former times, and of the golden little poem, which had its birthplace in this tower, that made me visit the old pile with more than common interest. The suit of armor hanging up in the hall, richly gilt and embellished, as if to figure in the tournay, brought the image of the gallant and romantic prince vividly before my imagination. I paced the deserted chambers where he had composed his poem; I leaned upon the window, and endeavored to persuade myself it was the very one where he had been visited by his vision; I looked out upon the spot where he had first seen the Lady Jane. It was the same genial and joyous month: the birds were again vying with each other in strains of liquid melody; everything was bursting into vegetation, and budding forth the tender promise of the year. Time, which delights to obliterate the sterner memorials of human pride, seems to have passed lightly over this little scene of poetry and love, and to have withheld his desolating hand. Several centuries have gone by, yet the garden still flourishes at the foot of the tower. It occupies what was once the moat of the keep, and though some parts have been separated by dividing walls, yet others have still their arbors and shaded walks, as in the days of James; and the whole is sheltered, blooming, and retired. There is a charm about the spot that has been printed by the footsteps of departed beauty, and consecrated by the inspirations of the poet, which is heightened, rather than impaired, by the lapse of ages. It is, indeed, the gift of poetry, to hallow every place in which it moves; to breathe round nature an odor more exquisite than the perfume of the rose, and to shed over it a tint more magical than the blush of morning.

Others may dwell on the illustrious deeds of James as a warrior and a legislator; but I have delighted to view him merely as the companion of his fellowmen, the benefactor of the human heart, stooping from his high estate to sow the sweet flowers of poetry and song in the paths of common life. He was the first to cultivate the vigorous and hardy plant of Scottish genius, which has since been so prolific of the most wholesome and highly flavored fruit. He carried with him into the sterner regions of the north all the fertilizing arts of southern refinement. He did everything in his power to win his countrymen to the gay, the elegant, and gentle arts which

soften and refine the character of a people, and wreathe a
grace round the loftiness of a proud and warlike spirit. He
wrote many poems, which, unfortunately for the fullness of
his fame, are now lost to the world; one, which is still preserved, called "Christ's Kirk of the Green," shows how diligently he had made himself acquainted with the rustic sports
and pastimes, which constitute such a source of kind and
social feeling among the Scottish peasantry; and with what
simple and happy humor he could enter into their enjoyments. He contributed greatly to improve the national
music; and traces of his tender sentiment and elegant taste
are said to exist in those witching airs, still piped among the
wild mountains and lonely glens of Scotland. He has thus
connected his image with whatever is most gracious and endearing in the national character; he has embalmed his
memory in song, and floated his name down to after-ages
in the rich stream of Scottish melody. The recollection of
these things was kindling at my heart, as I paced the silent
scene of his imprisonment. I have visited Vaucluse with as
much enthusiasm as a pilgrim would visit the shrine at Loretto; but I have never felt more poetical devotion than when
contemplating the old tower and the little garden at Windsor,
and musing over the romantic loves of the Lady Jane and
the Royal Poet of Scotland.

THE COUNTRY CHURCH

"A gentleman!
What o' the woolpack? or the sugar-chest?
Or lists of velvet? which is't, pound, or yard,
You vend your gentry by?"—BEGGAR'S BUSH

THERE are few places more favorable to the study of
character than an English country church. I was once passing a few weeks at the seat of a friend, who resided in the
vicinity of one, the appearance of which particularly struck

my fancy. It was one of those rich morsels of quaint antiquity which give such a peculiar charm to English landscape. It stood in the midst of a county filled with ancient families, and contained, within its cold and silent aisles, the congregated dust of many noble generations. The interior walls were incrusted with monuments of every age and style. The light streamed through windows dimmed with armorial bearings, richly emblazoned in stained glass. In various parts of the church were tombs of knights, and high-born dames, of gorgeous workmanship, with their effigies in colored marble. On every side, the eye was struck with some instance of aspiring mortality; some haughty memorial which human pride had erected over its kindred dust, in this temple of the most humble of all religions.

The congregation was composed of the neighboring people of rank, who sat in pews sumptuously lined and cushioned, furnished with richly-gilded prayer-books, and decorated with their arms upon the pew doors; of the villagers and peasantry, who filled the back seats, and a small gallery beside the organ; and of the poor of the parish, who were ranged on benches in the aisles.

The service was performed by a snuffling, well-fed vicar, who had a snug dwelling near the church. He was a privileged guest at all the tables of the neighborhood, and had been the keenest fox-hunter in the country, until age and good living had disabled him from doing anything more than ride to see the hounds throw off, and make one at the hunting dinner.

Under the ministry of such a pastor, I found it impossible to get into the train of thought suitable to the time and place; so having, like many other feeble Christians, compromised with my conscience, by laying the sin of my own delinquency at another person's threshold, I occupied myself by making observations on my neighbors.

I was as yet a stranger in England, and curious to notice the manners of its fashionable classes. I found, as usual, that there was the least pretension where there was the most

acknowledged title to respect. I was particularly struck, for
instance, with the family of a nobleman of high rank, consisting of several sons and daughters. Nothing could be
more simple and unassuming than their appearance. They
generally came to church in the plainest equipage, and often
on foot. The young ladies would stop and converse in the
kindest manner with the peasantry, caress the children, and
listen to the stories of the humble cottagers. Their countenances were open and beautifully fair, with an expression of
high refinement, but at the same time a frank cheerfulness
and engaging affability. Their brothers were tall, and ele-
gantly formed. They were dressed fashionably, but simply;
with strict neatness and propriety, but without any manner-
ism or foppishness. Their whole demeanor was easy and
natural, with that lofty grace and noble frankness which bespeak free-born souls that have never been checked in their
growth by feelings of inferiority. There is a healthful hardi-
ness about real dignity that never dreads contact and communion with others, however humble. It is only spurious
pride that is morbid and sensitive, and shrinks from every
touch. I was pleased to see the manner in which they would
converse with the peasantry about those rural concerns and
field sports in which the gentlemen of this country so much
delight. In these conversations, there was neither haughti-
ness on the one part, nor servility on the other; and you were
only reminded of the difference of rank by the habitual respect of the peasant.

In contrast to these was the family of a wealthy citizen,
who had amassed a vast fortune, and, having purchased the
estate and mansion of a ruined nobleman in the neighborhood, was endeavoring to assume all the style and dignity
of a hereditary lord of the soil. The family always came to
church *en prince*. They were rolled majestically along in a
carriage emblazoned with arms. The crest glittered in silver
radiance from every part of the harness where a crest could
possibly be placed. A fat coachman in a three-cornered hat,
richly laced, and a flaxen wig, curling close round his rosy

face, was seated on the box, with a sleek Danish dog beside
him.   Two footmen in gorgeous liveries, with huge bouquets,
and gold-headed canes, lolled behind.   The carriage rose and
sunk on its long springs with a peculiar stateliness of motion.
The very horses champed their bits, arched their necks, and
glanced their eyes more proudly than common horses; either
because they had got a little of the family feeling, or were
reined up more tightly than ordinary.

I could not but admire the style with which this splendid
pageant was brought up to the gate of the churchyard.
There was a vast effect produced at the turning of an angle
of the wall;—a great smacking of the whip; straining and
scrambling of the horses; glistening of harness, and flashing
of wheels through gravel.   This was the moment of triumph
and vainglory to the coachman.   The horses were urged
and checked, until they were fretted into a foam.   They
threw out their feet in a prancing trot, dashing about pebbles
at every step.   The crowd of villagers sauntering quietly to
church opened precipitately to the right and left, gaping in
vacant admiration.   On reaching the gate, the horses were
pulled up with a suddenness that produced an immediate
stop, and almost threw them on their haunches.

There was an extraordinary hurry of the footmen to
alight, open the door, pull down the steps, and prepare
everything for the descent on earth of this august family.
The old citizen first emerged his round red face from out the
door, looking about him with the pompous air of a man accustomed to rule on 'change, and shake the stock-market with a
nod.   His consort, a fine, fleshy, comfortable dame, followed
him.   There seemed, I must confess, but little pride in her
composition.   She was the picture of broad, honest, vulgar
enjoyment.   The world went well with her; and she liked
the world.   She had fine clothes, a fine house, a fine carriage, fine children, everything was fine about her: it was
nothing but driving about, and visiting and feasting.   Life
was to her a perpetual revel; it was one long Lord Mayor's
day.

Two daughters succeeded to this goodly couple. They certainly were handsome; but had a supercilious air that chilled admiration, and disposed the spectator to be critical. They were ultra-fashionables in dress, and, though no one could deny the richness of their decorations, yet their appropriateness might be questioned amid the simplicity of a country church. They descended loftily from the carriage, and moved up the line of peasantry with a step that seemed dainty of the soil it trod on. They cast an excursive glance around, that passed coldly over the burly faces of the peasantry, until they met the eyes of the nobleman's family, when their countenances immediately brightened into smiles, and they made the most profound and elegant courtesies, which were returned in a manner that showed they were but slight acquaintances.

I must not forget the two sons of this aspiring citizen, who came to church in a dashing curricle, with outriders. They were arrayed in the extremity of the mode with all that pedantry of dress which marks the man of questionable pretensions to style. They kept entirely by themselves, eying every one askance that came near them, as if measuring his claims to respectability; yet they were without conversation, except the exchange of an occasional cant phrase. They even moved artificially, for their bodies, in compliance with the caprice of the day, had been disciplined into the absence of all ease and freedom. Art had done everything to accomplish them as men of fashion, but Nature had denied them the nameless grace. They were vulgarly shaped, like men formed for the common purposes of life, and had that air of supercilious assumption which is never seen in the true gentleman.

I have been rather minute in drawing the pictures of these two families, because I considered them specimens of what is often to be met with in this country—the unpretending great, and the arrogant little. I have no respect for titled rank, unless it be accompanied by true nobility of soul; but I have remarked, in all countries where these artificial

distinctions exist, that the very highest classes are always
the most courteous and unassuming. Those who are well
assured of their own standing, are least apt to trespass on
that of others: whereas, nothing is so offensive as the aspirings of vulgarity, which thinks to elevate itself by humiliating its neighbor.

As I have brought these families into contrast, I must
notice their behavior in church. That of the nobleman's
family was quiet, serious, and attentive. Not that they appeared to have any fervor of devotion, but rather a respect
for sacred things and sacred places, inseparable from good-
breeding. The others, on the contrary, were in a perpetual
flutter and whisper; they betrayed a continual consciousness
of finery, and the sorry ambition of being the wonders of a
rural congregation.

The old gentleman was the only one really attentive to
the service. He took the whole burden of family devotion
upon himself; standing bolt upright, and uttering the responses with a loud voice that might be heard all over the
church. It was evident that he was one of these thorough
church and king men, who connect the idea of devotion and
loyalty; who consider the Deity, somehow or other, of the
government party, and religion "a very excellent sort of
thing, that ought to be countenanced and kept up."

When he joined so loudly in the service it seemed more
by way of example to the lower orders, to show them, that
though so great and wealthy, he was not above being religious; as I have seen a turtle-fed alderman swallow publicly
a basin of charity soup, smacking his lips at every mouthful,
and pronouncing it "excellent food for the poor."

When the service was at an end, I was curious to witness
the several exits of my groups. The young noblemen and
their sisters, as the day was fine, preferred strolling home
across the fields, chatting with the country people as they
went. The others departed as they came, in grand parade.
Again were the equipages wheeled up to the gate. There
was again the smacking of whips, the clattering of hoofs,

* * *7

and the glittering of harness. The horses started off almost
at a bound; the villagers again hurried to right and left; the
wheels threw up a cloud of dust, and the aspiring family was
wrapped out of sight in a whirlwind.

THE WIDOW AND HER SON

"Pittie olde age, within whose silver haires
Honour and reverence evermore have raigned."
—MARLOWE'S *Tamburlaine*

DURING my residence in the country I used frequently
to attend at the old village church. Its shadowy aisles, its
mouldering monuments, its dark oaken paneling, all reverend
with the gloom of departed years, seemed to fit it for the
haunt of solemn meditation. A Sunday, too, in the country,
is so holy in its repose—such a pensive quiet reigns over the
face of Nature that every restless passion is charmed down,
and we feel all the natural religion of the soul gently springing up within us.

"Sweet day, so pure, so calm, so bright,
The bridal of the earth and sky!"

I cannot lay claim to the merit of being a devout man;
but there are feelings that visit me in a country church, amid
the beautiful serenity of Nature, which I experience nowhere
else; and if not a more religious, I think I am a better man
on Sunday than on any other day of the seven.

But in this church I felt myself continually thrown back
upon the world, by the frigidity and pomp of the poor worms
around me. The only being that seemed thoroughly to feel
the humble and prostrate piety of a true Christian was a
poor decrepit old woman, bending under the weight of years
and infirmities. She bore the traces of something better than
abject poverty. The lingerings of decent pride were visible
in her appearance. Her dress, though humble in the ex-

treme, was scrupulously clean. Some trivial respect, too, had been awarded her, for she did not take her seat among the village poor, but sat alone on the steps of the altar. She seemed to have survived all love, all friendship, all society; and to have nothing left her but the hopes of heaven. When I saw her feebly rising and bending her aged form in prayer; habitually conning her prayer-book, which her palsied hand and failing eyes could not permit her to read, but which she evidently knew by heart, I felt persuaded that the faltering voice of that poor woman arose to heaven far before the responses of the clerk, the swell of the organ, or the chanting of the choir.

I am fond of loitering about country churches; and this was so delightfully situated that it frequently attracted me. It stood on a knoll, round which a small stream made a beautiful bend, and then wound its way through a long reach of soft meadow scenery. The church was surrounded by yew trees, which seemed almost coeval with itself. Its tall gothic spire shot up lightly from among them, with rooks and crows generally wheeling about it. I was seated there one still sunny morning, watching two laborers who were digging a grave. They had chosen one of the most remote and neglected corners of the churchyard, where, by the number of nameless graves around, it would appear that the indigent and friendless were huddled into the earth. I was told that the new-made grave was for the only son of a poor widow. While I was meditating on the distinctions of worldly rank, which extend thus down into the very dust, the toll of the bell announced the approach of the funeral. They were the obsequies of poverty, with which pride had nothing to do. A coffin of the plainest materials, without pall or other covering, was borne by some of the villagers. The sexton walked before with an air of cold indifference. There were no mock mourners in the trappings of affected woe, but there was one real mourner who feebly tottered after the corpse. It was the aged mother of the deceased— the poor old woman whom I had seen seated on the steps of the altar. She was supported by a humble friend, who was endeavoring to comfort her. A few of the neighboring poor had joined the train, and some children of the village were running hand in hand, now shouting with unthinking mirth, and now pausing to gaze, with childish curiosity, on the grief of the mourner.

As the funeral train approached the grave, the parson issued from the church porch, arrayed in the surplice, with prayer-book in hand, and attended by the clerk. The service, however, was a mere act of charity. The deceased had been destitute, and the survivor was penniless. It was shuffled through, therefore, in form, but coldly and unfeelingly. The well-fed priest moved but a few steps from the church door; his voice could scarcely be heard at the grave; and never did I hear the funeral service, that sublime and touching ceremony, turned into such a frigid mummery of words.

I approached the grave. The coffin was placed on the ground. On it were inscribed the name and age of the deceased—"George Somers, aged 26 years." The poor mother had been assisted to kneel down at the head of it. Her withered hands were clasped, as if in prayer; but I could perceive, by a feeble rocking of the body, and a convulsive motion of the lips, that she was gazing on the last relics of her son with the yearnings of a mother's heart.

Preparations were made to deposit the coffin in the earth. There was that bustling stir which breaks so harshly on the feelings of grief and affection: directions given in the cold tones of business; the striking of spades into sand and gravel; which, at the grave of those we love, is of all sounds the most withering. The bustle around seemed to waken the mother from a wretched reverie. She raised her glazed eyes, and looked about with a faint wildness. As the men approached with cords to lower the coffin into the grave, she wrung her hands, and broke into an agony of grief. The poor woman who attended her took her by the arm, endeavored to raise her from the earth, and to whisper something like consolation—"Nay, now—nay, now—don't take it so sorely to heart." She could only shake her head, and wring her hands, as one not to be comforted.

As they lowered the body into the earth the creaking of the cords seemed to agonize her; but when, on some accidental obstruction, there was a jostling of the coffin, all the tenderness of the mother burst forth; as if any harm could come to him who was far beyond the reach of worldly suffering.

I could see no more—my heart swelled into my throat—my eyes filled with tears—I felt as if I were acting a barbarous part in standing by and gazing idly on this scene of maternal anguish. I wandered to another part of the churchyard, where I remained until the funeral train had dispersed.

When I saw the mother slowly and painfully quitting the grave, leaving behind her the remains of all that was dear to her on earth, and returning to silence and destitution, my heart ached for her. What, thought I, are the distresses of the rich? They have friends to soothe—pleasures to beguile—a world to divert and dissipate their griefs. What are the sorrows of the young? Their growing minds soon close above the wound—their elastic spirits soon rise beneath the pressure—their green and ductile affections soon twine around new objects. But the sorrows of the poor, who have no outward appliances to soothe—the sorrows of the aged, with whom life at best is but a wintry day, and who can look for no after-growth of joy—the sorrows of a widow, aged, solitary, destitute, mourning over an only son, the last solace of her years;—these are indeed sorrows which make us feel the impotency of consolation.

It was some time before I left the churchyard. On my way homeward I met with the woman who had acted as comforter: she was just returning from accompanying her mother to her lonely habitation, and I drew from her some particulars connected with the affecting scene I had witnessed.

The parents of the deceased had resided in the village

from childhood. They had inhabited one of the neatest cottages, and by various rural occupations, and the assistance
of a small garden, had supported themselves creditably and
comfortably, and led a happy and a blameless life.   They
had one son, who had grown up to be the staff and pride of
their age.—"Oh, sir!" said the good woman, "he was such
a comely lad, so sweet-tempered, so kind to every one around
him, so dutiful to his parents!   It did one's heart good to see
him of a Sunday, dressed out in his best, so tall, so straight,
so cheery, supporting his old mother to church—for she was
always fonder of leaning on George's arm than on her good
man's; and, poor soul, she might well be proud of him, for
a finer lad there was not in the country round."

Unfortunately, the son was tempted, during a year of
scarcity and agricultural hardship, to enter into the service of
one of the small craft that plied on a neighboring river.   He
had not been long in this employ when he was entrapped by
a press-gang and carried off to sea.   His parents received
tidings of his seizure, but beyond that they could learn nothing.   It was the loss of their main prop.   The father, who
was already infirm, grew heartless and melancholy, and sunk
into his grave.   The widow, left lonely in her age and feeble-
ness, could no longer support herself, and came upon the parish.   Still there was a kind of feeling toward her throughout
the village, and a certain respect as being one of the oldest
inhabitants.   As no one applied for the cottage in which she
had passed so many happy days, she was permitted to remain in it, where she lived solitary and almost helpless.   The
few wants of nature were chiefly supplied from the scanty
productions of her little garden, which the neighbors would
now and then cultivate for her.   It was but a few days before the time at which these circumstances were told me,
that she was gathering some vegetables for her repast, when
she heard the cottage door which faced the garden suddenly
opened.   A stranger came out, and seemed to be looking
eagerly and wildly around.   He was dressed in seamen's
clothes, was emaciated and ghastly pale, and bore the air

of one broken by sickness and hardships. He saw her, and
hastened toward her, but his steps were faint and faltering;
he sank on his knees before her, and sobbed like a child.
The poor woman gazed upon him with a vacant and wandering eye—"Oh, my dear, dear mother! don't you know your
son? your poor boy George?" It was, indeed, the wreck of
her once noble lad; who, shattered by wounds, by sickness,
and foreign imprisonment, had, at length, dragged his
wasted limbs homeward, to repose among the scenes of
his childhood.

I will not attempt to detail the particulars of such a meeting, where sorrow and joy were so completely blended: still
he was alive!—he was come home!—he might yet live to
comfort and cherish her old age! Nature, however, was exhausted in him; and if anything had been wanting to finish
the work of fate, the desolation of his native cottage would
have been sufficient. He stretched himself on the pallet on
which his widowed mother had passed many a sleepless
night, and he never rose from it again.

The villagers, when they heard that George Somers had
returned, crowded to see him, offering every comfort and
assistance that their humble means afforded. He was too
weak, however, to talk—he could only look his thanks. His
mother was his constant attendant; and he seemed unwilling
to be helped by any other hand.

There is something in sickness that breaks down the pride
of manhood; that softens the heart, and brings it back to the
feelings of infancy. Who that has languished, even in advanced life, in sickness and despondency; who that has pined
on a weary bed in the neglect and loneliness of a foreign land;
but has thought on the mother "that looked on his childhood," that smoothed his pillow, and administered to his
helplessness? Oh! there is an enduring tenderness in the
love of a mother to a son that transcends all other affections
of the heart. It is neither to be chilled by selfishness, nor
daunted by danger, nor weakened by worthlessness, nor
stifled by ingratitude. She will sacrifice every comfort to

his convenience; she will surrender every pleasure to his enjoyment, she will glory in his fame, and exult in his prosperity;—and, if misfortune overtake him, he will be the dearer to her from misfortune; and if disgrace settle upon his name, she will still love and cherish him in spite of his disgrace; and if all the world beside cast him off, she will be all the world to him.

Poor George Somers had known what it was to be in sickness, and none to soothe—lonely and in prison, and none to visit him. He could not endure his mother from his sight; if she moved away, his eye would follow her. She would sit for hours by his bed, watching him as he slept. Sometimes he would start from a feverish dream, and looking anxiously up until he saw her bending over him, when he would take her hand, lay it on his bosom, and fall asleep with the tranquillity of a child. In this way he died.

My first impulse, on hearing this humble tale of affliction, was to visit the cottage of the mourner, and administer pecuniary assistance, and, if possible, comfort. I found, however, on inquiry, that the good feelings of the villagers had prompted them to do everything that the case admitted; and as the poor know best how to console each other's sorrows, I did not venture to intrude.

The next Sunday I was at the village church; when, to my surprise, I saw the poor old woman tottering down the aisle to her accustomed seat on the steps of the altar.

She had made an effort to put on something like mourning for her son; and nothing could be more touching than this struggle between pious affection and utter poverty: a black ribbon or so—a faded black handkerchief—and one or two more such humble attempts to express by outward signs that grief which passes show.—When I looked round upon the storied monuments, the stately hatchments, the cold marble pomp, with which grandeur mourned magnificently over departed pride, and turned to this poor widow, bowed down by age and sorrow at the altar of her God, and offering up the prayers and praises of a pious, though a broken heart, I felt that this living monument of real grief was worth them all.

I related her story to some of the wealthy members of the congregation, and they were moved by it. They exerted themselves to render her situation more comfortable, and to lighten her afflictions. It was, however, but smoothing a few steps to the grave. In the course of a Sunday or two after she was missed from her usual seat at church, and before I left the neighborhood I heard, with a feeling of satisfaction, that she had quietly breathed her last, and had gone to rejoin those she loved, in that world where sorrow is never known and friends are never parted.

THE BOAR'S HEAD TAVERN, EAST-CHEAP

A SHAKESPEARIAN RESEARCH

"A tavern is the rendezvous, the exchange, the staple of good fellows. I have heard my great-grandfather tell, how his great-great-grandfather should say, that it was an old proverb when his great-grandfather was a child, that 'it was a good wind that blew a man to the wine.'"—MOTHER BOMBIE

IT is a pious custom, in some Catholic countries, to honor the memory of saints by votive lights burned before their pictures. The popularity of a saint, therefore, may be known by the number of these offerings. One, perhaps, is left to moulder in the darkness of his little chapel; another may have a solitary lamp to throw its blinking rays athwart his effigy; while the whole blaze of adoration is lavished at the shrine of some beatified father of renown. The wealthy devotee brings his huge luminary of wax; the eager zealot, his seven-branched candlestick; and even the mendicant pilgrim is by no means satisfied that sufficient light is thrown upon the deceased, unless he hangs up his little lamp of smoking oil. The consequence is, in the eagerness to enlighten, they are often apt to obscure; and I have occasionally seen an unlucky saint almost smoked out of countenance by the officiousness of his followers.

In like manner has it fared with the immortal Shakespeare. Every writer considers it his bounden duty to light up some portion of his character or works, and to rescue some merit from oblivion. The commentator, opulent in words, produces vast tomes of dissertations; the common herd of editors send up mists of obscurity from their notes at the bottom of each page; and every casual scribbler brings his farthing rush-light of eulogy or research, to swell the cloud of incense and of smoke.

As I honor all established usages of my brethren of the quill, I thought it but proper to contribute my mite of homage to the memory of the illustrious bard. I was for some time, however, sorely puzzled in what way I should discharge this duty. I found myself anticipated in every attempt at a new reading; every doubtful line had been explained a dozen different ways, and perplexed beyond the reach of elucidation; and as to fine passages, they had all been amply praised by previous admirers: nay, so completely had the bard, of late, been overlarded with panegyric by a great German critic that it was difficult now to find even a fault that had not been argued into a beauty.

In this perplexity, I was one morning turning over his pages, when I casually opened upon the comic scenes of Henry IV., and was, in a moment, completely lost in the madcap revelry of the Boar's Head Tavern. So vividly and naturally are these scenes of humor depicted, and with such force and consistency are the characters sustained, that they become mingled up in the mind with the facts and personages of real life. To few readers does it occur that these are all ideal creations of a poet's brain, and that, in sober truth, no such knot of merry roisterers ever enlivened the dull neighborhood of Eastcheap.

For my part, I love to give myself up to the illusions of

poetry. A hero of fiction that never existed is just as valuable to me as a hero of history that existed a thousand years
since; and, if I may be excused such an insensibility to the
common ties of human nature, I would not give up fat Jack
for half the great men of ancient chronicle. What have the
heroes of yore done for me, or men like me? They have
conquered countries of which I do not enjoy an acre; or they
have gained laurels of which I do not inherit a leaf; or they
have furnished examples of hare-brained prowess which I
have neither the opportunity nor the inclination to follow.
But old Jack Falstaff!—kind Jack Falstaff!—sweet Jack
Falstaff! has enlarged the boundaries of human enjoyment;
he has added vast regions of wit and good-humor, in which
the poorest man may revel; and has bequeathed a never-failing inheritance of jolly laughter to make mankind merrier
and better to the latest posterity.

A thought suddenly struck me: "I will make a pilgrimage to Eastcheap," said I, closing the book, "and see if the
old Boar's Head Tavern still exists. Who knows but I may
light upon some legendary traces of Dame Quickly and her
guests; at any rate, there will be a kindred pleasure, in
treading the halls once vocal with their mirth, to that the
toper enjoys in smelling to the empty cask, once filled with
generous wine."

The resolution was no sooner formed than put in execution. I forbear to treat of the various adventures and wonders I encountered in my travels, of the haunted regions of
Cock Lane; of the faded glories of Little Britain, and the
parts adjacent; what perils I ran in Cateaton Street and Old
Jewry; of the renowned Guildhall and its two stunted
giants, the pride and wonder of the city, and the terror of all
unlucky urchins; and how I visited London Stone, and
struck my staff upon it, in imitation of that arch-rebel, Jack
Cade.

Let it suffice to say that I at length arrived in merry Eastcheap, that ancient region of wit and wassail, where the very
names of the streets relished of good cheer, as Pudding Lane

bears testimony even at the present day. For Eastcheap, says old Stow, "was always famous for its convivial doings. The cookes cried hot ribbes of beef roasted, pies well baked, and other victuals; there was clattering of pewter pots, harpe, pipe, and sawtrie." Alas! how sadly is the scene changed since the roaring days of Falstaff and old Stow! The madcap roisterer has given place to the plodding tradesman; the clattering of pots and the sound of "harpe and sawtrie," to the din of carts and the accursed dinging of the dustman's bell; and no song is heard, save, haply, the strain of some siren from Billingsgate, chanting the eulogy of deceased mackerel.

I sought, in vain, for the ancient abode of Dame Quickly. The only relic of it is a boar's head, carved in relief stone, which formerly served as the sign, but, at present, is built into the parting line of two houses which stand on the site of the renowned old tavern.

For the history of this little empire of good fellowship, I was referred to a tallow-chandler's widow, opposite, who had been born and brought up on the spot, and was looked up to as the indisputable chronicler of the neighborhood. I found her seated in a little back parlor, the window of which looked out upon a yard about eight feet square, laid out as a flower-garden; while a glass door opposite afforded a distant peep of the street, through a vista of soap and tallow candles; the two views, which comprised, in all probability, her prospects in life, and the little world in which she had lived, and moved, and had her being, for the better part of a century.

To be versed in the history of Eastcheap, great and little, from London Stone even unto the Monument, was, doubtless, in her opinion, to be acquainted with the history of the universe. Yet, with all this, she possessed the simplicity of true wisdom, and that liberal, communicative disposition which I have generally remarked in intelligent old ladies, knowing in the concerns of their neighborhood.

Her information, however, did not extend far back into antiquity. She could throw no light upon the history of the

Boar's Head, from the time that Dame Quickly espoused the valiant Pistol, until the great fire of London, when it was unfortunately burned down. It was soon rebuilt, and continued to flourish under the old name and sign, until a dying landlord, struck with remorse for double scores, bad measures, and other iniquities which are incident to the sinful race of publicans, endeavored to make his peace with Heaven, by bequeathing the tavern to St. Michael's Church, Crooked Lane, toward the supporting of a chaplain. For some time the vestry meetings were regularly held there; but it was observed that the old Boar never held up his head under church government. He gradually declined, and finally gave his last gasp about thirty years since. The tavern was then turned into shops; but she informed me that a picture of it was still preserved in St. Michael's Church, which stood just in the rear. To get a sight of this picture was now my determination; so, having informed myself of the abode of the sexton, I took my leave of the venerable chronicler of Eastcheap, my visit having doubtless raised greatly her opinion of her legendary lore, and furnished an important incident in the history of her life.

It cost me some difficulty, and much curious inquiry, to ferret out the humble hanger-on to the church. I had to explore Crooked Lane, and divers little alleys, and elbows, and dark passages, with which this old city is perforated, like an ancient cheese or a worm-eaten chest of drawers. At length I traced him to a corner of a small court, surrounded by lofty houses, where the inhabitants enjoy about as much of the face of heaven as a community of frogs at the bottom of a well. The sexton was a meek, acquiescing little man, of a bowing, lowly habit; yet he had a pleasant twinkling in his eye, and if encouraged, would now and then venture a small pleasantry; such as a man of his low estate might venture to make in the company of high church wardens, and other mighty men of the earth. I found him in company with the deputy organist, seated apart, like Milton's angels; discoursing, no doubt, on high doctrinal points, and settling the affairs of the church over a friendly pot of ale; for the lower classes of English seldom deliberate on any weighty matter without the assistance of a cool tankard to clear their understandings. I arrived at the moment when they had finished their ale and their argument, and were about to repair to the church to put it in order; so, having made known my wishes, I received their gracious permission to accompany them.

The church of St. Michael's, Crooked Lane, standing a short distance from Billingsgate, is enriched with the tombs of many fishmongers of renown; and as every profession has its galaxy of glory, and its constellation of great men, I presume the monument of a mighty fishmonger of the olden time is regarded with as much reverence by succeeding generations of the craft as poets feel on contemplating the tomb of Virgil, or soldiers the monument of a Marlborough or Turenne.

I cannot but turn aside, while thus speaking of illustrious men, to observe that St. Michael's, Crooked Lane, contains also the ashes of that doughty champion, William Walworth, Knight, who so manfully clove down the sturdy wight, Wat Tyler, in Smithfield; a hero worthy of honorable blazon, as almost the only Lord Mayor on record famous for deeds of arms; the sovereigns of Cockney being generally renowned as the most pacific of all potentates.[*]

---

[*] The following was the ancient inscription on the monument of this worthy, which, unhappily, was destroyed in the great conflagration:

> "Hereunder lyth a man of fame,
> William Walworth callyd by name;
> Fishmonger he was in lyfftime here,
> And twise Lord Maior, as in books appeare;
> Who, with courage stout and manly myght,
> Slew Jack Straw in Kyng Richard's sight,
> For which act done, and trew entent,
> The Kyng made him knyght incontinent;
> And gave him armes, as here you see,
> To declare his fact and chivaldrie:

Adjoining the church, in a small cemetery, immediately under the back windows of what was once the Boar's Head, stands the tombstone of Robert Preston, whilom drawer at the tavern. It is now nearly a century since this trusty drawer of good liquor closed his bustling career, and was thus quietly deposited within call of his customers. As I was clearing away the weeds from his epitaph, the little sexton drew me on one side with a mysterious air, and informed me, in a low voice, that once upon a time, on a dark wintry night, when the wind was unruly, howling and whistling, banging about doors and windows, and twirling weathercocks, so that the living were frightened out of their beds, and even the dead could not sleep quietly in their graves, the ghost of honest Preston, which happened to be airing itself in the churchyard, was attracted by the well-known call of "waiter," from the Boar's Head, and made its sudden appearance in the midst of a roaring club, just as the parish clerk was singing a stave from the "mirrie garland of Captain Death"; to the discomfiture of sundry train-band captains, and the conversion of an infidel attorney, who became a zealous Christian on the spot, and was never known to twist the truth afterward, except in the way of business.

I beg it may be remembered that I do not pledge myself for the authenticity of this anecdote; though it is well known that the churchyards and by-corners of this old metropolis are very much infested with perturbed spirits; and every one

---

He left this lyff the year of our God
Thirteen hondred fourscore and three odd."

An error in the foregoing inscription has been corrected by the venerable Stow: "Whereas," saith he, "it hath been far spread abroad by vulgar opinion, that the rebel smitten down so manfully by Sir William Walworth, the then worthy Lord Maior, was named Jack Straw, and not Wat Tyler, I thought good to reconcile this rash conceived doubt by such testimony as I find in ancient and good records. The principal leaders, or captains, of the commons, were Wat Tyler, as the first man; the second was John, or Jack Straw, etc., etc."—STOW's London.

must have heard of the Cock Lane ghost, and the apparition that guards the regalia in the Tower, which has frightened so many bold sentinels almost out of their wits.

Be all this as it may, this Robert Preston seems to have been a worthy successor to the nimble-tongued Francis, who attended upon the revels of Prince Hal; to have been equally prompt with his "anon, anon, sir," and to have transcended his predecessor in honesty; for Falstaff, the veracity of whose taste no man will venture to impeach, flatly accuses Francis of putting lime in his sack; whereas, honest Preston's epitaph lauds him for the sobriety of his conduct, the soundness of his wine, and the fairness of his measure.* The worthy dignitaries of the church, however, did not appear much captivated by the sober virtues of the tapster: the deputy organist, who had a moist look out of the eye, made some shrewd remark on the abstemiousness of a man brought up among full hogsheads; and the little sexton corroborated his opinion by a significant wink and a dubious shake of the head.

Thus far my researches, though they threw much light on the history of tapsters, fishmongers, and Lord Mayors, yet disappointed me in the great object of my quest, the picture of the Boar's Head Tavern. No such painting was to be found in the church of St. Michael's. "Marry and amen!" said I, "here endeth my research!" So I was giv-

---

* As this inscription is rife with excellent morality, I transcribe it for the admonition of delinquent tapsters. It is, no doubt, the production of some choice spirit who once frequented the Boar's Head.

"Bacchus, to give the toping world surprise,
Produced one sober son, and here he lies.
Though rear'd among full hogsheads, he defied
The charms of wine, and every one beside.
O reader, if to justice thou'rt inclined,
Keep honest Preston daily in thy mind.
He drew good wine, took care to fill his pots,
Had sundry virtues that excused his faults.
You that on Bacchus have the like dependence,
Pray copy Bob, in measure and attendance."

ing the matter up, with the air of a baffled antiquary, when my friend the sexton, perceiving me to be curious in everything relative to the old tavern, offered to show me the choice vessels of the vestry, which had been handed down from remote times, when the parish meetings were held at the Boar's Head. These were deposited in the parish club-room, which had been transferred, on the decline of the ancient establishment, to a tavern in the neighborhood.

A few steps brought us to the house, which stands No. 12, Mile Lane, bearing the title of The Mason's Arms, and is kept by Master Edward Honeyball, the "bully-rock" of the establishment. It is one of those little taverns which abound in the heart of the city, and form the center of gossip and intelligence of the neighborhood. We entered the bar-room, which was narrow and darkling; for in these close lanes but few rays of reflected light are enabled to struggle down to the inhabitants, whose broad day is at best but a tolerable twilight. The room was partitioned into boxes, each containing a table spread with a clean white cloth, ready for dinner. This showed that the guests were of the good old stamp, and divided their day equally, for it was but just one o'clock. At the lower end of the room was a clear coal fire, before which a breast of lamb was roasting. A row of bright brass candlesticks and pewter mugs glistened along the mantel-piece, and an old-fashioned clock ticked in one corner. There was something primitive in this medley of kitchen, parlor, and hall, that carried me back to earlier times, and pleased me. The place, indeed, was humble, but everything had that look of order and neatness which be-speaks the superintendence of a notable English housewife. A group of amphibious-looking beings, who might be either fishermen or sailors, were regaling themselves in one of the boxes. As I was a visitor of rather higher pretensions, I was ushered into a little misshapen back room, having at least nine corners. It was lighted by a skylight, furnished with antiquated leathern chairs, and ornamented with the portrait of a fat pig. It was evidently appropriated to par-

ticular customers, and I found a shabby gentleman, in a red
nose and oil-cloth hat, seated in one corner, meditating on a
half-empty pot of porter.

The old sexton had taken the landlady aside, and with an
air of profound importance imparted to her my errand.   Dame
Honeyball was a likely, plump, bustling little woman, and
no bad substitute for that paragon of hostesses, Dame
Quickly.   She seemed delighted with an opportunity to
oblige; and hurrying upstairs to the archives of her house,
where the precious vessels of the parish club were deposited,
she returned, smiling and courtesying, with them in her
hands.

The first she presented me was a japanned iron tobacco-
box, of gigantic size, out of which, I was told, the vestry
had smoked at their stated meetings since time immemorial;
and which was never suffered to be profaned by vulgar
hands, or used on common occasions.   I received it with becoming reverence; but what was my delight at beholding on
its cover the identical painting of which I was in quest!
There was displayed the outside of the Boar's Head Tavern,
and before the door was to be seen the whole convivial group,
at table, in full revel, pictured with that wonderful fidelity
and force with which the portraits of renowned generals and
commodores are illustrated on tobacco-boxes, for the benefit
of posterity.   Lest, however, there should be any mistake,
the cunning limner had warily inscribed the names of Prince
Hal and Falstaff on the bottoms of their chairs.

On the inside of the cover was an inscription, nearly obliterated, recording that this box was the gift of Sir Richard
Gore, for the use of the vestry meetings at the Boar's Head
Tavern, and that it was "repaired and beautified by his successor, Mr. John Packard, 1767."   Such is a faithful description of this august and venerable relic, and I question whether
the learned Scriblerius contemplated his Roman shield, or the
Knights of the Round Table the long-sought sangreal, with
more exultation.

While I was meditating on it with enraptured gaze, Dame

Honeyball, who was highly gratified by the interest it excited, put in my hands a drinking cup or goblet, which also
belonged to the vestry, and was descended from the old
Boar's Head. It bore the inscription of having been the gift
of Francis Wythers, Knight, and was held, she told me, in
exceeding great value, being considered very "antyke."
This last opinion was strengthened by the shabby gentleman
with the red nose and oil-cloth hat, and whom I strongly suspected of being a lineal descendant from the valiant Bar-
dolph. He suddenly aroused from his meditation on the pot
of porter, and, casting a knowing look at the goblet, exclaimed, "Ay, ay, the head don't ache now that made that
there article."

The great importance attached to this memento of ancient revelry by modern churchwardens at first puzzled me;
but there is nothing sharpens the apprehension so much as
antiquarian research; for I immediately perceived that this
could be no other than the identical "parcel-gilt goblet" on
which Falstaff made his loving but faithless vow to Dame
Quickly; and which would, of course, be treasured up with
care among the regalia of her domains as a testimony of that
solemn contract.*

Mine hostess, indeed, gave me a long history how the
goblet had been handed down from generation to generation.
She also entertained me with many particulars concerning
the worthy vestrymen who have seated themselves thus
quietly on the stools of the ancient roisterers of Eastcheap,
and, like so many commentators, utter clouds of smoke in
honor of Shakespeare. These I forbear to relate, lest my
readers should not be as curious in these matters as myself.
Suffice it to say, the neighbors, one and all, about Eastcheap,

---

* "Thou didst swear to me upon a *parcel-gilt goblet*, sitting in my
Dolphin Chamber, at the round table, by a sea-coal fire, on Wednesday
in Whitsun-week, when the Prince broke thy head for likening his
father to a singing man of Windsor; thou didst swear to me then, as I
was washing thy wound, to marry me, and make me my lady, thy
wife. Canst thou deny it?"—*Henry IV., Part 2.*

believe that Falstaff and his merry crew actually lived and reveled there. Nay, there are several legendary anecdotes concerning him still extant among the oldest frequenters of the Mason's Arms, which they give as transmitted down from their forefathers; and Mr. M'Kash, an Irish hairdresser, whose shop stands on the site of the old Boar's Head, has several dry jokes of Fat Jack's, not laid down in the books, with which he makes his customers ready to die of laughter.

I now turned to my friend the sexton to make some further inquiries, but I found him sunk in pensive meditation. His head had declined a little on one side; a deep sigh heaved from the very bottom of his stomach, and, though I could not see a tear trembling in his eye, yet a moisture was evidently stealing from a corner of his mouth. I followed the direction of his eye through the door which stood open, and found it fixed wistfully on the savory breast of lamb, roasting in dripping richness before the fire.

I now called to mind, that in the eagerness of my recondite investigation I was keeping the poor man from his dinner. My bowels yearned with sympathy, and, putting in his hand a small token of my gratitude and good-will, I departed with a hearty benediction on him, Dame Honeyball, and the parish club of Crooked Lane—not forgetting my shabby but sententious friend in the oil-cloth hat and copper nose.

Thus have I given a "tedious brief" account of this interesting research; for which, if it prove too short and unsatisfactory, I can only plead my inexperience in this branch of literature, so deservedly popular at the present day. I am aware that a more skillful illustrator of the immortal bard would have swelled the materials I have touched upon to a good merchantable bulk, comprising the biographies of William Walworth, Jack Straw, and Robert Preston; some notice of the eminent fishmongers of St. Michael's; the history of Eastcheap, great and little; private anecdotes of Dame Honeyball and her pretty daughter, whom I have not even mentioned: to say nothing of a damsel tending the breast of lamb (and whom, by the way, I remarked to be a comely lass, with a neat foot and ankle); the whole enlivened by the riots of Wat Tyler, and illuminated by the great fire of London.

All this I leave as a rich mine, to be worked by future commentators; nor do I despair of seeing the tobacco-box and the "parcel-gilt goblet," which I have thus brought to light, the subject of future engravings, and almost as fruitful of voluminous dissertations and disputes as the shield of Achilles, or the far-famed Portland vase.

THE MUTABILITY OF LITERATURE

A COLLOQUY IN WESTMINSTER ABBEY

> "I know that all beneath the moon decays,
> And what by mortals in this world is brought,
> In time's great periods shall return to naught,
> I know that all the muses' heavenly layes,
> With toil of sprite which are so dearly bought,
> As idle sounds of few or none are sought,
> That there is nothing lighter than mere praise."
> —DRUMMOND OF HAWTHORNDEN

THERE are certain half-dreaming moods of mind, in which we naturally steal away from noise and glare, and seek some quiet haunt, where we may indulge our reveries and build our air castles undisturbed. In such a mood, I was loitering about the old gray cloisters of Westminster Abbey, enjoying that luxury of wandering thought which one is apt to dignify with the name of reflection; when suddenly an irruption of madcap boys from Westminster school, playing at football, broke in upon the monastic stillness of the place, making the vaulted passages and mouldering tombs echo with their merriment. I sought to take refuge from their noise by penetrating still deeper into the solitudes of

the pile, and applied to one of the vergers for admission to
the library. He conducted me through a portal rich with
the crumbling sculpture of former ages, which opened upon
a gloomy passage leading to the Chapter House, and the
chamber in which Doomsday Book is deposited. Just within
the passage is a small door on the left. To this the verger
applied a key; it was double locked, and opened with some
difficulty, as if seldom used. We now ascended a dark narrow staircase, and passing through a second door, entered
the library.

I found myself in a lofty antique hall, the roof supported
by massive joists of old English oak. It was soberly lighted
by a row of gothic windows at a considerable height from
the floor, and which apparently opened upon the roofs of the
cloisters. An ancient picture of some reverend dignitary of
the church in his robes hung over the fireplace. Around the
hall and in a small gallery were the books, arranged in carved
oaken cases. They consisted principally of old polemical
writers, and were much more worn by time than use. In
the center of the library was a solitary table, with two or
three books on it, an inkstand without ink, and a few pens
parched by long disuse. The place seemed fitted for quiet
study and profound meditation. It was buried deep among
the massive walls of the abbey, and shut up from the tumult
of the world. I could only hear now and then the shouts of
the schoolboys faintly swelling from the cloisters, and the
sound of a bell tolling for prayers, that echoed soberly along
the roofs of the abbey. By degrees the shouts of merriment
grew fainter and fainter, and at length died away. The bell
ceased to toll, and a profound silence reigned through the
dusky hall.

I had taken down a little thick quarto, curiously bound
in parchment, with brass clasps, and seated myself at the
table in a venerable elbow-chair. Instead of reading, however, I was beguiled by the solemn monastic air and lifeless
quiet of the place, into a train of musing. As I looked
around upon the old volumes in their mouldering covers, thus

ranged on the shelves, and apparently never disturbed in
their repose, I could not but consider the library a kind of
literary catacomb, where authors, like mummies, are piously
entombed, and left to blacken and moulder in dusty oblivion.

How much, thought I, has each of these volumes, now
thrust aside with such indifference, cost some aching head—
how many weary days! how many sleepless nights! How
have their authors buried themselves in the solitude of
cells and cloisters; shut themselves up from the face of
man, and the still more blessed face of Nature; and devoted
themselves to painful research and intense reflection! And
all for what? to occupy an inch of dusty shelf—to have the
titles of their works read now and then in a future age, by
some drowsy churchman, or casual straggler like myself;
and in another age to be lost even to remembrance. Such is
the amount of this boasted immortality. A mere temporary
rumor, a local sound; like the tone of that bell which has
just tolled among these towers, filling the ear for a moment
—lingering transiently in echo—and then passing away, like
a thing that was not!

While I sat half-murmuring, half-meditating these unprofitable speculations, with my head resting on my hand, I
was thrumming with the other hand upon the quarto, until
I accidentally loosened the clasps; when, to my utter astonishment, the little book gave two or three yawns, like one
awaking from a deep sleep; then a husky hem, and at length
began to talk. At first its voice was very hoarse and broken,
being much troubled by a cobweb which some studious spider
had woven across it; and having probably contracted a cold
from long exposure to the chills and damps of the abbey. In
a short time, however, it became more distinct, and I soon
found it an exceedingly fluent conversable little tome. Its
language, to be sure, was rather quaint and obsolete, and its
pronunciation what in the present day would be deemed barbarous; but I shall endeavor, as far as I am able, to render
it in modern parlance.

It began with railings about the neglect of the world—

about merit being suffered to languish in obscurity, and other such commonplace topics of literary repining, and complained bitterly that it had not been opened for more than two centuries;—that the Dean only looked now and then into the library, sometimes took down a volume or two, trifled with them for a few moments, and then returned them to their shelves.

"What a plague do they mean," said the little quarto, which I began to perceive was somewhat choleric, "what a plague do they mean by keeping several thousand volumes of us shut up here, and watched by a set of old vergers, like so many beauties in a harem, merely to be looked at now and then by the Dean? Books were written to give pleasure and to be enjoyed; and I would have a rule passed that the Dean should pay each of us a visit at least once a year; or if he is not equal to the task, let them once in a while turn loose the whole school of Westminster among us, that at any rate we may now and then have an airing."

"Softly, my worthy friend," replied I, "you are not aware how much better you are off than most books of your generation. By being stored away in this ancient library you are like the treasured remains of those saints and monarchs which lie enshrined in the adjoining chapels; while the remains of their contemporary mortals, left to the ordinary course of nature, have long since returned to dust."

"Sir," said the little tome, ruffling his leaves and looking big, "I was written for all the world, not for the bookworms of an abbey. I was intended to circulate from hand to hand, like other great contemporary works; but here have I been clasped up for more than two centuries, and might have silently fallen a prey to these worms that are playing the very vengeance with my intestines, if you had not by chance given me an opportunity of uttering a few last words before I go to pieces."

"My good friend," rejoined I, "had you been left to the circulation of which you speak you would long ere this have been no more. To judge from your physiognomy, you are now well stricken in years; very few of your contemporaries can be at present in existence; and those few owe their longevity to being immured like yourself in old libraries; which, suffer me to add, instead of likening to harems, you might more properly and gratefully have compared to those infirmaries attached to religious establishments for the benefit of the old and decrepit, and where, by quiet fostering and no employment, they often endure to an amazingly good-for-nothing old age. You talk of your contemporaries as if in circulation—where do we meet with their works?—what do we hear of Robert Groteste of Lincoln? No one could have toiled harder than he for immortality. He is said to have written nearly two hundred volumes. He built, as it were, a pyramid of books to perpetuate his name; but, alas! the pyramid has long since fallen, and only a few fragments are scattered in various libraries, where they are scarcely disturbed even by the antiquarian. What do we hear of Giraldus Cambrensis, the historian, antiquary, philosopher, theologian, and poet? He declined two bishoprics that he might shut himself up and write for posterity; but posterity never inquires after his labors. What of Henry of Huntingdon, who, besides a learned history of England, wrote a treatise on the contempt of the world, which the world has revenged by forgetting him? What is quoted of Joseph of Exeter, styled the miracle of his age in classical composition? Of his three great heroic poems, one is lost forever, excepting a mere fragment; the others are known only to a few of the curious in literature; and as to his love verses and epigrams, they have entirely disappeared. What is in current use of John Wallis, the Franciscan, who acquired the name of the tree of life?—of William of Malmsbury; of Simeon of Durham; of Benedict of Peterborough; of John Hanvill of St. Albans; of—"

"Prithee, friend," cried the quarto in a testy tone, "how old do you think me? You are talking of authors that lived long before my time, and wrote either in Latin or French, so that they in a manner expatriated themselves, and de-

served to be forgotten;* but I, sir, was ushered into the
world from the press of the renowned Wynkyn de Worde.
I was written in my own native tongue, at a time when the
language had become fixed; and, indeed, I was considered
a model of pure and elegant English."

[I should observe that these remarks were couched in
such intolerably antiquated terms that I have had infinite
difficulty in rendering them into modern phraseology.]

"I cry you mercy," said I, "for mistaking your age; but
it matters little; almost all the writers of your time have
likewise passed into forgetfulness; and De Worde's publica-
tions are mere literary rarities among book-collectors. The
purity and stability of language, too, on which you found
your claims to perpetuity, have been the fallacious dependence of authors of every age, even back to the times of the
worthy Robert of Gloucester, who wrote his history in
rhymes of mongrel Saxon.† Even now many talk of
Spenser's 'well of pure English undefiled,' as if the language ever sprang from a well or fountain-head, and was
not rather a mere confluence of various tongues, perpetually
subject to changes and intermixtures. It is this which has
made English literature so extremely mutable, and the reputation built upon it so fleeting. Unless thought can be committed to something more permanent and unchangeable than

---

* "In Latin and French hath many soueraine wittes had great delyte
to endyte, and haue many noble things fulfilde, but certes there ben
some that speaken their poisye in French, of which speche the Frenchmen have as good a fantasye as we have in hearing of Frenchmen's
Englishe."—CHAUCER'S *Testament of Love*.

† Holinshed, in his "Chronicle," observes, "afterwards, also, by diligent travell of Geffry Chaucer and John Gowrie, in the time of Richard
the Second, and after them of John Scogan and John Lydgate, monke
of Berrie, our said toong was brought to an excellent passe, notwithstanding that it never came unto the type of perfection until the
time of Queen Elizabeth, wherein John Jewell, Bishop of Sarum, John
Fox, and sundrie learned and excellent writers, have fully accomplished
the ornature of the same, to their great praise and immortal commen-
dation."

such a medium, even thought must share the fate of everything else, and fall into decay. This should serve as a check upon the vanity and exultation of the most popular writer. He finds the language in which he has embarked his fame gradually altering, and subject to the dilapidations of time and the caprice of fashion. He looks back, and beholds the early authors of his country, once the favorites of their day, supplanted by modern writers: a few short ages have covered them with obscurity, and their merits can only be relished by the quaint taste of the bookworm. And such, he anticipates, will be the fate of his own work, which, however it may be admired in its day, and held up as a model of purity, will, in the course of years, grow antiquated and obsolete, until it shall become almost as unintelligible in its native land as an Egyptian obelisk, or one of those Runic inscriptions, said to exist in the deserts of Tartary. I declare," added I, with some emotion, "when I contemplate a modern library, filled with new works in all the bravery of rich gilding and binding, I feel disposed to sit down and weep; like the good Xerxes, when he surveyed his army, pranked out in all the splendor of military array, and reflected that in one hundred years not one of them would be in existence!"

"Ah," said the little quarto, with a heavy sigh, "I see how it is; these modern scribblers have superseded all the good old authors. I suppose nothing is read nowadays but Sir Philip Sidney's "Arcadia," Sackville's stately plays and "Mirror for Magistrates," or the fine spun euphuisms of the 'unparalleled John Lyly.' "

"There you are again mistaken," said I; "the writers whom you suppose in vogue, because they happened to be so when you were last in circulation, have long since had their day. Sir Philip Sidney's "Arcadia," the immortality of which was so fondly predicted by his admirers,* and which, in

---

* "Live ever sweete booke; the simple image of his gentle witt and the golden pillar of his noble courage; and ever notify unto the world that thy writer was the secretary of eloquence, the breath of the muses,

truth, was full of noble thoughts, delicate images, and grace-ful turns of language, is now scarcely ever mentioned. Sack-ville has strutted into obscurity; and even Lyly, though his writings were once the delight of a court, and apparently perpetuated by a proverb, is now scarcely known even by name. A whole crowd of authors who wrote and wrangled at the time have likewise gone down with all their writings and their controversies. Wave after wave of succeeding literature has rolled over them, until they are buried so deep that it is only now and then that some industrious diver after fragments of antiquity brings up a specimen for the gratifi-cation of the curious.

"For my part," I continued, "I consider this mutability of language a wise precaution of Providence for the benefit of the world at large, and of authors in particular. To rea-son from analogy: we daily behold the varied and beautiful tribes of vegetables springing up, flourishing, adorning the fields for a short time, and then fading into dust, to make way for their successors. Were not this the case, the fecun-dity of nature would be a grievance instead of a blessing: the earth would groan with rank and excessive vegetation, and its surface become a tangled wilderness. In like man-ner the works of genius and learning decline and make way for subsequent productions. Language gradually varies, and with it fade away the writings of authors who have flourished their allotted time; otherwise the creative powers of genius would overstock the world, and the mind would be completely bewildered in the endless mazes of literature. Formerly there were some restraints on this excessive multi-plication: works had to be transcribed by hand, which was a slow and laborious operation; they were written either on parchment, which was expensive, so that one work was often

---

the honey bee of the daintyest flowers of witt and arte, the pith of morale and the intellectual virtues, the arme of Bellona in the field, the tongue of Suada in the chamber, the spirite of Practise in esse, and the paragon of excellency in print."—HARVEY's *Pierce's Supererogation*.

erased to make way for another; or on papyrus, which was
fragile and extremely perishable. Authorship was a limited
and unprofitable craft, pursued chiefly by monks in the leisure
and solitude of their cloisters. The accumulation of manuscripts was slow and costly, and confined almost entirely to
monasteries. To these circumstances it may, in some measure, be owing that we have not been inundated by the intellect of antiquity; that the fountains of thought have not
been broken up, and modern genius drowned in the deluge.
But the inventions of paper and the press have put an end to
all these restraints: they have made every one a writer, and
enabled every mind to pour itself into print, and diffuse itself
over the whole intellectual world. The consequences are
alarming. The stream of literature has swollen into a torrent—augmented into a river—expanded into a sea. A few
centuries since five or six hundred manuscripts constituted a
great library; but what would you say to libraries, such as
actually exist, containing three or four hundred thousand
volumes; legions of authors at the same time busy; and a
press going on with fearfully increasing activity, to double
and quadruple the number? Unless some unforeseen mortality should break out among the progeny of the Muse, now
that she has become so prolific, I tremble for posterity. I
fear the mere fluctuation of language will not be sufficient.
Criticism may do much; it increases with the increase of
literature, and resembles one of those salutary checks on
population spoken of by economists. All possible encouragement, therefore, should be given to the growth of critics,
good or bad. But I fear all will be in vain; let criticism do
what it may, writers will write, printers will print, and the
world will inevitably be overstocked with good books. It will
soon be the employment of a lifetime merely to learn their
names. Many a man of passable information at the present
day reads scarcely anything but reviews, and before long a
man of erudition will be little better than a mere walking
catalogue."

"My very good sir," said the little quarto, yawning most

drearily in my face, "excuse my interrupting you, but I perceive you are rather given to prose. I would ask the fate of an author who was making some noise just as I left the world. His reputation, however, was considered quite temporary. The learned shook their heads at him, for he was a poor, half-educated varlet that knew little of Latin, and nothing of Greek, and had been obliged to run the country for deer-stealing. I think his name was Shakespeare. I presume he soon sunk into oblivion."

"On the contrary," said I, "it is owing to that very man that the literature of his period has experienced a duration beyond the ordinary term of English literature. There arise authors now and then who seem proof against the mutability of language, because they have rooted themselves in the unchanging principles of human nature. They are like gigantic trees that we sometimes see on the banks of a stream, which, by their vast and deep roots, penetrating through the mere surface, and laying hold on the very foundations of the earth, preserve the soil around them from being swept away by the overflowing current, and hold up many a neighboring plant, and, perhaps, worthless weed, to perpetuity. Such is the case with Shakespeare, whom we behold, defying the encroachments of time, retaining in modern use the language and literature of his day, and giving duration to many an indifferent author merely from having flourished in his vicinity. But even he, I grieve to say, is gradually assuming the tint of age, and his whole form is overrun by a profusion of commentators, who, like clambering vines and creepers, almost bury the noble plant that upholds them."

Here the little quarto began to heave his sides and chuckle, until at length he broke out into a plethoric fit of laughter that had wellnigh choked him, by reason of his excessive corpulency. "Mighty well!" cried he, as soon as he could recover breath, "mighty well! and so you would persuade me that the literature of an age is to be perpetuated by a vagabond deer-stealer! by a man without learning! by a poet! forsooth—a poet!" And here he wheezed forth another fit of laughter.

I confess that I felt somewhat nettled at this rudeness, which, however, I pardoned on account of his having flourished in a less polished age. I determined, nevertheless, not to give up my point.

"Yes," resumed I, positively, "a poet; for of all writers he has the best chance for immortality. Others may write from the head, but he writes from the heart, and the heart will always understand him. He is the faithful portrayer of Nature, whose features are always the same, and always interesting. Prose writers are voluminous and unwieldy; their pages crowded with commonplaces, and their thoughts expanded into tediousness. But with the true poet everything is terse, touching, or brilliant. He gives the choicest thoughts in the choicest language. He illustrates them by everything that he sees most striking in nature and art. He enriches them by pictures of human life, such as it is, passing before him. His writings, therefore, contain the spirit, the aroma, if I may use the phrase, of the age in which he lives. They are caskets which inclose within a small compass the wealth of the language—its family jewels, which are thus transmitted in a portable form to posterity. The setting may occasionally be antiquated, and require now and then to be renewed, as in the case of Chaucer; but the brilliancy and intrinsic value of the gems continue unaltered. Cast a look back over the long reach of literary history. What vast valleys of dullness, filled with monkish legends and academical controversies! What bogs of theological speculations! What dreary wastes of metaphysics! Here and there only do we behold the heaven-illumined bards, elevated like beacons on their widely-separated heights, to transmit the pure light of poetical intelligence from age to age." *

---

* "Thorow earth, and waters deepe,
  The pen by skill doth passe:
  And featly nyps the worldes abuse,
  And shoes us in a glasse,

I was just about to launch forth into eulogiums upon the poets of the day, when the sudden opening of the door caused me to turn my head. It was the verger, who came to inform me that it was time to close the library. I sought to have a parting word with the quarto, but the worthy little tome was silent; the clasps were closed; and it looked perfectly unconscious of all that had passed. I have been to the library two or three times since, and have endeavored to draw it into further conversation, but in vain: and whether all this rambling colloquy actually took place, or whether it was another of those odd day-dreams to which I am subject, I have never, to this moment, been able to discover.

RURAL FUNERALS

"Here's a few flowers! but about midnight more;
  The herbs that have on them cold dew o' the night
  Are strewings fitt'st for graves—
  You were as flowers now withered: even so
  These herblets shall, which we upon you strow."
                                   —*Cymbeline*

AMONG the beautiful and simple-hearted customs of rural life which still linger in some parts of England are those of strewing flowers before the funerals and planting them at the graves of departed friends. These, it is said, are the remains of some of the rites of the primitive church; but they are of still higher antiquity, having been observed among the

---

The vertu and the vice
  Of every wight alyve;
The honey combe that bee doth make,
  Is not so sweet in hyve,
As are the golden leves
  That drops from poet's head;
Which doth surmount our common talke,
  As farre as dross doth lead."—CHURCHYARD

Greeks and Romans, and frequently mentioned by their writers, and were, no doubt, the spontaneous tributes of unlettered affection, originating long before art had tasked itself to modulate sorrow into song, or story it on the monument. They are now only to be met with in the most distant and retired places of the kingdom, where fashion and innovation have not been able to throng in, and trample out all the curious and interesting traces of the olden time.

In Glamorganshire, we are told, the bed whereon the corpse lies is covered with flowers, a custom alluded to in one of the wild and plaintive ditties of Ophelia:

> "White his shroud as the mountain snow,
>   Larded all with sweet flowers;
> Which be-wept to the grave did go,
>   With true love showers."

There is also a most delicate and beautiful rite observed in some of the remote villages of the south, at the funeral of a female who has died young and unmarried. A chaplet of white flowers is borne before the corpse by a young girl, nearest in age, size, and resemblance, and is afterward hung up in the church over the accustomed seat of the deceased. These chaplets are sometimes made of white paper, in imitation of flowers, and inside of them is generally a pair of white gloves. They are intended as emblems of the purity of the deceased, and the crown of glory which she has received in heaven.

In some parts of the country, also, the dead are carried to the grave with the singing of psalms and hymns; a kind of triumph, "to show," says Bourne, "that they have finished their course with joy, and are become conquerors." This, I am informed, is observed in some of the northern counties, particularly in Northumberland, and it has a pleasing, though melancholy effect, to hear, of a still evening, in some lonely country scene, the mournful melody of a funeral dirge swelling from a distance, and to see the train slowly moving along the landscape.

"Thus, thus, and thus, we compass round
Thy harmless and unhaunted ground,
And as we sing thy dirge, we will
                    The Daffodill
And other flowers lay upon
The altar of our love, thy stone."—HERRICK.

There is also a solemn respect paid by the traveler to the
passing funeral in these sequestered places; for such spectacles, occurring among the quiet abodes of Nature, sink deep
into the soul.   As the mourning train approaches, he pauses,
uncovered, to let it go by; he then follows silently in the
rear; sometimes quite to the grave, at other times for a few
hundred yards, and having paid this tribute of respect to the
deceased, turns and resumes his journey.

The rich vein of melancholy which runs through the English character, and gives it some of its most touching and
ennobling graces, is finely evidenced in these pathetic customs, and in the solicitude shown by the common people for
an honored and a peaceful grave.   The humblest peasant,
whatever may be his lowly lot while living, is anxious that
some little respect may be paid to his remains.   Sir Thomas
Overbury, describing the "faire and happy milkmaid," observes, "thus lives she, and all her care is that she may die
in the springtime, to have store of flowers stucke upon her
winding-sheet."   The poets, too, who always breathe the
feeling of a nation, continually advert to this fond solicitude
about the grave.   In "The Maid's Tragedy," by Beaumont
and Fletcher, there is a beautiful instance of the kind, describing the capricious melancholy of a broken-hearted girl.

"When she sees a bank
Stuck full of flowers, she, with a sigh, will tell
Her servants, what a pretty place it were
To bury lovers in; and make her maids
Pluck 'em, and strew her over like a corse."

The custom of decorating graves was once universally
prevalent: osiers were carefully bent over them to keep the

turf uninjured, and about them were planted evergreens and flowers. "We adorn their graves," says Evelyn, in his "Sylva," "with flowers and redolent plants, just emblems of the life of man, which has been compared in Holy Scriptures to those fading beauties, whose roots, being buried in dishonor, rise again in glory." This usage has now become extremely rare in England; but it may still be met with in the churchyards of retired villages among the Welsh mountains; and I recollect an instance of it at the small town of Ruthven, which lies at the head of the beautiful vale of Clewyd. I have been told also by a friend, who was present at the funeral of a young girl in Glamorganshire, that the female attendants had their aprons full of flowers, which, as soon as the body was interred, they stuck about the grave.

He noticed several graves which had been decorated in the same manner. As the flowers had been merely stuck in the ground, and not planted, they had soon withered, and might be seen in various states of decay; some drooping, others quite perished. They were afterward to be supplanted by holly, rosemary, and other evergreens; which on some graves had grown to great luxuriance, and overshadowed the tombstones.

There was formerly a melancholy fancifulness in the arrangement of these rustic offerings that had something in it truly poetical. The rose was sometimes blended with the lily, to form a general emblem of frail mortality. "This sweet flower," said Evelyn, "borne on a branch set with thorns, and accompanied with the lily, are natural hieroglyphics of our fugitive, umbratile, anxious, and transitory life, which, making so fair a show for a time, is not yet without its thorns and crosses." The nature and color of the flowers, and of the ribbons with which they were tied, had often a particular reference to the qualities or story of the deceased, or were expressive of the feelings of the mourner. In an old poem, entitled "Corydon's Doleful Knell," a lover specifies the decorations he intends to use:

"A garland shall be framed
    By Art and Nature's skill,
Of sundry-colored flowers,
    In token of good will.

"And sundry-colored ribands
    On it I will bestow;
But chiefly blacke and yellowe
    With her to grave shall go.

"I'll deck her tomb with flowers
    The rarest ever seen;
And with my tears as showers
    I'll keep them fresh and green."

The white rose, we are told, was planted at the grave of a virgin; her chaplet was tied with white ribbons, in token of her spotless innocence; though sometimes black ribbons were intermingled, to bespeak the grief of the survivors. The red rose was occasionally used, in remembrance of such as had been remarkable for benevolence; but roses in general were appropriated to the graves of lovers. Evelyn tells us that the custom was not altogether extinct in his time, near his dwelling in the county of Surrey, "where the maidens yearly planted and decked the graves of their defunct sweethearts with rose-bushes." And Camden likewise remarks, in his "Britannia": "Here is also a certain custom, observed time out of mind, of planting rose-trees upon the graves, especially by the young men and maids who have lost their loves; so that this churchyard is now full of them."

When the deceased had been unhappy in their loves, emblems of a more gloomy character were used, such as the yew and cypress; and if flowers were strewn, they were of the most melancholy colors. Thus, in poems by Thomas Stanley, Esq. (published in 1651), is the following stanza:

"Yet strew
Upon my dismal grave
Such offerings as you have,
    Forsaken cypresse and yewe;
For kinder flowers can take no birth
Or growth from such unhappy earth."

In "The Maid's Tragedy," a pathetic little air is introduced, illustrative of this mode of decorating the funerals of females who have been disappointed in love:

"Lay a garland on my hearse
  Of the dismal yew,
Maidens willow branches wear,
  Say I died true.

"My love was false, but I was firm,
  From my hour of birth,
Upon my buried body lie
  Lightly, gentle earth."

The natural effect of sorrow over the dead is to refine and elevate the mind; and we have a proof of it in the purity of sentiment, and the unaffected elegance of thought, which pervaded the whole of these funeral observances. Thus, it was an especial precaution that none but sweet-scented evergreens and flowers should be employed. The intention seems to have been to soften the horrors of the tomb, to beguile the mind from brooding over the disgraces of perishing mortality, and to associate the memory of the deceased with the most delicate and beautiful objects in Nature. There is a dismal process going on in the grave, ere dust can return to its kindred dust, which the imagination shrinks from contemplating; and we seek still to think of the form we have loved with those refined associations which it awakened when blooming before us in youth and beauty. "Lay her i' the earth," says Laertes of his virgin sister,

"And from her fair and unpolluted flesh
  May violets spring."

Herrick, also, in his "Dirge of Jephtha," pours forth a fragrant flow of poetical thought and image which in a manner embalms the dead in the recollections of the living.

"Sleep in thy peace, thy bed of spice,
And make this place all Paradise:
May sweets grow here! and smoke from hence
            Fat frankincense.

Let balme and cassia send their scent
From out thy maiden monument.

.   .   .   .

"May all shie maids at wonted hours
Come forth to strew thy tombe with flowers!
May virgins, when they come to mourn,
            Male incense burn
Upon thine altar! then return
And leave thee sleeping in thy urn."

I might crowd my pages with extracts from the older British poets, who wrote when these rites were more prevalent, and delighted frequently to allude to them; but I have already quoted more than is necessary. I cannot, however, refrain from giving a passage from Shakespeare, even though it should appear trite, which illustrates the emblematical meaning often conveyed in these floral tributes, and at the same time possesses that magic of language and appositeness of imagery for which he stands pre-eminent.

"With fairest flowers,
Whilst summer lasts, and I live here, Fidele,
I'll sweeten thy sad grave; thou shalt not lack
The flower that's like thy face, pale primrose; nor
The azured harebell like thy veins; no, nor
The leaf of eglantine; whom not to slander,
Outsweetened not thy breath."

There is certainly something more affecting in these prompt and spontaneous offerings of nature than in the most costly monuments of art; the hand strews the flower while the heart is warm, and the tear falls on the grave as affection is binding the osier round the sod; but pathos expires under the slow labor of the chisel, and is chilled among the cold conceits of sculptured marble.

It is greatly to be regretted that a custom so truly elegant and touching has disappeared from general use, and exists only in the most remote and insignificant villages. But it seems as if poetical custom always shuns the walks of cultivated society. In proportion as people grow polite they cease

to be poetical. They talk of poetry, but they have learned
to check its free impulses, to distrust its sallying emotions,
and to supply its most affecting and picturesque usages by
studied form and pompous ceremonial. Few pageants can
be more stately and frigid than an English funeral in town.
It is made up of show and gloomy parade: mourning car-
riages, mourning horses, mourning plumes, and hireling
mourners, who make a mockery of grief. "There is a grave
digged," says Jeremy Taylor, "and a solemn mourning, and
a great talk in the neighborhood, and when the daies are finished, they shall be, and they shall be remembered no more."
The associate in the gay and crowded city is soon forgotten;
the hurrying succession of new intimates and new pleasures
effaces him from our minds, and the very scenes and circles
in which he moved are incessantly fluctuating. But funerals
in the country are solemnly impressive. The stroke of death
makes a wider space in the village circle, and is an awful
event in the tranquil uniformity of rural life. The passing
bell tolls its knell in every ear; it steals with its pervading
melancholy over hill and vale, and saddens all the landscape.

The fixed and unchanging features of the country, also,
perpetuate the memory of the friend with whom we once
enjoyed them; who was the companion of our most retired
walks, and gave animation to every lonely scene. His idea
is associated with every charm of Nature: we hear his voice
in the echo which he once delighted to awaken; his spirit
haunts the grove which he once frequented; we think of him
in the wild upland solitude, or amid the pensive beauty of
the valley. In the freshness of joyous morning, we remember his beaming smiles and bounding gayety; and when
sober evening returns, with its gathering shadows and sub-
duing quiet, we call to mind many a twilight hour of gentle
talk and sweet-souled melancholy.

> "Each lonely place shall him restore,
>   For him the tear be duly shed,
> Beloved, till life can charm no more,
>   And mourn'd till pity's self be dead."

Another cause that perpetuates the memory of the deceased in the country is, that the grave is more immediately in sight of the survivors. They pass it on their way to prayer; it meets their eyes when their hearts are softened by the exercise of devotion; they linger about it on the Sabbath, when the mind is disengaged from worldly cares, and most disposed to turn aside from present pleasures and present loves, and to sit down among the solemn mementos of the past. In North Wales, the peasantry kneel and pray over the graves of their deceased friends for several Sundays after the interment; and where the tender rite of strewing and planting flowers is still practiced, it is always renewed on Easter, Whitsuntide, and other festivals, when the season brings the companion of former festivity more vividly to mind. It is also invariably performed by the nearest relatives and friends; no menials nor hirelings are employed, and if a neighbor yields assistance, it would be deemed an insult to offer compensation.

I have dwelt upon this beautiful rural custom, because, as it is one of the last, so is it one of the holiest offices of love. The grave is the ordeal of true affection. It is there that the divine passion of the soul manifests its superiority to the instinctive impulse of mere animal attachment. The latter must be continually refreshed and kept alive by the presence of its object; but the love that is seated in the soul can live on long remembrance. The mere inclinations of sense languish and decline with the charms which excited them, and turn with shuddering and disgust from the dismal precincts of the tomb; but it is thence that truly spiritual affection rises purified from every sensual desire, and returns, like a holy flame, to illumine and sanctify the heart of the survivor.

The sorrow for the dead is the only sorrow from which we refuse to be divorced. Every other wound we seek to heal—every other affliction to forget; but this wound we consider it a duty to keep open—this affliction we cherish and brood over in solitude. Where is the mother who would willingly forget the infant that perished like a blossom from her arms, though every recollection is a pang? Where is the child that would willingly forget the most tender of parents, though to remember be but to lament? Who, even in the hour of agony, would forget the friend over whom he mourns? Who, even when the tomb is closing upon the remains of her he most loved; when he feels his heart, as it were, crushed in the closing of its portal; would accept of consolation that must be bought by forgetfulness?—No, the love which survives the tomb is one of the noblest attributes of the soul. If it has its woes, it has likewise its delights; and when the overwhelming burst of grief is calmed into the gentle tear of recollection—when the sudden anguish and the convulsive agony over the present ruins of all that we most loved is softened away into pensive meditation on all that it was in the days of its loveliness—who would root out such a sorrow from the heart? Though it may sometimes throw a passing cloud over the bright hour of gayety, or spread a deeper sadness over the hour of gloom; yet who would exchange it even for the song of pleasure, or the burst of revelry? No, there is a voice from the tomb sweeter than song. There is a remembrance of the dead, to which we turn even from the charms of the living. Oh, the grave!—the grave!—It buries every error—covers every defect—extinguishes every resentment! From its peaceful bosom spring none but fond regrets and tender recollections. Who can look down upon the grave even of an enemy and not feel a compunctious throb that he should ever have warred with the poor handful of earth that lies mouldering before him?

But the grave of those we love—what a place for meditation! There it is that we call up in long review the whole history of virtue and gentleness, and the thousand endearments lavished upon us almost unheeded in the daily intercourse of intimacy;—there it is that we dwell upon the tenderness, the solemn, awful tenderness of the parting scene. The bed of death, with all its stifled griefs—its noiseless attendance—its mute, watchful assiduities. The last testimonies of expiring love! The feeble, fluttering, thrilling—oh! how thrilling!—pressure of the hand. The last fond look of the glazing eye, turning upon us even from the threshold of existence. The faint, faltering accents, struggling in death to give one more assurance of affection!

Ay, go to the grave of buried love, and meditate! There settle the account with thy conscience for every past benefit unrequited, every past endearment unregarded, of that departed being, who can never—never—never return to be soothed by thy contrition!

If thou art a child, and hast ever added a sorrow to the soul or a furrow to the silvered brow of an affectionate parent—if thou art a husband, and hast ever caused the fond bosom that ventured its whole happiness in thy arms to doubt one moment of thy kindness or thy truth—if thou art a friend, and hast ever wronged, in thought, or word, or deed, the spirit that generously confided in thee—if thou art a lover, and hast ever given one unmerited pang to that true heart which now lies cold and still beneath thy feet; then be sure that every unkind look, every ungracious word, every ungentle action, will come thronging back upon thy memory, and knocking dolefully at thy soul—then be sure that thou wilt lie down sorrowing and repentant on the grave, and utter the unheard groan, and pour the unavailing tear—more deep, more bitter, because unheard and unavailing.

Then weave thy chaplet of flowers, and strew the beauties of nature about the grave; console thy broken spirit, if thou canst, with these tender, yet futile tributes of regret;—but take warning by the bitterness of this thy contrite affliction over the dead, and henceforth be more faithful and affectionate in the discharge of thy duties to the living.

————

In writing the preceding article, it was not intended to give a full detail of the funeral customs of the English peasantry, but merely to furnish a few hints and quotations illustrative of particular rites, to be appended, by way of note, to another paper, which has been withheld. The article swelled insensibly into its present form, and this is mentioned as an apology for so brief and casual a notice of these usages, after they have been amply and learnedly investigated in other works.

I must observe, also, that I am well aware that this custom of adorning graves with flowers prevails in other countries besides England. Indeed, in some it is much more general, and is observed even by the rich and fashionable; but it is then apt to lose its simplicity, and to degenerate into affectation. Bright, in his travels in Lower Hungary, tells of monuments of marble, and recesses formed for retirement, with seats placed among bowers of green-house plants; and that the graves generally are covered with the gayest flowers of the season. He gives a casual picture of final piety, which I cannot but describe, for I trust it is as useful as it is delightful to illustrate the amiable virtues of the sex. "When I was at Berlin," says he, "I followed the celebrated Iffland to the grave. Mingled with some pomp, you might trace much real feeling. In the midst of the ceremony my attention was attracted by a young woman who stood on a mound of earth, newly covered with turf, which she anxiously protected from the feet of the passing crowd. It was the tomb of her parent; and the figure of this affectionate daughter presented a monument more striking than the most costly work of art."

I will barely add an instance of sepulchral decoration that I once met with among the mountains of Switzerland. It was at the village of Gersau, which stands on the borders of the lake of Luzerne, at the foot of Mount Rigi. It was once the capital of a miniature republic, shut up between the Alps and the lake, and accessible on the land side only by footpaths. The whole force of the republic did not exceed six hundred fighting men; and a few miles of circumference, scooped out, as it were, from the bosom of the mountains, comprised its territory. The village of Gersau seemed sepa-

rated from the rest of the world, and retained the golden
simplicity of a purer age. It had a small church, with a
burying-ground adjoining. At the heads of the graves were
placed crosses of wood or iron. On some were affixed minia-
tures, rudely executed, but evidently attempts at likenesses
of the deceased. On the crosses were hung chaplets of flowers, some withering, others fresh, as if occasionally renewed.
I paused with interest at this scene; I felt that I was at the
source of poetical description, for these were the beautiful
but unaffected offerings of the heart, which poets are fain to
record. In a gayer and more populous place I should have
suspected them to have been suggested by factitious sentiment, derived from books; but the good people of Gersau
knew little of books; there was not a novel nor a love poem
in the village; and I question whether any peasant of the
place dreamed, while he was twining a fresh chaplet for the
grave of his mistress, that he was fulfilling one of the most
fanciful rites of poetical devotion, and that he was practically
a poet.

THE INN KITCHEN

"Shall I not take mine ease in mine inn?"—Falstaff

DURING a journey that I once made through the Nether-
lands, I had arrived one evening at the Pomme d'Or, the
principal inn of a small Flemish village. It was after the
hour of the *table d'hote*, so that I was obliged to make a
solitary supper from the relics of its ampler board. The
weather was chilly; I was seated alone in one end of a great
gloomy dining-room, and my repast being over, I had the
prospect before me of a long dull evening, without any visible means of enlivening it. I summoned mine host, and re-
quested something to read; he brought me the whole literary
stock of his household, a Dutch family Bible, an almanac in
the same language, and a number of old Paris newspapers.
As I sat dozing over one of the latter, reading old news and

stale criticisms, my ear was now and then struck with bursts of laughter which seemed to proceed from the kitchen. Every one that has traveled on the Continent must know how favorite a resort the kitchen of a country inn is to the middle and inferior order of travelers; particularly in that equivocal kind of weather when a fire becomes agreeable toward evening. I threw aside the newspaper, and explored my way to the kitchen, to take a peep at the group that appeared to be so merry. It was composed partly of travelers who had arrived some hours before in a diligence, and partly of the usual attendants and hangers-on of inns. They were seated round a great burnished stove, that might have been mistaken for an altar at which they were worshiping. It was covered with various kitchen vessels of resplendent brightness; among which steamed and hissed a huge copper tea-kettle. A large lamp threw a strong mass of light upon the group, bringing out many odd features in strong relief. Its yellow rays partially illumined the spacious kitchen, dying duskily away into remote corners; except where they settled in mellow radiance on the broad side of a flitch of bacon, or were reflected back from well-scoured utensils that gleamed from the midst of obscurity. A strapping Flemish lass, with long golden pendents in her ears, and a necklace with a golden heart suspended to it, was the presiding priestess of the temple.

Many of the company were furnished with pipes, and most of them with some kind of evening potation. I found their mirth was occasioned by anecdotes which a little swarthy Frenchman, with a dry weazen face and large whiskers, was giving of his love adventures; at the end of each of which there was one of those bursts of honest unceremonious laughter, in which a man indulges in that temple of true liberty, an inn.

As I had no better mode of getting through a tedious blustering evening, I took my seat near the stove, and listened to a variety of traveler's tales, some very extravagant, and most very dull. All of them, however, have faded from

my treacherous memory, except one, which I will endeavor
to relate. I fear, however, it derived its chief zest from the
manner in which it was told, and the peculiar air and appearance of the narrator. He was a corpulent old Swiss,
who had the look of a veteran traveler. He was dressed in
a tarnished green traveling-jacket, with a broad belt round
his waist, and a pair of overalls with buttons from the hips
to the ankles. He was of a full, rubicund countenance, with
a double chin, aquiline nose, and a pleasant twinkling eye.
His hair was light, and curled from under an old green velvet traveling-cap, stuck on one side of his head. He was
interrupted more than once by the arrival of guests, or the
remarks of his auditors; and paused, now and then, to re-
plenish his pipe; at which times he had generally a roguish
leer, and a sly joke, for the buxom kitchen maid.

I wish my reader could imagine the old fellow lolling in
a huge armchair, one arm akimbo, the other holding a curiously twisted tobacco-pipe, formed of genuine *écume de mer*,
decorated with silver chain and silken tassel—his head cocked
on one side, and a whimsical cut of the eye occasionally, as
he related the following story:

THE SPECTER BRIDEGROOM

A TRAVELER'S TALE *

"He that supper for is dight,
  He lyes full cold, I trow, this night!
  Yestreen to chamber I him led,
  This night Gray-steel has made his bed!"
        —SIR EGER, SIR GRAHAME, and SIR GRAY-STEEL

ON the summit of one of the heights of the Odenwald, a
wild and romantic tract of Upper Germany that lies not far

---

* The erudite reader, well versed in good-for-nothing lore, will
perceive that the above Tale must have been suggested to the old Swiss
by a little French anecdote, of a circumstance said to have taken place
at Paris.

from the confluence of the Maine and the Rhine, there stood,
many, many years since, the Castle of the Baron Von Landshort. It is now quite fallen to decay, and almost buried
among beech trees and dark firs; above which, however, its
old watch-tower may still be seen struggling, like the former
possessor I have mentioned, to carry a high head, and look
down upon a neighboring country.

The Baron was a dry branch of the great family of Katzenellenbogen,* and inherited the relics of the property and
all the pride of his ancestors. Though the warlike disposition of his predecessors had much impaired the family possessions, yet the Baron still endeavored to keep up some show
of former state. The times were peaceable, and the German
nobles, in general, had abandoned their inconvenient old castles, perched like eagles' nests among the mountains, and
had built more convenient residences in the valleys; still the
Baron remained proudly drawn up in his little fortress, cherishing with hereditary inveteracy all the old family feuds;
so that he was on ill terms with some of his nearest neighbors, on account of disputes that had happened between their
great-great-grandfathers.

The Baron had but one child, a daughter; but Nature,
when she grants but one child, always compensates by making it a prodigy; and so it was with the daughter of the
Baron. All the nurses, gossips, and country cousins, assured her father that she had not her equal for beauty in all
Germany; and who should know better than they? She
had, moreover, been brought up with great care, under the
superintendence of two maiden aunts, who had spent some
years of their early life at one of the little German courts,
and were skilled in all the branches of knowledge necessary
to the education of a fine lady. Under their instructions,
she became a miracle of accomplishments. By the time she
was eighteen she could embroider to admiration, and had

---

*I.e., CAT'S ELBOW—the name of a family of those parts, very
powerful in former times. The appellation, we are told, was given in
compliment to a peerless dame of the family, celebrated for a fine arm.

worked whole histories of the saints in tapestry with such strength of expression in their countenances that they looked like so many souls in purgatory. She could read without great difficulty, and had spelled her way through several church legends, and almost all the chivalric wonders of the Heldenbuch. She had even made considerable proficiency in writing, could sign her own name without missing a letter, and so legibly that her aunts could read it without spectacles. She excelled in making little good-for-nothing ladylike knickknacks of all kinds; was versed in the most abstruse dancing of the day; played a number of airs on the harp and guitar; and knew all the tender ballads of the Minnie-lieders by heart.

Her aunts, too, having been great flirts and coquettes in their younger days, were admirably calculated to be vigilant guardians and strict censors of the conduct of their niece; for there is no duenna so rigidly prudent, and inexorably decorous, as a superannuated coquette. She was rarely suffered out of their sight; never went beyond the domains of the castle, unless well attended, or, rather, well watched; had continual lectures read to her about strict decorum and implicit obedience; and, as to the men—pah! she was taught to hold them at such distance and distrust that, unless properly authorized, she would not have cast a glance upon the handsomest cavalier in the world—no, not if he were even dying at her feet.

The good effects of this system were wonderfully apparent. The young lady was a pattern of docility and correctness. While others were wasting their sweetness in the glare of the world, and liable to be plucked and thrown aside by every hand, she was coyly blooming into fresh and lovely womanhood under the protection of those immaculate spinsters, like a rose-bud blushing forth among guardian thorns. Her aunts looked upon her with pride and exultation, and vaunted that though all the other young ladies in the world might go astray, yet, thank Heaven, nothing of the kind could happen to the heiress of Katzenellenbogen.

But however scantily the Baron Von Landshort might be provided with children, his household was by no means a small one, for Providence had enriched him with abundance of poor relations. They, one and all, possessed the affectionate disposition common to humble relatives; were wonderfully attached to the Baron, and took every possible occasion to come in swarms and enliven the castle. All family festivals were commemorated by these good people at the Baron's expense; and when they were filled with good cheer, they would declare that there was nothing on earth so delightful as these family meetings, these jubilees of the heart.

The Baron, though a small man, had a large soul, and it swelled with satisfaction at the consciousness of being the greatest man in the little world about him. He loved to tell long stories about the stark old warriors whose portraits looked grimly down from the walls around, and he found no listeners equal to those who fed at his expense. He was much given to the marvelous, and a firm believer in all those supernatural tales with which every mountain and valley in Germany abounds. The faith of his guests even exceeded his own: they listened to every tale of wonder with open eyes and mouth, and never failed to be astonished, even though repeated for the hundredth time. Thus lived the Baron Von Landshort, the oracle of his table, the absolute monarch of his little territory, and happy, above all things, in the persuasion that he was the wisest man of the age.

At the time of which my story treats there was a great family-gathering at the castle, on an affair of the utmost importance: it was to receive the destined bridegroom of the Baron's daughter. A negotiation had been carried on between the father and an old nobleman of Bavaria, to unite the dignity of their houses by the marriage of their children. The preliminaries had been conducted with proper punctilio. The young people were betrothed without seeing each other, and the time was appointed for the marriage ceremony. The young Count Von Altenburg had been recalled from the army for the purpose, and was actually on his way to the

Baron's to receive his bride. Missives had even been received from him, from Wurtzburg, where he was accidentally detained, mentioning the day and hour when he might be expected to arrive.

The castle was in a tumult of preparation to give him a suitable welcome. The fair bride had been decked out with uncommon care. The two aunts had superintended her toilet, and quarreled the whole morning about every article of her dress. The young lady had taken advantage of their contest to follow the bent of her own taste; and fortunately it was a good one. She looked as lovely as youthful bridegroom could desire; and the flutter of expectation heightened the luster of her charms.

The suffusions that mantled her face and neck, the gentle heaving of the bosom, the eye now and then lost in reverie, all betrayed the soft tumult that was going on in her little heart. The aunts were continually hovering around her; for maiden aunts are apt to take great interest in affairs of this nature: they were giving her a world of staid counsel how to deport herself, what to say, and in what manner to receive the expected lover.

The Baron was no less busied in preparations. He had, in truth, nothing exactly to do; but he was naturally a fuming, bustling little man, and could not remain passive when all the world was in a hurry. He worried from top to bottom of the castle, with an air of infinite anxiety; he continually called the servants from their work to exhort them to be diligent, and buzzed about every hall and chamber, as idly restless and importunate as a blue-bottle fly of a warm summer's day.

In the meantime, the fatted calf had been killed; the forests had rung with the clamor of the huntsmen; the kitchen was crowded with good cheer; the cellars had yielded up whole oceans of *Rhein-wein* and *Ferne-wein*, and even the great Heidelberg Tun had been laid under contribution. Everything was ready to receive the distinguished guest with *Saus und Braus* in the true spirit of German hospital-

ity—but the guest delayed to make his appearance. Hour
rolled after hour. The sun that had poured his downward
rays upon the rich forests of the Odenwald, now just gleamed
along the summits of the mountains. The Baron mounted
the highest tower, and strained his eyes in hopes of catching
a distant sight of the Count and his attendants. Once he
thought he beheld them; the sound of horns came floating
from the valley, prolonged by the mountain echoes: a number
of horsemen were seen far below, slowly advancing along
the road; but when they had nearly reached the foot of the
mountain they suddenly struck off in a different direction.
The last ray of sunshine departed—the bats began to flit by
in the twilight—the road grew dimmer and dimmer to the
view; and nothing appeared stirring in it but now and then
a peasant lagging homeward from his labor.

While the old castle of Landshort was in this state of perplexity, a very interesting scene was transacting in a different
part of the Odenwald.

The young Count Von Altenburg was tranquilly pursuing his route in that sober jog-trot way in which a man
travels toward matrimony when his friends have taken all
the trouble and uncertainty of courtship off his hands, and a
bride is waiting for him, as certainly as a dinner, at the end
of his journey. He had encountered at Wurtzburg a youthful companion in arms, with whom he had seen some service
on the frontiers; Herman Von Starkenfaust, one of the stoutest hands and worthiest hearts of German chivalry, who was
now returning from the army. His father's castle was not
far distant from the old fortress of Landshort, although a
hereditary feud rendered the families hostile and strangers
to each others.

In the warm-hearted moment of recognition, the young
friends related all their past adventures and fortunes, and
the Count gave the whole history of his intended nuptials
with a young lady whom he had never seen, but of whose
charms he had received the most enrapturing descriptions.

As the route of the friends lay in the same direction, they

agreed to perform the rest of their journey together; and, that they might do it more leisurely, set off from Wurtzburg at an early hour, the Count having given directions for his retinue to follow and overtake him.

They beguiled their wayfaring with recollections of their military scenes and adventures; but the Count was apt to be a little tedious, now and then, about the reputed charms of his bride, and the felicity that awaited him.

In this way they had entered among the mountains of the Odenwald, and were traversing one of its most lonely and thickly wooded passes. It is well known that the forests of Germany have always been as much infested with robbers as its castles by specters; and, at this time, the former were particularly numerous, from the hordes of disbanded soldiers wandering about the country. It will not appear extraordinary, therefore, that the cavaliers were attacked by a gang of these stragglers in the midst of the forest. They defended themselves with bravery, but were nearly overpowered when the Count's retinue arrived to their assistance. At sight of them the robbers fled, but not until the Count had received a mortal wound. He was slowly and carefully conveyed back to the city of Wurtzburg, and a friar summoned from a neighboring convent, who was famous for his skill in administering to both soul and body. But half of his skill was superfluous; the moments of the unfortunate Count were numbered.

With his dying breath he entreated his friend to repair instantly to the castle of Landshort, and explain the fatal cause of his not keeping his appointment with his bride. Though not the most ardent of lovers, he was one of the most punctilious of men, and appeared earnestly solicitous that this mission should be speedily and courteously executed. "Unless this is done," said he, "I shall not sleep quietly in my grave!" He repeated these last words with peculiar solemnity. A request, at a moment so impressive, admitted no hesitation. Starkenfaust endeavored to soothe him to calmness; promised faithfully to execute his wish, and gave him his hand in solemn pledge. The dying man pressed it in acknowledgment, but soon lapsed into delirium—raved about his bride—his engagements—his plighted word; ordered his horse, that he might ride to the castle of Landshort, and expired in the fancied act of vaulting into the saddle.

Starkenfaust bestowed a sigh and a soldier's tear on the untimely fate of his comrade; and then pondered on the awkward mission he had undertaken. His heart was heavy, and his head perplexed; for he was to present himself an unbidden guest among hostile people, and to damp their festivity with tidings fatal to their hopes. Still there were certain whisperings of curiosity in his bosom to see this far-famed beauty of Katzenellenbogen so cautiously shut up from the world; for he was a passionate admirer of the sex, and there was a dash of eccentricity and enterprise in his character that made him fond of all singular adventure.

Previous to his departure, he made all due arrangements with the holy fraternity of the convent for the funeral solemnities of his friend, who was to be buried in the cathedral of Wurtzburg, near some of his illustrious relatives; and the mourning retinue of the Count took charge of his remains.

It is now high time that we should return to the ancient family of Katzenellenbogen, who were impatient for their guest, and still more for their dinner; and to the worthy little Baron, whom we left airing himself on the watch-tower.

Night closed in, but still no guest arrived. The Baron descended from the tower in despair. The banquet, which had been delayed from hour to hour, could no longer be postponed. The meats were already overdone, the cook in an agony, and the whole household had the look of a garrison that had been reduced by famine. The Baron was obliged reluctantly to give orders for the feast without the presence of the guest. All were seated at table, and just on the point of commencing, when the sound of a horn from without the gate gave notice of the approach of a stranger. Another long blast filled the old courts of the castle with its echoes, and was answered by the warder from the walls. The Baron hastened to receive his future son-in-law.

The drawbridge had been let down, and the stranger was before the gate. He was a tall gallant cavalier, mounted on a black steed. His countenance was pale, but he had a beaming, romantic eye, and an air of stately melancholy. The Baron was a little mortified that he should have come in this simple, solitary style. His dignity for a moment was ruffled, and he felt disposed to consider it a want of proper respect for the important occasion, and the important family with which he was to be connected. He pacified himself, however, with the conclusion that it must have been youthful impatience which had induced him thus to spur on sooner than his attendants.

"I am sorry," said the stranger, "to break in upon you thus unseasonably—"

Here the Baron interrupted him with a world of compliments and greetings; for, to tell the truth, he prided himself upon his courtesy and his eloquence. The stranger attempted, once or twice, to stem the torrent of words, but in vain; so he bowed his head and suffered it to flow on. By the time the Baron had come to a pause they had reached the inner court of the castle; and the stranger was again about to speak, when he was once more interrupted by the appearance of the female part of the family, leading forth the shrinking and blushing bride. He gazed on her for a moment as one entranced; it seemed as if his whole soul beamed forth in the gaze, and rested upon that lovely form. One of the maiden aunts whispered something in her ear; she made an effort to speak; her moist blue eye was timidly raised, gave a shy glance of inquiry on the stranger, and was cast again to the ground. The words died away; but there was a sweet smile playing about her lips, and a soft dimpling of the cheek, that showed her glance had not been unsatisfactory. It was impossible for a girl of the fond age of eighteen, highly predisposed for love and matrimony, not to be pleased with so gallant a cavalier.

The late hour at which the guest had arrived left no time for parley. The Baron was peremptory, and deferred all particular conversation until the morning, and led the way to the untasted banquet.

It was served up in the great hall of the castle. Around the walls hung the hard-favored portraits of the heroes of the house of Katzenellenbogen, and the trophies which they had gained in the field and in the chase. Hacked corselets, splintered jousting spears, and tattered banners, were mingled with the spoils of sylvan warfare: the jaws of the wolf, and the tusks of the boar, grinned horribly among crossbows and battle-axes, and a huge pair of antlers branched immediately over the head of the youthful bridegroom.

The cavalier took but little notice of the company or the entertainment. He scarcely tasted the banquet, but seemed absorbed in admiration of his bride. He conversed in a low tone, that could not be overheard—for the language of love is never loud; but where is the female ear so dull that it cannot catch the softest whisper of the lover? There was a mingled tenderness and gravity in his manner that appeared to have a powerful effect upon the young lady. Her color came and went, as she listened with deep attention. Now and then she made some blushing reply, and when his eye was turned away she would steal a sidelong glance at his romantic countenance, and heave a gentle sigh of tender happiness. It was evident that the young couple were completely enamored. The aunts, who were deeply versed in the mysteries of the heart, declared that they had fallen in love with each other at first sight.

The feast went on merrily, or at least noisily, for the guests were all blessed with those keen appetites that attend upon light purses and mountain air. The Baron told his best and longest stories, and never had he told them so well, or with such great effect. If there was anything marvelous, his auditors were lost in astonishment; and if anything facetious, they were sure to laugh exactly in the right place. The Baron, it is true, like most great men, was too dignified to utter any joke but a dull one: it was always enforced, however, by a bumper of excellent Hoch-heimer; and even a dull joke, at one's own table, served up with jolly old wine, is irresistible. Many good things were said by poorer and keener wits that would not bear repeating, except on similar occasions; many sly speeches whispered in ladies' ears that almost convulsed them with suppressed laughter; and a song or two roared out by a poor, but merry and broad-faced cousin of the Baron, that absolutely made the maiden aunts hold up their fans.

Amid all this revelry, the stranger-guest maintained a most singular and unseasonable gravity. His countenance assumed a deeper cast of dejection as the evening advanced, and, strange as it may appear, even the Baron's jokes seemed only to render him the more melancholy. At times he was lost in thought, and at times there was a perturbed and rest-less wandering of the eye that bespoke a mind but ill at ease. His conversation with the bride became more and more ear-nest and mysterious. Lowering clouds began to steal over the fair serenity of her brow, and tremors to run through her tender frame.

All this could not escape the notice of the company. Their gayety was chilled by the unaccountable gloom of the bridegroom; their spirits were infected; whispers and glances were interchanged, accompanied by shrugs and dubious shakes of the head. The song and the laugh grew less and less frequent: there were dreary pauses in the con-versation, which were at length succeeded by wild tales, and supernatural legends. One dismal story produced an-other still more dismal, and the Baron nearly frightened some of the ladies into hysterics with the history of the goblin horseman that carried away the fair Leonora — a dreadful, but true story, which has since been put into ex-cellent verse, and is read and believed by all the world.

The bridegroom listened to this tale with profound atten-tion. He kept his eyes steadily fixed on the Baron, and, as the story drew to a close, began gradually to rise from his seat, growing taller and taller, until, in the Baron's entranced eye, he seemed almost to tower into a giant. The moment the tale was finished, he heaved a deep sigh, and took a solemn farewell of the company. They were all amazement. The Baron was perfectly thunderstruck.

"What! going to leave the castle at midnight? Why, everything was prepared for his reception; a chamber was ready for him if he wished to retire."

The stranger shook his head mournfully and mysteriously: "I must lay my head in a different chamber tonight!"

There was something in this reply, and the tone in which it was uttered, that made the Baron's heart misgive him; but he rallied his forces, and repeated his hospitable entreaties. The stranger shook his head silently, but positively, at every offer; and, waving his farewell to the company, stalked slowly out of the hall. The maiden aunts were absolutely petrified—the bride hung her head, and a tear stole to her eye.

The Baron followed the stranger to the great court of the castle, where the black charger stood pawing the earth and snorting with impatience. When they had reached the portal, whose deep archway was dimly lighted by a cresset, the stranger paused, and addressed the Baron in a hollow tone of voice, which the vaulted roof rendered still more sepulchral. "Now that we are alone," said he, "I will impart to you the reason of my going. I have a solemn, an indispensable engagement—"

"Why," said the Baron, "cannot you send some one in your place?"

"It admits of no substitute—I must attend it in person—I must away to Wurtzburg cathedral—"

"Ay," said the Baron, plucking up spirit, "but not until to-morrow—to-morrow you shall take your bride there."

"No! no!" replied the stranger, with tenfold solemnity, "my engagement is with no bride—the worms! the worms expect me! I am a dead man—I have been slain by robbers

—my body lies at Wurtzburg—at midnight I am to be buried
—the grave is waiting for me—I must keep my appointment!''

He sprang on his black charger, dashed over the drawbridge, and the clattering of his horse's hoofs was lost in the
whistling of the night-blast.

The Baron returned to the hall in the utmost consterna-
tion, and related what had passed. Two ladies fainted outright; others sickened at the idea of having banqueted with
a specter. It was the opinion of some that this might be the
wild huntsman famous in German legend. Some talked of
mountain sprites, of wood-demons, and of other supernatural
beings, with which the good people of Germany have been
so grievously harassed since time immemorial. One of the
poor relations ventured to suggest that it might be some
sportive evasion of the young cavalier, and that the very
gloominess of the caprice seemed to accord with so melancholy a personage. This, however, drew on him the indignation of the whole company, and especially of the Baron,
who looked upon him as little better than an infidel; so that
he was fain to abjure his heresy as speedily as possible, and
come into the faith of the true believers.

But, whatever may have been the doubts entertained,
they were completely put to an end by the arrival, next day,
of regular missives confirming the intelligence of the young
Count's murder, and his interment in Wurtzburg cathedral.

The dismay at the castle may well be imagined. The
Baron shut himself up in his chamber. The guests who had
come to rejoice with him could not think of abandoning him
in his distress. They wandered about the courts, or collected
in groups in the hall, shaking their heads and shrugging
their shoulders at the troubles of so good a man; and sat
longer than ever at table, and ate and drank more stoutly
than ever, by way of keeping up their spirits. But the situation of the widowed bride was the most pitiable. To have
lost a husband before she had even embraced him—and such
a husband! if the very specter could be so gracious and noble,

what must have been the living man? She filled the house
with lamentations.

On the night of the second day of her widowhood, she
had retired to her chamber, accompanied by one of her aunts,
who insisted on sleeping with her. The aunt, who was one
of the best tellers of ghost stories in all Germany, had just
been recounting one of her longest, and had fallen asleep in
the very midst of it. The chamber was remote, and over-
looked a small garden. The niece lay pensively gazing at the
beams of the rising moon, as they trembled on the leaves of
an aspen tree before the lattice. The castle clock had just
told midnight, when a soft strain of music stole up from the
garden. She rose hastily from her bed and stepped lightly
to the window. A tall figure stood among the shadows of
the trees. As it raised its head, a beam of moonlight fell
upon the countenance. Heaven and earth! she beheld the
Specter Bridegroom! A loud shriek at that moment burst
upon her ear, and her aunt, who had been awakened by the
music, and had followed her silently to the window, fell into
her arms. When she looked again, the specter had disappeared.

Of the two females, the aunt now required the most
soothing, for she was perfectly beside herself with terror.
As to the young lady, there was something, even in the
specter of her lover, that seemed endearing. There was still
the semblance of manly beauty; and though the shadow of a
man is but little calculated to satisfy the affections of a love-
sick girl, yet, where the substance is not to be had, even that
is consoling. The aunt declared she would never sleep in
that chamber again; the niece, for once, was refractory, and
declared as strongly that she would sleep in no other in the
castle: the consequence was that she had to sleep in it alone;
but she drew a promise from her aunt not to relate the story
of the specter, lest she should be denied the only melancholy
pleasure left her on earth—that of inhabiting the chamber over
which the guardian shade of her lover kept its nightly vigils.

How long the good old lady would have observed this

promise is uncertain, for she dearly loved to talk of the marvelous, and there is a triumph in being the first to tell a frightful story; it is, however, still quoted in the neighborhood, as a memorable instance of female secrecy, that she kept it to herself for a whole week; when she was suddenly absolved from all further restraint by intelligence brought to the breakfast-table one morning that the young lady was not to be found. Her room was empty—the bed had not been slept in—the window was open—and the bird had flown!

The astonishment and concern with which the intelligence was received can only be imagined by those who have witnessed the agitation which the mishaps of a great man cause among his friends. Even the poor relations paused for a moment from the indefatigable labors of the trencher; when the aunt, who had at first been struck speechless, wrung her hands and shrieked out, "The goblin! the goblin! She's carried away by the goblin!"

In a few words she related the fearful scene of the garden, and concluded that the specter must have carried off his bride. Two of the domestics corroborated the opinion, for they had heard the clattering of a horse's hoofs down the mountain about midnight, and had no doubt that it was the specter on his black charger, bearing her away to the tomb. All present were struck with the direful probability; for events of the kind are extremely common in Germany, as many well-authenticated histories bear witness.

What a lamentable situation was that of the poor Baron! What a heartrending dilemma for a fond father, and a member of the great family of Katzenellenbogen! His only daughter had either been rapt away to the grave, or he was to have some wood-demon for a son-in-law, and, perchance, a troop of goblin grandchildren. As usual, he was completely bewildered, and all the castle in an uproar. The men were ordered to take horse and scour every road and path and glen of the Odenwald. The Baron himself had just drawn on his jack-boots, girded on his sword, and was about to mount his steed to sally forth on the doubtful quest, when he was brought to a pause by a new apparition. A lady was seen approaching the castle, mounted on a palfrey attended by a cavalier on horseback. She galloped up to the gate, sprang from her horse, and falling at the Baron's feet, embraced his knees. It was his lost daughter, and her companion—the Specter Bridegroom! The Baron was astounded. He looked at his daughter, then at the specter, and almost doubted the evidence of his senses. The latter, too, was wonderfully improved in his appearance, since his visit to the world of spirits. His dress was splendid, and set off a noble figure of manly symmetry. He was no longer pale and melancholy. His fine countenance was flushed with the glow of youth, and joy rioted in his large dark eye.

The mystery was soon cleared up. The cavalier (for, in truth, as you must have known all the while, he was no goblin) announced himself as Sir Herman Von Starkenfaust. He related his adventure with the young Count. He told how he had hastened to the castle to deliver the unwelcome tidings, but that the eloquence of the Baron had interrupted him in every attempt to tell his tale. How the sight of the bride had completely captivated him, and that to pass a few hours near her he had tacitly suffered the mistake to continue. How he had been sorely perplexed in what way to make a decent retreat, until the Baron's goblin stories had suggested his eccentric exit. How, fearing the feudal hostility of the family, he had repeated his visits by stealth—had haunted the garden beneath the young lady's window—had wooed—had won—had borne away in triumph—and, in a word, had wedded the fair.

Under any other circumstances the Baron would have been inflexible, for he was tenacious of paternal authority and devoutly obstinate in all family feuds; but he loved his daughter; he had lamented her as lost; he rejoiced to find her still alive; and, though her husband was of a hostile house, yet, thank Heaven, he was not a goblin. There was something, it must be acknowledged, that did not exactly accord with his notions of strict veracity, in the joke the knight had passed upon him of his being a dead man; but several old friends present, who had served in the wars, assured him that every stratagem was excusable in love, and that the cavalier was entitled to especial privilege, having lately served as a trooper.

Matters, therefore, were happily arranged. The Baron pardoned the young couple on the spot. The revels at the castle were resumed. The poor relations overwhelmed this new member of the family with loving-kindness; he was so gallant, so generous—and so rich. The aunts, it is true, were somewhat scandalized that their system of strict seclusion, and passive obedience, should be so badly exemplified, but attributed it all to their negligence in not having the windows grated. One of them was particularly mortified at having her marvelous story marred, and that the only specter she had ever seen should turn out a counterfeit; but the niece seemed perfectly happy at having found him substantial flesh and blood—and so the story ends.

WESTMINSTER ABBEY

"When I behold, with deep astonishment,
  To famous Westminster how there resorte,
  Living in brasse or stony monument,
  The princes and the worthies of all sorte;
  Doe not I see reformed nobilitie,
  Without contempt, or pride, or ostentation,
  And looke upon offenseless majesty,
  Naked of pomp or earthly domination?
  And how a play-game of a painted stone
  Contents the quiet now and silent sprites,
  Whome all the world which late they stood upon
  Could not content nor quench their appetites.
      Life is a frost of cold felicitie,
      And death the thaw of all our vanitie."
            —*Christolero's Epigrams*, by T. B., 1598.

ON one of those sober and rather melancholy days, in the latter part of autumn, when the shadows of morning and evening almost mingle together, and throw a gloom over the decline of the year, I passed several hours in rambling about Westminster Abbey.   There was something congenial to the season in the mournful magnificence of the old pile; and as I passed its threshold, it seemed like stepping back into the regions of antiquity, and losing myself among the shades of former ages.

I entered from the inner court of Westminster school, through a long, low, vaulted passage, that had an almost subterranean look, being dimly lighted in one part by circular perforations in the massive walls.   Through this dark avenue I had a distant view of the cloisters, with the figure of an old verger, in his black gown, moving along their shadowy vaults, and seeming like a specter from one of the neighboring tombs.

The approach to the abbey through these gloomy monastic remains prepares the mind for its solemn contemplation. The cloister still retains something of the quiet and seclusion of former days.   The gray walls are discolored by damps and crumbling with age; a coat of hoary moss has gathered over the inscriptions of the mural monuments, and obscured the death's heads, and other funeral emblems.   The sharp touches of the chisel are gone from the rich tracery of the arches; the roses which adorned the keystones have lost their leafy beauty; everything bears marks of the gradual dilapidations of time, which yet has something touching and pleasing in its very decay.

The sun was pouring down a yellow autumnal ray into the square of the cloisters; beaming upon a scanty plot of grass in the center, and lighting up an angle of the vaulted passage with a kind of dusty splendor.   From between the arcades, the eye glanced up to a bit of blue sky, or a passing cloud; and beheld the sun-gilt pinnacles of the abbey towering into the azure heaven.

As I paced the cloisters, sometimes contemplating this mingled picture of glory and decay, and sometimes endeavoring to decipher the inscriptions on the tombstones,

which formed the pavement beneath my feet, my eyes were
attracted to three figures, rudely carved in relief, but nearly
worn away by the footsteps of many generations. They
were the effigies of three of the early abbots; the epitaphs
were entirely effaced; the names alone remained, having no
doubt been renewed in later time (Vitalis. Abbas. 1082, and
Gislebertus Crispinus. Abbas. 1114, and Laurentius. Abbas.
1176). I remained some little while musing over these casual relics of antiquity, thus left like wrecks upon this distant
shore of time, telling no tale but that such beings had been
and had perished; teaching no moral but the futility of that
pride which hopes still to exact homage in its ashes, and to
live in an inscription. A little longer, and even these faint
records will be obliterated and the monument will cease to
be a memorial. While I was yet looking down upon the
gravestones, I was roused by the sound of the abbey clock,
reverberating from buttress to buttress, and echoing among
the cloisters. It is almost startling to hear this warning of
departed time sounding among the tombs, and telling the
lapse of the hour, which, like a billow, has rolled us onward
toward the grave.

I pursued my walk to an arched door opening to the interior of the abbey. On entering here, the magnitude of the
building breaks fully upon the mind, contrasted with the
vaults of the cloisters. The eye gazes with wonder at clus-
tered columns of gigantic dimensions, with arches springing
from them to such an amazing height; and man wandering
about their bases, shrunk into insignificance in comparison
with his own handiwork. The spaciousness and gloom of
this vast edifice produce a profound and mysterious awe.
We step cautiously and softly about, as if fearful of disturb-
ing the hallowed silence of the tomb; while every footfall
whispers along the walls and chatters among the sepulchers,
making us more sensible of the quiet we have interrupted.

It seems as if the awful nature of the place presses down
upon the soul, and hushes the beholder into noiseless reverence. We feel that we are surrounded by the congregated

bones of the great men of past times, who have filled history
with their deeds and the earth with their renown. And yet
it almost provokes a smile at the vanity of human ambition,
to see how they are crowded together, and justled in the
dust; what parsimony is observed in doling out a scanty
nook—a gloomy corner—a little portion of earth, to those
whom, when alive, kingdoms could not satisfy: and how
many shapes, and forms, and artifices, are devised to catch
the casual notice of the passenger, and save from forgetfulness, for a few short years, a name which once aspired to
occupy ages of the world's thought and admiration.

I passed some time in Poet's Corner, which occupies an
end of one of the transepts or cross aisles of the abbey. The
monuments are generally simple; for the lives of literary
men afford no striking themes for the sculptor. Shakespeare
and Addison have statues erected to their memories; but the
greater part have busts, medallions, and sometimes mere inscriptions. Notwithstanding the simplicity of these memorials, I have always observed that the visitors to the abbey
remain longest about them. A kinder and fonder feeling
takes place of that cold curiosity or vague admiration with
which they gaze on the splendid monuments of the great
and the heroic. They linger about these as about the tombs
of friends and companions; for indeed there is something of
companionship between the author and the reader. Other
men are known to posterity only through the medium of history, which is continually growing faint and obscure; but
the intercourse between the author and his fellowmen is ever
new, active, and immediate. He has lived for them more
than for himself; he has sacrificed surrounding enjoyments,
and shut himself up from the delights of social life, that he
might the more intimately commune with distant minds and
distant ages. Well may the world cherish his renown; for
it has been purchased, not by deeds of violence and blood,
but by the diligent dispensation of pleasure. Well may posterity be grateful to his memory; for he has left it an inheritance, not of empty names and sounding actions, but

whole treasures of wisdom, bright gems of thought, and golden veins of language.

From Poet's Corner I continued my stroll toward that part of the abbey which contains the sepulchers of the kings. I wandered among what once were chapels, but which are now occupied by the tombs and monuments of the great. At every turn, I met with some illustrious name, or the cognizance of some powerful house renowned in history. As the eye darts into these dusky chambers of death, it catches glimpses of quaint effigies: some kneeling in niches, as if in devotion; others stretched upon the tombs, with hands piously pressed together; warriors in armor, as if reposing after battle; prelates, with crosiers and miters; and nobles in robes and coronets, lying, as it were, in state. In glancing over this scene, so strangely populous, yet where every form is so still and silent, it seems almost as if we were treading a mansion of that fabled city where every being had been suddenly transmuted into stone.

I paused to contemplate a tomb on which lay the effigy of a knight in complete armor. A large buckler was on one arm; the hands were pressed together in supplication upon the breast; the face was almost covered by the morion; the legs were crossed in token of the warrior's having been engaged in the holy war. It was the tomb of a crusader; of one of those military enthusiasts who so strangely mingled religion and romance, and whose exploits form the connecting link between fact and fiction—between the history and the fairy tale. There is something extremely picturesque in the tombs of these adventurers, decorated, as they are, with rude armorial bearings and Gothic sculpture. They comport with the antiquated chapels in which they are generally found; and in considering them, the imagination is apt to kindle with the legendary associations, the romantic fictions, the chivalrous pomp and pageantry, which poetry has spread over the wars for the Sepulcher of Christ. They are the relics of times utterly gone by; of beings passed from recollection; of customs and manners with which ours have no affinity. They are like objects from some strange and distant land, of which we have no certain knowledge, and about which all our conceptions are vague and visionary. There is something extremely solemn and awful in those effigies on Gothic tombs, extended as if in the sleep of death or in the supplication of the dying hour. They have an effect infinitely more impressive on my feelings than the fanciful attitudes, the overwrought conceits and allegorical groups, which abound on modern monuments. I have been struck, also, with the superiority of many of the old sepulchral inscriptions. There was a noble way, in former times, of saying things simply, and yet saying them proudly; and I do not know an epitaph that breathes a loftier consciousness of family worth and honorable lineage than one which affirms, of a noble house, that "all the brothers were brave, and all the sisters virtuous."

In the opposite transept of Poet's Corner stands a monument which is among the most renowned achievements of modern art; but which, to me, appears horrible rather than sublime. It is the tomb of Mrs. Nightingale, by Roubillac. The bottom of the monument is represented as throwing open its marble doors, and a sheeted skeleton is starting forth. The shroud is falling from his fleshless frame as he lanches his dart at his victim. She is sinking into her affrighted husband's arms, who strives, with vain and frantic effort, to avert the blow. The whole is executed with terrible truth and spirit; we almost fancy we hear the gibbering yell of triumph bursting from the distended jaws of the specter.— But why should we thus seek to clothe death with unnecessary terrors, and to spread horrors round the tomb of those we love? The grave should be surrounded by everything that might inspire tenderness and veneration for the dead; or that might win the living to virtue. It is the place, not of disgust and dismay, but of sorrow and meditation.

While wandering about these gloomy vaults and silent aisles, studying the records of the dead, the sound of busy existence from without occasionally reaches the ear: the

rumbling of the passing equipage; the murmur of the multitude; or perhaps the light laugh of pleasure. The contrast
is striking with the deathlike repose around; and it has a
strange effect upon the feelings, thus to hear the surges of
active life hurrying along and beating against the very walls
of the sepulcher.

I continued in this way to move from tomb to tomb, and
from chapel to chapel. The day was gradually wearing
away; the distant tread of loiterers about the abbey grew less
and less frequent; the sweet-tongued bell was summoning
to evening prayers; and I saw at a distance the choristers, in
their white surplices, crossing the aisle and entering the choir.
I stood before the entrance to Henry the Seventh's chapel.
A flight of steps leads up to it, through a deep and gloomy,
but magnificent arch. Great gates of brass, richly and deli-
cately wrought, turn heavily upon their hinges, as if proudly
reluctant to admit the feet of common mortals into this most
gorgeous of sepulchers.

On entering, the eye is astonished by the pomp of architecture, and the elaborate beauty of sculptured detail. The
very walls are wrought into universal ornament, incrusted
with tracery, and scooped into niches, crowded with the
statues of saints and martyrs. Stone seems, by the cunning
labor of the chisel, to have been robbed of its weight and
density, suspended aloft, as if by magic, and the fretted roof
achieved with the wonderful minuteness and airy security of
a cobweb.

Along the sides of the chapel are the lofty stalls of the
Knights of the Bath, richly carved of oak, though with the
grotesque decorations of Gothic architecture. On the pinnacles of the stalls are affixed the helmets and crests of the
knights, with their scarfs and swords; and above them are
suspended their banners, emblazoned with armorial bearings,
and contrasting the splendor of gold and purple and crimson
with the cold gray fretwork of the roof. In the midst of this
grand mausoleum stands the sepulcher of its founder—his
effigy, with that of his queen, extended on a sumptuous

tomb, and the whole surrounded by a superbly wrought brazen railing.

There is a sad dreariness in this magnificence; this strange mixture of tombs and trophies; these emblems of living and aspiring ambition, close beside mementos which show the dust and oblivion in which all must sooner or later terminate. Nothing impresses the mind with a deeper feeling of loneliness than to tread the silent and deserted scene of former throng and pageant. On looking round on the vacant stalls of the knights and their esquires, and on the rows of dusty but gorgeous banners that were once borne before them, my imagination conjured up the scene when this hall was bright with the valor and beauty of the land; glittering with the splendor of jeweled rank and military array; alive with the tread of many feet, and the hum of an admiring multitude. All had passed away; the silence of death had settled again upon the place; interrupted only by the casual chirping of birds, which had found their way into the chapel, and built their nests among its friezes and pendents—sure signs of solitariness and desertion. When I read the names inscribed on the banners, they were those of men scattered far and wide about the world; some tossing upon distant seas; some under arms in distant lands; some mingling in the busy intrigues of courts and cabinets: all seeking to deserve one more distinction in this mansion of shadowy honors—the melancholy reward of a monument.

Two small aisles on each side of this chapel present a touching instance of the equality of the grave which brings down the oppressor to a level with the oppressed, and mingles the dust of the bitterest enemies together. In one is the sepulcher of the haughty Elizabeth; in the other is that of her victim, the lovely and unfortunate Mary. Not an hour in the day but some ejaculation of pity is uttered over the fate of the latter, mingled with indignation at her oppressor. The walls of Elizabeth's sepulcher continually echo with the sighs of sympathy heaved at the grave of her rival.

A peculiar melancholy reigns over the aisle where Mary

lies buried.   The light struggles dimly through windows
darkened by dust.   The greater part of the place is in deep
shadow, and the walls are stained and tinted by time and
weather.   A marble figure of Mary is stretched upon the
tomb, round which is an iron railing, much corroded, bearing her national emblem—the thistle.   I was weary with
wandering, and sat down to rest myself by the monument,
revolving in my mind the checkered and disastrous story of
poor Mary.

The sound of casual footsteps had ceased from the abbey.
I could only hear, now and then, the distant voice of the
priest repeating the evening service, and the faint responses
of the choir; these paused for a time, and all was hushed.
The stillness, the desertion and obscurity that were gradually prevailing around, gave a deeper and more solemn
interest to the place:

> "For in the silent grave no conversation,
> No joyful tread of friends, no voice of lovers,
> No careful father's counsel—nothing's heard,
> For nothing is, but all oblivion,
> Dust, and an endless darkness."

Suddenly the notes of the deep-laboring organ burst upon
the ear, falling with doubled and redoubled intensity, and
rolling, as it were, huge billows of sound.   How well do
their volume and grandeur accord with this mighty building!   With what pomp do they swell through its vast vaults,
and breathe their awful harmony through these caves of
death, and make the silent sepulcher vocal!—And now they
rise in triumphant acclamation, heaving higher and higher
their accordant notes, and piling sound on sound.—And now
they pause, and the soft voices of the choir break out into
sweet gushes of melody; they soar aloft, and warble along
the roof, and seem to play about these lofty vaults like the
pure airs of heaven.   Again the pealing organ heaves its
thrilling thunders, compressing air into music, and rolling
it forth upon the soul.   What long-drawn cadences!   What

solemn sweeping concords! It grows more and more dense and powerful—it fills the vast pile, and seems to jar the very walls—the ear is stunned—the senses are overwhelmed. And now it is winding up in full jubilee—it is rising from the earth to heaven—the very soul seems rapt away, and floated upward on this swelling tide of harmony!

I sat for some time lost in that kind of reverie which a strain of music is apt sometimes to inspire: the shadows of evening were gradually thickening around me; the monuments began to cast deeper and deeper gloom; and the distant clock again gave token of the slowly waning day.

I arose, and prepared to leave the abbey. As I descended the flight of steps which lead into the body of the building, my eye was caught by the shrine of Edward the Confessor, and I ascended the small staircase that conducts to it, to take from thence a general survey of this wilderness of tombs. The shrine is elevated upon a kind of platform, and close around it are the sepulchers of various kings and queens. From this eminence the eye looks down between pillars and funeral trophies to the chapels and chambers below, crowded with tombs; where warriors, prelates, courtiers, and statesmen, lie mouldering in "their beds of darkness." Close by me stood the great chair of coronation, rudely carved of oak, in the barbarous taste of a remote and Gothic age. The scene seemed almost as if contrived, with theatrical artifice, to produce an effect upon the beholder. Here was a type of the beginning and the end of human pomp and power; here it was literally but a step from the throne to the sepulcher. Would not one think that these incongruous mementos had been gathered together as a lesson to living greatness?—to show it, even in the moment of its proudest exaltation, the neglect and dishonor to which it must soon arrive? how soon that crown which encircles its brow must pass away; and it must lie down in the dust and disgraces of the tomb, and be trampled upon by the feet of the meanest of the multitude? For, strange to tell, even the grave is here no longer a sanctuary. There is a shocking levity in some natures which leads them to sport with awful and hallowed things; and there are base minds which delight to revenge on the illustrious dead the abject homage and groveling servility which they pay to the living. The coffin of Edward the Confessor has been broken open, and his remains despoiled of their funeral ornaments; the scepter has been stolen from the hand of the imperious Elizabeth, and the effigy of Henry the Fifth lies headless. Not a royal monument but bears some proof how false and fugitive is the homage of mankind. Some are plundered; some mutilated; some covered with ribaldry and insult—all more or less outraged and dishonored!

The last beams of day were now faintly streaming through the painted windows in the high vaults above me: the lower parts of the abbey were already wrapped in the obscurity of twilight. The chapels and aisles grew darker and darker. The effigies of the kings faded into shadows; the marble figures of the monuments assumed strange shapes in the uncertain light; the evening breeze crept through the aisles like the cold breath of the grave; and even the distant footfall of a verger, traversing the Poet's Corner, had something strange and dreary in its sound. I slowly retraced my morning's walk, and as I passed out at the portal of the cloisters, the door, closing with a jarring noise behind me, filled the whole building with echoes.

I endeavored to form some arrangement in my mind of the objects I had been contemplating, but found they were already falling into indistinctness and confusion. Names, inscriptions, trophies, had all become confounded in my recollection, though I had scarcely taken my foot from off the threshold. What, thought I, is this vast assemblage of sepulchers but a treasury of humiliation; a huge pile of reiterated homilies on the emptiness of renown and the certainty of oblivion? It is, indeed, the empire of Death; his great shadowy palace; where he sits in state, mocking at the relics of human glory, and spreading dust and forgetfulness on the monuments of princes. How idle a boast, after all, is the immortality of a name! Time is ever silently turning

over his pages; we are too much engrossed by the story of
the present to think of the characters and anecdotes that
gave interest to the past; and each age is a volume thrown
aside to be speedily forgotten. The idol of to-day pushes the
hero of yesterday out of our recollection; and will, in turn,
be supplanted by his successor of to-morrow. "Our fathers,"
says Sir Thomas Brown, "find their graves in our short
memories, and sadly tell us how we may be buried in our
survivors." History fades into fable; fact becomes clouded
with doubt and controversy; the inscription moulders from
the tablet; the statue falls from the pedestal. Columns,
arches, pyramids, what are they but heaps of sand—and
their epitaphs but characters written in the dust? What is
the security of the tomb, or the perpetuity of an embalm-
ment? The remains of Alexander the Great have been scattered to the wind, and his empty sarcophagus is now the
mere curiosity of a museum. "The Egyptian mummies
which Cambyses or time hath spared, avarice now con-
sumeth; Mizraim cures wounds, and Pharaoh is sold for
balsams." *

What then is to insure this pile, which now towers above
me, from sharing the fate of mightier mausoleums? The
time must come when its gilded vaults, which now spring so
loftily, shall lie in rubbish beneath the feet; when, instead
of the sound of melody and praise, the wind shall whistle
through the broken arches, and the owl hoot from the shattered tower—when the garish sunbeam shall break into these
gloomy mansions of death; and the ivy twine round the
fallen column; and the fox-glove hang its blossoms about
the nameless urn, as if in mockery of the dead. Thus man
passes away; his name perishes from record and recollection; his history is as a tale that is told, and his very
monument becomes a ruin.

* Sir Thomas Brown.

CHRISTMAS

"But is old, old, good old Christmas gone? Nothing but the hair of
his good, gray, old head and beard left? Well, I will have that, seeing
I cannot have more of him."—*Hue and Cry after Christmas*

"A man might then behold
        At Christmas, in each hall,
Good fires to curb the cold,
        And meat for great and small.
The neighbors were friendly bidden,
        And all had welcome true,
The poor from the gates were not chidden,
        When this old cap was new."—*Old Song*

THERE is nothing in England that exercises a more delightful spell over my imagination than the lingerings of the
holyday customs and rural games of former times. They
recall the pictures my fancy used to draw in the May morning of life, when as yet I only knew the world through
books, and believed it to be all that poets had painted it; and
they bring with them the flavor of those honest days of yore,
in which, perhaps with equal fallacy, I am apt to think the
world was more homebred, social, and joyous than at present. I regret to say that they are daily growing more and
more faint, being gradually worn away by time, but still
more obliterated by modern fashion. They resemble those
picturesque morsels of Gothic architecture, which we see
crumbling in various parts of the country, partly dilapidated
by the waste of ages, and partly lost in the additions and
alterations of latter days. Poetry, however, clings with
cherishing fondness about the rural game and holyday revel
from which it has derived so many of its themes—as the ivy
winds its rich foliage about the Gothic arch and mouldering

tower, gratefully repaying their support, by clasping together their tottering remains, and, as it were, embalming
them in verdure.

Of all the old festivals, however, that of Christmas
awakens the strongest and most heartfelt associations.
There is a tone of solemn and sacred feeling that blends
with our conviviality, and lifts the spirit to a state of hallowed and elevated enjoyment. The services of the church
about this season are extremely tender and inspiring: they
dwell on the beautiful story of the origin of our faith, and
the pastoral scenes that accompanied its announcement: they
gradually increase in fervor and pathos during the season of
Advent, until they break forth in full jubilee on the morning
that brought peace and good-will to men. I do not know a
grander effect of music on the moral feelings than to hear the
full choir and the pealing organ performing a Christmas
anthem in a cathedral, and filling every part of the vast pile
with triumphant harmony.

It is a beautiful arrangement, also, derived from days of
yore, that this festival, which commemorates the announcement of the religion of peace and love, has been made the
season for gathering together of family connections, and
drawing closer again those bands of kindred hearts which
the cares and pleasures and sorrows of the world are continually operating to cast loose; of calling back the children
of a family, who have launched forth in life, and wandered
widely asunder, once more to assemble about the paternal
hearth, that rallying-place of the affections, there to grow
young and loving again among the endearing mementos of
childhood.

There is something in the very season of the year that
gives a charm to the festivity of Christmas. At other times,
we derive a great portion of our pleasures from the mere
beauties of Nature. Our feelings sally forth and dissipate
themselves over the sunny landscape, and we "live abroad
and everywhere." The song of the bird, the murmur of the
stream, the breathing fragrance of spring, the soft voluptu-

ousness of summer, the golden pomp of autumn; earth with
its mantle of refreshing green, and heaven with its deep delicious blue and its cloudy magnificence—all fill us with mute
but exquisite delight, and we revel in the luxury of mere
sensation. But in the depth of winter, when Nature lies
despoiled of every charm, and wrapped in her shroud of
sheeted snow, we turn for our gratifications to moral sources.
The dreariness and desolation of the landscape, the short
gloomy days and darksome nights, while they circumscribe
our wanderings, shut in our feelings also from rambling
abroad, and make us more keenly disposed for the pleasures
of the social circle. Our thoughts are more concentrated;
our friendly sympathies more aroused. We feel more sensibly the charm of each other's society, and are brought more
closely together by dependence on each other for enjoyment.
Heart calleth unto heart, and we draw our pleasures from
the deep wells of living kindness which lie in the quiet recesses of our bosoms; and which, when resorted to, furnish
forth the pure element of domestic felicity.

The pitchy gloom without makes the heart dilate on entering the room filled with the glow and warmth of the evening fire. The ruddy blaze diffuses an artificial summer and
sunshine through the room, and lights up each countenance
into a kindlier welcome. Where does the honest face of hospitality expand into a broader and more cordial smile—where
is the shy glance of love more sweetly eloquent—than by the
winter fireside? and as the hollow blast of wintry wind rushes
through the hall, claps the distant door, whistles about the
casement, and rumbles down the chimney, what can be more
grateful than that feeling of sober and sheltered security
with which we look round upon the comfortable chamber,
and the scene of domestic hilarity?

The English, from the great prevalence of rural habits
throughout every class of society, have always been fond of
those festivals and holydays which agreeably interrupt the
stillness of country life; and they were in former days particularly observant of the religious and social rights of Christ-

mas. It is inspiring to read even the dry details which some antiquaries have given of the quaint humors, the burlesque pageants, the complete abandonment to mirth and good fellowship, with which this festival was celebrated. It seemed to throw open every door and unlock every heart. It brought the peasant and the peer together, and blended all ranks in one warm generous flow of joy and kindness. The old halls of castles and manor-houses resounded with the harp and the Christmas carol, and their ample boards groaned under the weight of hospitality. Even the poorest cottage welcomed the festive season with green decorations of bay and holly; the cheerful fire glanced its rays through the lattice, inviting the passenger to raise the latch and join the gossip knot huddled round the hearth, beguiling the long evening with legendary jokes and oft-told Christmas tales.

One of the least pleasing effects of modern refinement is the havoc it has made among the hearty old holyday customs. It has completely taken off the sharp touchings and spirited reliefs of these embellishments of life, and has worn down society into a more smooth and polished, but certainly a less characteristic surface. Many of the games and ceremonials of Christmas have entirely disappeared, and, like the sherris sack of old Falstaff, are become matters of speculation and dispute among commentators. They flourished in times full of spirit and lustihood, when men enjoyed life roughly, but heartily and vigorously: times wild and picturesque, which have furnished poetry with its richest materials, and the drama with its most attractive variety of characters and manners. The world has become more worldly. There is more of dissipation and less of enjoyment. Pleasure has expanded into a broader, but a shallower stream, and has forsaken many of those deep and quiet channels, where it flowed sweetly through the calm bosom of domestic life. Society has acquired a more enlightened and elegant tone; but it has lost many of its strong local peculiarities, its home-bred feelings, its honest fireside delights. The traditionary customs of golden-hearted antiquity, its feudal hospitalities,

and lordly wassailings, have passed away with the baronial
castles and stately manor-houses in which they were celebrated. They comported with the shadowy hall, the great
oaken gallery, and the tapestried parlor, but are unfitted for
the light showy saloons and gay drawing-rooms of the modern villa.

Shorn, however, as it is, of its ancient and festive honors,
Christmas is still a period of delightful excitement in England. It is gratifying to see that home feeling completely
aroused which holds so powerful a place in every English
bosom. The preparations making on every side for the
social board that is again to unite friends and kindred—the
presents of good cheer passing and repassing, those tokens
of regard and quickeners of kind feelings—the evergreens
distributed about houses and churches, emblems of peace and
gladness—all these have the most pleasing effect in producing fond associations, and kindling benevolent sympathies.
Even the sound of the waits, rude as may be their minstrelsy, breaks upon the midwatches of a winter night with
the effect of perfect harmony. As I have been awakened by
them in that still and solemn hour "when deep sleep falleth
upon man," I have listened with a hushed delight, and connecting them with the sacred and joyous occasion, have almost fancied them into another celestial choir, announcing
peace and good-will to mankind. How delightfully the imagination, when wrought upon by these moral influences, turns
everything to melody and beauty! The very crowing of the
cock, heard sometimes in the profound repose of the country,
"telling the nightwatches to his feathery dames," was thought
by the common people to announce the approach of the sacred
festival:

> "Some say that ever 'gainst that season comes
> Wherein our Saviour's birth was celebrated,
> This bird of dawning singeth all night long:
> And then, they say, no spirit dares stir abroad;
> The nights are wholesome—then no planets strike,
> No fairy takes, no witch hath power to charm,
> So hallowed and so gracious is the time."

Amid the general call to happiness, the bustle of the spirits, and stir of the affections, which prevail at this period, what bosom can remain insensible? It is, indeed, the season of regenerated feeling—the season for kindling not merely the fire of hospitality in the hall, but the genial flame of charity in the heart. The scene of early love again rises green to memory beyond the sterile waste of years, and the idea of home, fraught with the fragrance of home-dwelling joys, reanimates the drooping spirit—as the Arabian breeze will sometimes waft the freshness of the distant fields to the weary pilgrim of the desert.

Stranger and sojourner as I am in the land—though for me no social hearth may blaze, no hospitable roof throw open its doors, nor the warm grasp of friendship welcome me at the threshold—yet I feel the influence of the season beaming into my soul from the happy looks of those around me. Surely happiness is reflective, like the light of heaven; and every countenance bright with smiles, and glowing with innocent enjoyment, is a mirror transmitting to others the rays of a supreme and ever-shining benevolence. He who can turn churlishly away from contemplating the felicity of his fellow-beings, and can sit down darkling and repining in his loneliness when all around is joyful, may have his moments of strong excitement and selfish gratification, but he wants the genial and social sympathies which constitute the charm of a merry Christmas.

THE STAGE–COACH

"Omne benê
Sine pœnâ
Tempus est ludendi
Venit hora
Absque morâ
Libros deponendi."
—*Old Holyday School Song*

In the preceding paper, I have made some general observations on the Christmas festivities of England, and am tempted to illustrate them by some anecdotes of a Christmas passed in the country; in perusing which, I would most courteously invite my reader to lay aside the austerity of wisdom, and to put on that genuine holyday spirit which is tolerant of folly and anxious only for amusement.

In the course of a December tour in Yorkshire, I rode for a long distance in one of the public coaches, on the day preceding Christmas. The coach was crowded, both inside and out, with passengers, who, by their talk, seemed principally bound to the mansions of relations or friends to eat the Christmas dinner. It was loaded also with hampers of game, and baskets and boxes of delicacies; and hares hung dangling their long ears about the coachman's box, presents from distant friends for the impending feast. I had three fine rosy-cheeked schoolboys for my fellow-passengers inside, full of the buxom health and manly spirit which I have observed in the children of this country. They were returning home for the holydays, in high glee, and promising themselves a world of enjoyment. It was delightful to hear the gigantic plans of pleasure of the little rogues, and the impracticable feats they were to perform during their six weeks' emancipation from the abhorred thralldom of book, birch, and pedagogue. They were full of the anticipations of the meeting with the family and household, down to the very cat and dog; and of the joy they were to give their little sisters, by the presents with which their pockets were crammed; but the meeting to which they seemed to look forward with the greatest impatience was with Bantam, which I found to be a pony, and, according to their talk, possessed of more virtues than any steed since the days of Bucephalus. How he could trot! how he could run! and then such leaps as he would take—there was not a hedge in the whole country that he could not clear.

They were under the particular guardianship of the coachman, to whom, whenever an opportunity presented, they addressed a host of questions, and pronounced him one of the best fellows in the whole world. Indeed, I could not but notice the more than ordinary air of bustle and importance of the coachman, who wore his hat a little on one side, and had a large bunch of Christmas greens stuck in the buttonhole of his coat. He is always a personage full of mighty care and business; but he is particularly so during this season, having so many commissions to execute in consequence of the great interchange of presents. And here, perhaps, it may not be unacceptable to my untraveled readers, to have a sketch that may serve as a general representation of this very numerous and important class of functionaries, who have a dress, a manner, a language, an air, peculiar to themselves, and prevalent throughout the fraternity; so that, wherever an English stage-coachman may be seen, he cannot be mistaken for one of any other craft or mystery.

He has commonly a broad full face, curiously mottled with red, as if the blood had been forced by hard feeding into every vessel of the skin; he is swelled into jolly dimensions by frequent potations of malt liquors, and his bulk is still further increased by a multiplicity of coats, in which he is buried like a cauliflower, the upper one reaching to his heels. He wears a broad-brimmed low-crowned hat, a huge roll of colored handkerchief about his neck, knowingly knotted and tucked in at the bosom; and has in summer-time a large bouquet of flowers in his buttonhole, the present, most probably, of some enamored country lass. His waistcoat is commonly of some bright color, striped, and his smallclothes extend far below the knees, to meet a pair of jockey boots which reach about half-way up his legs.

All this costume is maintained with much precision; he has a pride in having his clothes of excellent materials, and, notwithstanding the seeming grossness of his appearance, there is still discernible that neatness and propriety of person which is almost inherent in an Englishman. He enjoys great consequence and consideration along the road; has frequent conferences with the village housewives, who look upon him as a man of great trust and dependence; and he seems to have a good understanding with every bright eyed country lass. The moment he arrives where the horses are to be changed, he throws down the reins with something of an air, and abandons the cattle to the care of the hostler, his duty being merely to drive them from one stage to another. When off the box, his hands are thrust in the pockets of his greatcoat, and he rolls about the inn-yard with an air of the most absolute lordliness. Here he is generally surrounded by an admiring throng of hostlers, stable-boys, shoeblacks, and those nameless hangers-on that infest inns and taverns, and run errands, and do all kinds of odd jobs, for the privilege of battening on the drippings of the kitchen and the leakage of the tap-room. These all look up to him as to an oracle; treasure up his cant phrases; echo his opinions about horses and other topics of jockey lore; and, above all, endeavor to imitate his air and carriage. Every ragamuffin that has a coat to his back, thrusts his hands in the pockets, rolls in his gait, talks slang, and is an embryo Coachey.

Perhaps it might be owing to the pleasing serenity that reigned in my own mind that I fancied I saw cheerfulness in every countenance throughout the journey. A Stage-Coach, however, carries animation always with it, and puts

the world in motion as it whirls along. The horn, sounded
at the entrance of a village, produces a general bustle. Some
hasten forth to meet friends; some with bundles and band-
boxes to secure places, and in the hurry of the moment can
hardly take leave of the group that accompanies them. In
the meantime, the coachman has a world of small commissions to execute; sometimes he delivers a hare or pheasant;
sometimes jerks a small parcel or newspaper to the door of a
public house; and sometimes, with knowing leer and words
of sly import, hands to some half-blushing, half-laughing
housemaid an odd-shaped billet-doux from some rustic admirer. As the coach rattles through the village, every one
runs to the window, and you have glances on every side of
fresh country faces, and blooming giggling girls. At the
corners are assembled juntos of village idlers and wise men,
who take their stations there for the important purpose of
seeing company pass; but the sagest knot is generally at the
blacksmith's, to whom the passing of the coach is an event
fruitful of much speculation. The smith, with the horse's
heel in his lap, pauses as the vehicle whirls by; the cyclops
round the anvil suspend their ringing hammers, and suffer
the iron to grow cool; and the sooty specter in brown paper
cap, laboring at the bellows, leans on the handle for a moment, and permits the asthmatic engine to heave a long-
drawn sigh, while he glares through the murky smoke and
sulphurous gleams of the smithy.

Perhaps the impending holyday might have given a more
than usual animation to the country, for it seemed to me as
if everybody was in good looks and good spirits. Game,
poultry, and other luxuries of the table, were in brisk circulation in the villages; the grocers, butchers, and fruiterers'
shops were thronged with customers. The housewives were
stirring briskly about, putting their dwellings in order; and
the glossy branches of holly, with their bright red berries,
began to appear at the windows. The scene brought to
mind an old writer's account of Christmas preparations.
"Now capons and hens, besides turkeys, geese, and ducks,

with beef and mutton—must all die—for in twelve days a
multitude of people will not be fed with a little. Now plums
and spice, sugar and honey, square it among pies and broth.
Now or never must music be in tune, for the youth must
dance and sing to get them a-heat, while the aged sit by the
fire. The country maid leaves half her market, and must be
sent again, if she forgets a pair of cards on Christmas eve.
Great is the contention of Holly and Ivy, whether master or
dame wears the breeches. Dice and cards benefit the butler;
and if the cook do not lack wit, he will sweetly lick his
fingers."

I was roused from this fit of luxurious meditation by a
shout from my little traveling companions. They had been
looking out of the coach-windows for the last few miles, rec-
ognizing every tree and cottage as they approached home,
and now there was a general burst of joy—"There's John!
and there's old Carlo! and there's Bantam!" cried the happy
little rogues, clapping their hands.

At the end of a lane there was an old sober-looking servant in livery waiting for them; he was accompanied by a
superannuated pointer, and by the redoubtable Bantam,
a little old rat of a pony, with a shaggy mane and long
rusty tail, who stood dozing quietly by the roadside, little
dreaming of the bustling times that awaited him.

I was pleased to see the fondness with which the little
fellows leaped about the steady old footman, and hugged the
pointer, who wriggled his whole body for joy. But Bantam
was the great object of interest; all wanted to mount at
once, and it was with some difficulty that John arranged
that they should ride by turns, and the eldest should ride
first.

Off they set at last; one on the pony, with the dog bounding and barking before him, and the others holding John's
hands; both talking at once and overpowering him with questions about home, and with school anecdotes. I looked after
them with a feeling in which I do not know whether pleasure
or melancholy predominated; for I was reminded of those

days when, like them, I had neither known care nor sorrow,
and a holyday was the summit of earthly felicity. We
stopped a few moments afterward to water the horses; and
on resuming our route, a turn of the road brought us in
sight of a neat country-seat. I could just distinguish the
forms of a lady and two young girls in the portico, and I
saw my little comrades, with Bantam, Carlo, and old John,
trooping along the carriage road. I leaned out of the coach-
window, in hopes of witnessing the happy meeting, but a
grove of trees shut it from my sight.

In the evening we reached a village where I had determined to pass the night. As we drove into the great gateway of the inn, I saw, on one side, the light of a rousing
kitchen fire beaming through a window. I entered, and admired, for the hundredth time, that picture of convenience,
neatness, and broad honest enjoyment, the kitchen of an
English inn. It was of spacious dimensions, hung round
with copper and tin vessels highly polished, and decorated
here and there with a Christmas green. Hams, tongues,
and flitches of bacon were suspended from the ceiling; a
smoke-jack made its ceaseless clanking beside the fireplace,
and a clock ticked in one corner. A well-scoured deal table
extended along one side of the kitchen, with a cold round of
beef and other hearty viands upon it, over which two foaming tankards of ale seemed mounting guard. Travelers of
inferior order were preparing to attack this stout repast,
while others sat smoking and gossiping over their ale on two
high-backed oaken settles beside the fire. Trim housemaids
were hurrying backward and forward, under the directions
of a fresh bustling landlady; but still seizing an occasional
moment to exchange a flippant word, and have a rallying
laugh, with the group round the fire. The scene completely
realized Poor Robin's humble idea of the comforts of mid-
winter

"Now trees their leafy hats do bare
To reverence Winter's silver hair;
A handsome hostess, merry host,

A pot of ale and now a toast,
Tobacco and a good coal fire,
Are things this season doth require." *

I had not been long at the inn, when a post-chaise drove
up to the door.   A young gentleman stepped out, and by the
light of the lamps I caught a glimpse of a countenance which
I thought I knew.   I moved forward to get a nearer view,
when his eye caught mine.   I was not mistaken; it was
Frank Bracebridge, a sprightly good-humored young fellow,
with whom I had once traveled on the Continent.   Our
meeting was extremely cordial, for the countenance of an
old fellow-traveler always brings up the recollection of a
thousand pleasant scenes, odd adventures, and excellent
jokes.   To discuss all these in a transient interview at an
inn was impossible; and finding that I was not pressed for
time, and was merely making a tour of observation, he insisted that I should give him a day or two at his father's
country-seat, to which he was going to pass the holydays,
and which lay at a few miles' distance.   "It is better than
eating a solitary Christmas dinner at an inn," said he, "and
I can assure you of a hearty welcome, in something of
the old-fashioned style."   His reasoning was cogent, and I
must confess the preparation I had seen for universal festivity and social enjoyment had made me feel a little impatient
of my loneliness.   I closed, therefore, at once, with his invitation; the chaise drove up to the door, and in a few
moments I was on my way to the family mansion of the
Bracebridges.

* Poor Robin's Almanack, 1694.

CHRISTMAS EVE

"Saint Francis and Saint Benedight
Blesse this house from wicked wight;
From the night-mare and the goblin,
That is hight good fellow Robin;
Keep it from all evil spirits,
Fairies, weazles, rats, and ferrets:
From curfew-time
To the next prime."—CARTWRIGHT

IT was a brilliant moonlight night, but extremely cold;
our chaise whirled rapidly over the frozen ground; the post-
boy smacked his whip incessantly, and a part of the time his
horses were on a gallop. "He knows where he is going."
said my companion, laughing, "and is eager to arrive in time
for some of the merriment and good cheer of the servants'
hall. My father, you must know, is a bigoted devotee of the
old school, and prides himself upon keeping up something of
old English hospitality. He is a tolerable specimen of what
you will rarely meet with nowadays in its purity—the old
English country gentleman; for our men of fortune spend so
much of their time in town, and fashion is carried so much
into the country, that the strong rich peculiarities of ancient
rural life are almost polished away. My father, however,
from early years, took honest Peacham * for his text-book,
instead of Chesterfield; he determined in his own mind that
there was no condition more truly honorable and enviable
than that of a country gentleman on his paternal lands, and,
therefore, passes the whole of his time on his estate. He is
a strenuous advocate for the revival of the old rural games
and holyday observances, and is deeply read in the writers,

---

* Peacham's "Complete Gentleman," 1622.

ancient and modern, who have treated on the subject.   Indeed, his favorite range of reading is among the authors who
flourished at least two centuries since; who, he insists, wrote
and thought more like true Englishmen than any of their
successors.   He even regrets sometimes that he had not been
born a few centuries earlier, when England was itself, and
had its peculiar manners and customs.   As he lives at some
distance from the main road, in rather a lonely part of the
country, without any rival gentry near him, he has that
most enviable of all blessings to an Englishman, an opportunity of indulging the bent of his own humor without molestation.   Being representative of the oldest family in the neighborhood, and a great part of the peasantry being his tenants,
he is much looked up to, and, in general, is known simply
by the appellation of 'The Squire'; a title which has been
accorded to the head of the family since time immemorial.
I think it best to give you these hints about my worthy old
father, to prepare you for any little eccentricities that might
otherwise appear absurd."

We had passed for some time along the wall of a park,
and at length the chaise stopped at the gate.   It was in a
heavy magnificent old style of iron bars, fancifully wrought
at top into flourishes and flowers.   The huge square columns
that supported the gate were surmounted by the family crest.
Close adjoining was the porter's lodge, sheltered under dark
fir trees, and almost buried in shrubbery.

The post-boy rang a large porter's bell, which resounded
through the still frosty air, and was answered by the distant
barking of dogs, with which the mansion-house seemed garrisoned.   An old woman immediately appeared at the gate.
As the moonlight fell strongly upon her, I had a full view
of a little primitive dame, dressed very much in antique
taste, with a neat kerchief and stomacher, and her silver
hair peeping from under a cap of snowy whiteness.   She
came courtesying forth with many expressions of simple
joy at seeing her young master.   Her husband, it seemed,
was up at the house, keeping Christmas eve in the servants'

hall; they could not do without him, as he was the best hand at a song and story in the household.

My friend proposed that we should alight, and walk through the park to the Hall, which was at no great distance, while the chaise should follow on. Our road wound through a noble avenue of trees, among the naked branches of which the moon glittered as she rolled through the deep vault of a cloudless sky. The lawn beyond was sheeted with a slight covering of snow, which here and there sparkled as the moonbeams caught a frosty crystal; and at a distance might be seen a thin transparent vapor, stealing up from the low grounds, and threatening gradually to shroud the landscape.

My companion looked round him with transport—"How often," said he, "have I scampered up this avenue, on returning home on school vacations! How often have I played under these trees when a boy! I feel a degree of filial reverence for them, as we look up to those who have cherished us in childhood. My father was always scrupulous in exacting our holydays, and having us around him on family festivals. He used to direct and superintend our games with the strictness that some parents do the studies of their children. He was very particular that we should play the old English games according to their original form; and consulted old books for precedent and authority for every 'merrie disport'; yet, I assure you, there never was pedantry so delightful. It was the policy of the good old gentleman to make his children feel that home was the happiest place in the world, and I value this delicious home-feeling as one of the choicest gifts a parent could bestow."

We were interrupted by the clamor of a troop of dogs of all sorts and sizes, "mongrel, puppy, whelp, and hound, and curs of low degree" that, disturbed by the ringing of the porter's bell and the rattling of the chaise, came bounding open-mouthed across the lawn.

> " '—The little dogs and all,
>   Tray, Blanche, and Sweetheart, see, they bark at me!' "

cried Bracebridge, laughing. At the sound of his voice, the
bark was changed into a yelp of delight, and in a moment
he was surrounded and almost overpowered by the caresses
of the faithful animals.

We had now come in full view of the old family mansion, partly thrown in deep shadow, and partly lighted up
by the cold moonshine. It was an irregular building of
some magnitude, and seemed to be of the architecture of
different periods. One wing was evidently very ancient,
with heavy stone-shafted bow windows jutting out and overrun with ivy, from among the foliage of which the small dia-
mond-shaped panes of glass glittered with the moonbeams.
The rest of the house was in the French taste of Charles the
Second's time, having been repaired and altered, as my friend
told me, by one of his ancestors, who returned with that
monarch at the Restoration. The grounds about the house
were laid out in the old formal manner of artificial flower-
beds, clipped shrubberies, raised terraces, and heavy stone
balustrades, ornamented with urns, a leaden statue or two,
and a jet of water. The old gentleman, I was told, was extremely careful to preserve this obsolete finery in all its original state. He admired this fashion in gardening; it had an
air of magnificence, was courtly and noble, and befitting
good old family style. The boasted imitation of nature and
modern gardening had sprung up with modern republican
notions, but did not suit a monarchical government—it
smacked of the leveling system. I could not help smiling
at this introduction of politics into gardening, though I expressed some apprehension that I should find the old gentleman rather intolerant in his creed. Frank assured me, however, that it was almost the only instance in which he had
ever heard his father meddle with politics; and he believed
he had got this notion from a member of Parliament, who
once passed a few weeks with him. The Squire was glad
of any argument to defend his clipped yew trees and formal
terraces, which had been occasionally attacked by modern
landscape gardeners.

As we approached the house, we heard the sound of music, and now and then a burst of laughter, from one end of the building. This, Bracebridge said, must proceed from the servants' hall, where a great deal of revelry was permitted, and even encouraged, by the Squire, throughout the twelve days of Christmas, provided everything was done conformably to ancient usage. Here were kept up the old games of hoodman blind, shoe the wild mare, hot cockles, steal the white loaf, bob-apple, and snap-dragon; the Yule clog, and Christmas candle, were regularly burned, and the mistletoe, with its white berries, hung up, to the imminent peril of all the pretty housemaids.*

So intent were the servants upon their sports that we had to ring repeatedly before we could make ourselves heard. On our arrival being announced, the Squire came out to receive us, accompanied by his two other sons; one a young officer in the army, home on leave of absence; the other an Oxonian, just from the university. The Squire was a fine healthy-looking old gentleman, with silver hair curling lightly round an open florid countenance; in which a physiognomist, with the advantage, like myself, of a previous hint or two, might discover a singular mixture of whim and benevolence.

The family meeting was warm and affectionate; as the evening was far advanced, the Squire would not permit us to change our traveling dresses, but ushered us at once to the company, which was assembled in a large old-fashioned hall. It was composed of different branches of a numerous family connection, where there were the usual proportions of old uncles and aunts, comfortable married dames, super-annuated spinsters, blooming country cousins, half-fledged striplings, and bright-eyed boarding-school hoydens. They were variously occupied; some at a round game of cards; others conversing round the fireplace; at one end of the hall

---

* The mistletoe is still hung up in farmhouses and kitchens, at Christmas; and the young men have the privilege of kissing the girls under it, plucking each time a berry from the bush. When the berries are all plucked, the privilege ceases.

was a group of the young folks, some nearly grown up, others of a more tender and budding age, fully engrossed by a merry game; and a profusion of wooden horses, penny trumpets, and tattered dolls about the floor, showed traces of a troop of little fairy beings, who, having frolicked through a happy day, had been carried off to slumber through a peaceful night.

While the mutual greetings were going on between young Bracebridge and his relatives, I had time to scan the apartment. I have called it a hall, for so it had certainly been in old times, and the Squire had evidently endeavored to restore it to something of its primitive state. Over the heavy projecting fireplace was suspended a picture of a warrior in armor, standing by a white horse, and on the opposite wall hung a helmet, buckler, and lance. At one end an enormous pair of antlers were inserted in the wall, the branches serving as hooks on which to suspend hats, whips, and spurs; and in the corners of the apartment were fowling-pieces, fishing-rods, and other sporting implements. The furniture was of the cumbrous workmanship of former days, though some articles of modern convenience had been added, and the oaken floor had been carpeted; so that the whole presented an odd mixture of parlor and hall.

The grate had been removed from the wide overwhelming fireplace, to make way for a fire of wood, in the midst of which was an enormous log, glowing and blazing, and sending forth a vast volume of light and heat; this I understood was the yule clog, which the Squire was particular in having brought in and illumined on a Christmas eve, according to ancient custom.*

---

* The *yule clog* is a great log of wood, sometimes the root of a tree, brought into the house with great ceremony on Christmas eve, laid in the fireplace, and lighted with the brand of last year's clog. While it lasted, there was great drinking, singing, and telling of tales. Sometimes it was accompanied by Christmas candles; but in the cottages, the only light was from the ruddy blaze of the great wood fire. The yule clog was to burn all night; if it went out, it was considered a sign of ill luck.

Herrick mentions it in one of his songs:

It was really delightful to see the old Squire, seated in his hereditary elbow-chair, by the hospitable fireside of his ancestors, and looking around him like the sun of a system, beaming warmth and gladness to every heart. Even the very dog that lay stretched at his feet, as he lazily shifted his position and yawned, would look fondly up in his master's face, wag his tail against the floor, and stretch himself again to sleep, confident of kindness and protection. There is an emanation from the heart in genuine hospitality which cannot be described, but is immediately felt, and puts the stranger at once at his ease. I had not been seated many minutes by the comfortable hearth of the worthy old cavalier, before I found myself as much at home as if I had been one of the family.

Supper was announced shortly after our arrival. It was served up in a spacious oaken chamber, the panels of which shone with wax, and around which were several family portraits decorated with holly and ivy. Besides the accustomed lights, two great wax tapers, called Christmas candles, wreathed with greens, were placed on a highly polished beaufet among the family plate. The table was abundantly spread with substantial fare; but the Squire made his supper of frumenty, a dish made of wheat cakes boiled in milk with rich spices, being a standing dish in old times for Christmas eve. I was happy to find my old friend, minced pie, in

---

"Come bring with a noise,
　My merrie, merrie boys,
　　The Christmas Log to the firing;
　While my good dame she
　Bids ye all be free,
　　And drink to your hearts desiring."

The yule clog is still burned in many farmhouses and kitchens in England, particularly in the north; and there are several superstitions connected with it among the peasantry. If a squinting person come to the house while it is burning, or a person barefooted, it is considered an ill omen. The brand remaining from the yule clog is carefully put away to light the next year's Christmas fire.

the retinue of the feast; and finding him to be perfectly or-
thodox, and that I need not be ashamed of my predilection,
I greeted him with all the warmth wherewith we usually
greet an old and very genteel acquaintance.

The mirth of the company was greatly promoted by the
humors of an eccentric personage, whom Mr. Bracebridge
always addressed with the quaint appellation of Master
Simon. He was a tight brisk little man, with the air of
an arrant old bachelor. His nose was shaped like the bill
of a parrot; his face slightly pitted with the small-pox, with
a dry perpetual bloom on it, like a frost-bitten leaf in autumn.
He had an eye of great quickness and vivacity, with a droll-
ery and lurking waggery of expression that was irresistible.
He was evidently the wit of the family, dealing very much
in sly jokes and innuendoes with the ladies, and making infinite merriment by harpings upon old themes; which, unfortunately, my ignorance of the family chronicles did not
permit me to enjoy. It seemed to be his great delight, during supper, to keep a young girl next him in a continual
agony of stifled laughter, in spite of her awe of the reprov-
ing looks of her mother, who sat opposite. Indeed, he was
the idol of the younger part of the company, who laughed at
everything he said or did, and at every turn of his countenance. I could not wonder at it; for he must have been a
miracle of accomplishments in their eyes. He could imitate
Punch and Judy; make an old woman of his hand, with the
assistance of a burned cork and pocket-handkerchief; and
cut an orange into such a ludicrous caricature that the young
folks were ready to die with laughing.

I was let briefly into his history by Frank Bracebridge.
He was an old bachelor, of a small independent income,
which, by careful management, was sufficient for all his
wants. He revolved through the family system like a vagrant comet in its orbit, sometimes visiting one branch, and
scmetimes another quite remote, as is often the case with
gentlemen of extensive connections and small fortunes in
England. He had a chirping, buoyant disposition, always

enjoying the present moment; and his frequent change of
scene and company prevented his acquiring those rusty,
unaccommodating habits with which old bachelors are so
uncharitably charged. He was a complete family chronicle,
being versed in the genealogy, history, and intermarriages
of the whole house of Bracebridge, which made him a great
favorite with the old folks; he was a beau of all the elder
ladies and superannuated spinsters, among whom he was
habitually considered rather a young fellow, and he was
master of the revels among the children; so that there
was not a more popular being in the sphere in which he
moved than Mr. Simon Bracebridge. Of late years he had
resided almost entirely with the Squire, to whom he had
become a factotum, and whom he particularly delighted by
jumping with his humor in respect to old times, and by having a scrap of an old song to suit every occasion. We had
presently a specimen of his last-mentioned talent; for no
sooner was supper removed, and spiced wines and other
beverages peculiar to the season introduced, than Master
Simon was called on for a good old Christmas song. He
bethought himself for a moment, and then, with a sparkle
of the eye, and a voice that was by no means bad, excepting that it ran occasionally into a falsetto, like the notes of
a split reed, he quavered forth a quaint old ditty:

> "Now Christmas is come,
> Let us beat up the drum,
> And call all our neighbors together;
> And when they appear,
> Let us make such a cheer,
> As will keep out the wind and the weather," etc.

The supper had disposed every one to gayety, and an old
harper was summoned from the servants' hall, where he had
been strumming all the evening, and to all appearance comforting himself with some of the Squire's home-brewed. He
was a kind of hanger-on, I was told, of the establishment,
and though ostensibly a resident of the village, was oftener

to be found in the Squire's kitchen than his own home; the old gentleman being fond of the sound of "Harp in hall."

The dance, like most dances after supper, was a merry one: some of the older folks joined in it, and the Squire himself figured down several couple with a partner with whom he affirmed he had danced at every Christmas for nearly half a century. Master Simon, who seemed to be a kind of connecting link between the old times and the new, and to be withal a little antiquated in the taste of his accomplishments, evidently piqued himself on his dancing, and was endeavoring to gain credit by the heel and toe, rigadoon, and other graces of the ancient school; but he had unluckily assorted himself with a little romping girl from boarding-school, who, by her wild vivacity, kept him continually on the stretch, and defeated all his sober attempts at elegance: —such are the ill-sorted matches to which antique gentlemen are unfortunately prone!

The young Oxonian, on the contrary, had led out one of his maiden aunts, on whom the rogue played a thousand little knaveries with impunity; he was full of practical jokes, and his delight was to tease his aunts and cousins; yet, like all madcap youngsters, he was a universal favorite among the women. The most interesting couple in the dance was the young officer and a ward of the Squire's, a beautiful blushing girl of seventeen. From several shy glances which I had noticed in the course of the evening, I suspected there was a little kindness growing up between them; and, indeed, the young soldier was just the hero to captivate a romantic girl. He was tall, slender, and handsome; and, like most young British officers of late years, had picked up various small accomplishments on the Continent—he could talk French and Italian—draw landscapes—sing very tolerably —dance divinely; but, above all, he had been wounded at Waterloo:—what girl of seventeen, well read in poetry and romance, could resist such a mirror of chivalry and perfection?

The moment the dance was over he caught up a guitar,

and lolling against the old marble fireplace, in an attitude
which I am half inclined to suspect was studied, began the
little French air of the Troubadour. The Squire, however,
exclaimed against having anything on Christmas eve but
good old English; upon which the young minstrel, casting
up his eye for a moment, as if an effort of memory, struck
into another strain, and, with a charming air of gallantry,
gave Herrick's "Night-Piece to Julia."

> "Her eyes the glow-worm lend thee,
>   The shooting stars attend thee,
>   And the elves also,
>   Whose little eyes glow
>   Like the sparks of fire, befriend thee.
>
> "No Will-o'-the-Wisp mislight thee;
>   Nor snake or slow-worm bite thee;
>   But on, on thy way,
>   Not making a stay,
>   Since ghost there is none to affright thee.
>
> "Then let not the dark thee cumber;
>   What though the moon does slumber,
>   The stars of the night
>   Will lend thee their light,
>   Like tapers clear without number.
>
> "Then, Julia, let me woo thee,
>   Thus, thus to come unto me:
>   And when I shall meet
>   Thy silvery feet,
>   My soul I'll pour into thee."

The song might or might not have been intended in compliment to the fair Julia, for so I found his partner was
called; she, however, was certainly unconscious of any such
application; for she never looked at the singer, but kept her
eyes cast upon the floor; her face was suffused, it is true,
with a beautiful blush, and there was a gentle heaving of
the bosom, but all that was doubtless caused by the exercise
of the dance: indeed, so great was her indifference that she
was amusing herself with plucking to pieces a choice bouquet

of hothouse flowers, and by the time the song was concluded the nosegay lay in ruins on the floor.

The party now broke up for the night with the kind-hearted old custom of shaking hands. As I passed through the hall on my way to my chamber, the dying embers of the yule clog still sent forth a dusky glow; and had it not been the season when "no spirit dares stir abroad," I should have been half tempted to steal from my room at midnight, and peep whether the fairies might not be at their revels about the hearth.

My chamber was in the old part of the mansion, the ponderous furniture of which might have been fabricated in the days of the giants. The room was paneled with cornices of heavy carved work, in which flowers and grotesque faces were strangely intermingled, and a row of black-looking portraits stared mournfully at me from the walls. The bed was of rich, though faded damask, with a lofty tester, and stood in a niche opposite a bow-window. I had scarcely got into bed when a strain of music seemed to break forth in the air just below the window: I listened, and found it proceeded from a band, which I concluded to be the waits from some neighboring village. They went round the house, playing under the windows. I drew aside the curtains to hear them more distinctly. The moonbeams fell through the upper part of the casement, partially lighting up the antiquated apartment. The sounds, as they receded, became more soft and aerial, and seemed to accord with quiet and moonlight. I listened and listened—they became more and more tender and remote, and, as they gradually died away, my head sunk upon the pillow, and I fell asleep.

CHRISTMAS DAY

"Dark and dull night flie hence away
And give the honor to this day
That sees December turn'd to May.

. . . .

Why does the chilling winter's morne
Smile like a field beset with corn?
Or smell like to a meade new-shorne,
Thus on a sudden?—come and see
The cause, why things thus fragrant be."
—HERRICK

WHEN I woke the next morning, it seemed as if all the events of the preceding evening had been a dream, and nothing but the identity of the ancient chamber convinced me of their reality. While I lay musing on my pillow, I heard the sound of little feet pattering outside of the door, and a whispering consultation. Presently a choir of small voices chanted forth an old Christmas carol, the burden of which was—

"Rejoice, our Saviour He was born
On Christmas day in the morning."

I rose softly, slipped on my clothes, opened the door suddenly, and beheld one of the most beautiful little fairy groups that a painter could imagine. It consisted of a boy and two girls, the eldest not more than six, and lovely as seraphs. They were going the rounds of the house, singing at every chamber door, but my sudden appearance frightened them into mute bashfulness. They remained for a moment playing on their lips with their fingers, and now and then stealing a shy glance from under their eyebrows, until, as if by one impulse, they scampered away, and as they turned an angle of the gallery, I heard them laughing in triumph at their escape.

Everything conspired to produce kind and happy feelings, in this stronghold of old-fashioned hospitality. The window of my chamber looked out upon what in summer would have been a beautiful landscape. There was a sloping lawn, a fine stream winding at the foot of it, and a tract of park beyond, with noble clumps of trees and herds of deer. At a distance was a neat hamlet, with the smoke from the cottage chimneys hanging over it; and a church, with its dark spire in strong relief against the clear cold sky. The house was surrounded with evergreens, according to the English custom, which would have given almost an appearance of summer; but the morning was extremely frosty; the light vapor of the preceding evening had been precipitated by the cold, and covered all the trees and every blade of grass with its fine crystallizations. The rays of a bright morning sun had a dazzling effect among the glittering foliage. A robin, perched upon the top of a mountain ash that hung its clusters of red berries just before my window, was basking himself in the sunshine, and piping a few querulous notes; and a peacock was displaying all the glories of his train, and strutting with the pride and gravity of a Spanish grandee on the terrace-walk below.

I had scarcely dressed myself, when a servant appeared to invite me to family prayers. He showed me the way to a small chapel in the old wing of the house, where I found the principal part of the family already assembled in a kind of gallery, furnished with cushions, hassocks, and large prayer-books; the servants were seated on benches below. The old gentleman read prayers from a desk in front of the gallery, and Master Simon acted as clerk and made the responses; and I must do him the justice to say that he acquitted himself with great gravity and decorum.

The service was followed by a Christmas carol which Mr. Bracebridge himself had constructed from a poem of his favorite author, Herrick; and it had been adapted to a church melody by Master Simon. As there were several good voices among the household, the effect was extremely

pleasing; but I was particularly gratified by the exaltation
of heart, and sudden sally of grateful feeling, with which
the worthy Squire delivered one stanza; his eye glistening,
and his voice rambling out of all the bounds of time and tune:

> " 'Tis Thou that crown'st my glittering hearth
>   With guiltless mirth,
> And giv'st me Wassaile bowles to drink
>   Spic'd to the brink:

> "Lord, 'tis Thy plenty-dropping hand
>   That soiles my land:
> And giv'st me for my bushell sowne,
>   Twice ten for one."

I afterward understood that early morning service was
read on every Sunday and saint's day throughout the year,
either by Mr. Bracebridge or some member of the family. It
was once almost universally the case at the seats of the nobility and gentry of England, and it is much to be regretted
that the custom is falling into neglect; for the dullest observer must be sensible of the order and serenity prevalent in
those households where the occasional exercise of a beautiful form of worship in the morning gives, as it were, the
keynote to every temper for the day, and attunes every
spirit to harmony.

Our breakfast consisted of what the Squire denominated
true old English fare. He indulged in some bitter lamentations over modern breakfasts of tea and toast, which he censured as among the causes of modern effeminacy and weak
nerves, and the decline of old English heartiness; and though
he admitted them to his table to suit the palates of his guests,
yet there was a brave display of cold meats, wine, and ale,
on the sideboard.

After breakfast, I walked about the grounds with Frank
Bracebridge and Master Simon, or Mr. Simon, as he was
called by everybody but the Squire. We were escorted by a
number of gentlemen-like dogs that seemed loungers about
the establishment; from the frisking spaniel to the steady
old stag-hound—the last of which was of a race that had

been in the family time out of mind—they were all obedient
to a dog-whistle which hung to Master Simon's buttonhole,
and in the midst of their gambols would glance an eye occasionally upon a small switch he carried in his hand.

The old mansion had a still more venerable look in the
yellow sunshine than by pale moonlight; and I could not but
feel the force of the Squire's idea that the formal terraces,
heavily molded balustrades, and clipped yew trees, carried
with them an air of proud aristocracy.

There appeared to be an unusual number of peacocks
about the place, and I was making some remarks upon what
I termed a flock of them that were basking under a sunny
wall, when I was gently corrected in my phraseology by
Master Simon, who told me that according to the most ancient and approved treatise on hunting, I must say a *muster*
of peacocks. "In the same way," added he, with a slight
air of pedantry, "we say a flight of doves or swallows, a
bevy of quails, a herd of deer, of wrens, or cranes, a skulk
of foxes, or a building of rooks." He went on to inform me
that, according to Sir Anthony Fitzherbert, we ought to
ascribe to this bird "both understanding and glory; for, being praised, he will presently set up his tail, chiefly against
the sun, to the intent you may the better behold the beauty
thereof. But at the fall of the leaf, when his tail falleth,
he will mourn and hide himself in corners, till his tail come
again as it was."

I could not help smiling at this display of small erudition
on so whimsical a subject; but I found that the peacocks
were birds of some consequence at the Hall; for Frank
Bracebridge informed me that they were great favorites
with his father, who was extremely careful to keep up the
breed, partly because they belonged to chivalry, and were in
great request at the stately banquets of the olden time; and
partly because they had a pomp and magnificence about
them highly becoming an old family mansion. Nothing, he
was accustomed to say, had an air of greater state and dignity than a peacock perched upon an antique stone balustrade.

Master Simon had now to hurry off, having an appointment at the parish church with the village choristers, who were to perform some music of his selection. There was something extremely agreeable in the cheerful flow of animal spirits of the little man; and I confess I had been somewhat surprised at his apt quotations from authors who certainly were not in the range of every-day reading. I mentioned this last circumstance to Frank Bracebridge, who told me with a smile that Master Simon's whole stock of erudition was confined to some half a dozen old authors, which the Squire had put into his hands, and which he read over and over, whenever he had a studious fit; as he sometimes had on a rainy day or a long winter evening. Sir Anthony Fitzherbert's "Book of Husbandry"; Markham's "Country Contentments"; the "Tretyse of Hunting," by Sir Thomas Cockayne, Knight; Isaac Walton's "Angler," and two or three more such ancient worthies of the pen, were his standard authorities; and, like all men who know but a few books, he looked up to them with a kind of idolatry, and quoted them on all occasions. As to his songs, they were chiefly picked out of old books in the Squire's library, and adapted to tunes that were popular among the choice spirits of the last century. His practical application of scraps of literature, however, had caused him to be looked upon as a prodigy of book-knowledge by all the grooms, huntsmen, and small sportsmen of the neighborhood.

While we were talking, we heard the distant toll of the village bell, and I was told that the Squire was a little particular in having his household at church on a Christmas morning; considering it a day of pouring out of thanks and rejoicing; for, as old Tusser observed—

> "At Christmas be merry, *and thankful withal*,
> And feast thy poor neighbors, the great with the small."

"If you are disposed to go to church," said Frank Bracebridge, "I can promise you a specimen of my cousin Simon's musical achievements. As the church is destitute of an organ, he has formed a band from the village amateurs, and established a musical club for their improvement; he has also sorted a choir, as he sorted my father's pack of hounds, according to the directions of Jervaise Markham, in his 'Country Contentments'; for the bass he has sought out all the 'deep, solemn mouths,' and for the tenor the 'loud ringing mouth,' among the country bumpkins; and for 'sweet mouths,' he has culled with curious taste among the prettiest lasses in the neighborhood; though these last, he affirms, are the most difficult to keep in tune; your pretty female singer being exceedingly wayward and capricious, and very liable to accident."

As the morning, though frosty, was remarkably fine and clear, the most of the family walked to the church, which was a very old building of gray stone, and stood near a village, about half a mile from the park gate. Adjoining it was a low snug parsonage, which seemed coeval with the church. The front of it was perfectly matted with a yew tree that had been trained against its walls, through the dense foliage of which apertures had been formed to admit light into the small antique lattices. As we passed this sheltered nest, the parson issued forth and preceded us.

I had expected to see a sleek well conditioned pastor, such as is often found in a snug living in the vicinity of a rich patron's table, but I was disappointed. The parson was a little, meager, black-looking man, with a grizzled wig that was too wide, and stood off from each ear; so that his head seemed to have shrunk away within it, like a dried filbert in its shell. He wore a rusty coat, with great skirts, and pockets that would have held the church Bible and prayer-book: and his small legs seemed still smaller, from being planted in large shoes, decorated with enormous buckles.

I was informed by Frank Bracebridge that the parson had been a chum of his father's at Oxford, and had received this living shortly after the latter had come to his estate. He was a complete black-letter hunter, and would scarcely read a work printed in the Roman character. The editions

of Caxton and Wynkin de Worde were his delight; and ne
was indefatigable in his researches after such old English
writers as have fallen into oblivion from their worthlessness.
In deference, perhaps, to the notions of Mr. Bracebridge, he
had made diligent investigations into the festive rites and
holyday customs of former times; and had been as zealous
in the inquiry as if he had been a boon companion; but it
was merely with that plodding spirit with which men of
adust temperament follow up any track of study, merely because it is denominated learning; indifferent to its intrinsic
nature, whether it be the illustration of the wisdom or of the
ribaldry and obscenity of antiquity. He had pored over
these old volumes so intensely that they seemed to have been
reflected into his countenance; which, if the face be indeed
an index of the mind, might be compared to a title page of
black-letter.

On reaching the church porch, we found the parson re-
buking the gray-headed sexton for having used mistletoe
among the greens with which the church was decorated. It
was, he observed, an unholy plant, profaned by having been
used by the Druids in their mystic ceremonies; and though
it might be innocently employed in the festive ornamenting
of halls and kitchens, yet it had been deemed by the Fathers
of the Church as unhallowed, and totally unfit for sacred
purposes. So tenacious was he on this point, that the poor
sexton was obliged to strip down a great part of the humble
trophies of his taste, before the parson would consent to enter
upon the service of the day.

The interior of the church was venerable, but simple; on
the walls were several mural monuments of the Bracebridges,
and just beside the altar was a tomb of ancient workmanship, on which lay the effigy of a warrior in armor, with his
legs crossed, a sign of his having been a crusader. I was
told it was one of the family who had signalized himself in
the Holy Land, and the same whose picture hung over the
fireplace in the hall.

During service, Master Simon stood up in the pew and

repeated the responses very audibly; evincing that kind of ceremonious devotion punctually observed by a gentleman of the old school, and a man of old family connections. I observed, too, that he turned over the leaves of a folio prayer-book with something of a flourish, possibly to show off an enormous seal-ring which enriched one of his fingers, and which had the look of a family relic. But he was evidently most solicitous about the musical part of the service, keeping his eye fixed intently on the choir, and beating time with much gesticulation and emphasis.

The orchestra was in a small gallery, and presented a most whimsical grouping of heads, piled one above the other, among which I particularly noticed that of the village tailor, a pale fellow with a retreating forehead and chin, who played on the clarionet, and seemed to have blown his face to a point; and there was another, a short pursy man, stooping and laboring at a bass viol, so as to show nothing but the top of a round bald head, like the egg of an ostrich. There were two or three pretty faces among the female singers, to which the keen air of a frosty morning had given a bright rosy tint; but the gentlemen choristers had evidently been chosen, like old Cremona fiddles, more for tone than looks; and as several had to sing from the same book, there were clusterings of odd physiognomies, not unlike those groups of cherubs we sometimes see on country tombstones.

The usual services of the choir were managed tolerably well, the vocal parts generally lagging a little behind the instrumental, and some loitering fiddler now and then making up for lost time by traveling over a passage with prodigious celerity, and clearing more bars than the keenest fox-hunter, to be in at the death. But the great trial was an anthem that had been prepared and arranged by Master Simon, and on which he had founded great expectation. Unluckily there was a blunder at the very outset—the musicians became flurried; Master Simon was in a fever; everything went on lamely and irregularly, until they came to a chorus beginning, "Now let us sing with one accord," which seemed to be a signal for parting company: all became discord and confusion; each shifted for himself, and got to the end as well, or, rather, as soon as he could; excepting one old chorister, in a pair of horn spectacles, bestriding and pinching a long sonorous nose; who, happening to stand a little apart, and being wrapped up in his own melody, kept on a quavering course, wriggling his head, ogling his book, and winding all up by a nasal solo of at least three bars' duration.

The parson gave us a most erudite sermon on the rites and ceremonies of Christmas, and the propriety of observing it, not merely as a day of thanksgiving, but of rejoicing; supporting the correctness of his opinions by the earliest usages of the church, and enforcing them by the authorities of Theophilus of Cesarea, St. Cyprian, St. Chrysostom, St. Augustine, and a cloud more of Saints and Fathers, from whom he made copious quotations. I was a little at a loss to perceive the necessity of such a mighty array of forces to maintain a point which no one present seemed inclined to dispute; but I soon found that the good man had a legion of ideal adversaries to contend with; having, in the course of his researches on the subject of Christmas, got completely embroiled in the sectarian controversies of the Revolution, when the Puritans made such a fierce assault upon the ceremonies of the church and poor old Christmas was driven out of the land by proclamation of Parliament.* The worthy

---

* From the "Flying Eagle," a small Gazette, published December 24th, 1652—"The House spent much time this day about the business of the Navy, for settling the affairs at sea, and before they rose were presented with a terrible remonstrance against Christmas day, grounded upon divine Scriptures, 2 Cor. v. 16, 1 Cor. xv. 14, 17; and in honor of the Lord's Day, grounded upon these Scriptures, John xx. 1, Rev. i. 10, Psalms cxviii. 24, Lev. xx. iii. 7, 11, Mark xv. 8, Psalms lxxxiv. 10; in which Christmas is called Anti-christ's masse, and those Massemongers and Papists who observe it, etc. In consequence of which Parliament spent some time in consultation about the abolition of Christmas day, passed orders to that effect, and resolved to sit on the following day which was commonly called Christmas day."

parson lived but with times past, and knew but little of the present.

Shut up among worm-eaten tomes in the retirement of his antiquated little study, the pages of old times were to him as the gazettes of the day; while the era of the Revolution was mere modern history. He forgot that nearly two centuries had elapsed since the fiery persecution of poor mince-pie throughout the land; when plum porridge was denounced as "mere popery," and roast beef as anti-Christian; and that Christmas had been brought in again triumphantly with the merry court of King Charles at the Restoration. He kindled into warmth with the ardor of his contest, and the host of imaginary foes with whom he had to combat, he had a stubborn conflict with old Prynne and two or three other forgotten champions of the Round Heads, on the subject of Christmas festivity, and concluded by urging his hearers, in the most solemn and affecting manner, to stand to the traditional customs of their fathers, and feast and make merry on this joyful anniversary of the church.

I have seldom known a sermon attended apparently with more immediate effects; for on leaving the church, the congregation seemed one and all possessed with the gayety of spirit so earnestly enjoined by their pastor. The elder folks gathered in knots in the churchyard, greeting and shaking hands; and the children ran about crying, "Ule! Ule!" and repeating some uncouth rhymes,* which the parson, who had joined us, informed me had been handed down from days of yore. The villagers doffed their hats to the Squire as he passed, giving him the good wishes of the season with every appearance of heartfelt sincerity, and were invited by him to the hall, to take something to keep out the cold of the weather; and I heard blessings uttered by several of the poor, which convinced me that, in the midst of his enjoyments, the worthy

---

* "Ule! Ule!
Three puddings in a pule;
Crack nuts and cry ule!"

old cavalier had not forgotten the true Christmas virtue of
charity.

On our way homeward, his heart seemed overflowing
with generous and happy feelings. As we passed over a
rising ground which commanded something of a prospect,
the sounds of rustic merriment now and then reached our
ears; the Squire paused for a few moments, and looked
around with an air of inexpressible benignity. The beauty
of the day was, of itself, sufficient to inspire philanthropy.
Notwithstanding the frostiness of the morning, the sun in
his cloudless journey had acquired sufficient power to melt
away the thin covering of snow from every southern decliv-
ity, and to bring out the living green which adorns an English landscape even in mid-winter. Large tracts of smiling
verdure contrasted with the dazzling whiteness of the shaded
slopes and hollows. Every sheltered bank, on which the
broad rays rested, yielded its silver rill of cold and limpid
water, glittering through the dripping grass; and sent up
slight exhalations to contribute to the thin haze that hung
just above the surface of the earth. There was something
truly cheering in this triumph of warmth and verdure over
the frosty thralldom of winter; it was, as the Squire observed, an emblem of Christmas hospitality, breaking
through the chills of ceremony and selfishness, and thaw-
ing every heart into a flow. He pointed with pleasure to
the indications of good cheer reeking from the chimneys of
the comfortable farmhouses and low thatched cottages. "I
love," said he, "to see this day well kept by rich and poor;
it is a great thing to have one day in the year, at least, when
you are sure of being welcome wherever you go, and of having, as it were, the world all thrown open to you; and I am
almost disposed to join with poor Robin, in his malediction on
every churlish enemy to this honest festival:

> " 'Those who at Christmas do repine,
> And would fain hence dispatch him,
> May they with old Duke Humphry dine,
> Or else may Squire Ketch catch him.' "

The Squire went on to lament the deplorable decay of the games and amusements which were once prevalent at this season among the lower orders, and countenanced by the higher; when the old halls of castles and manor-houses were thrown open at daylight; when the tables were covered with brawn, and beef, and humming ale; when the harp and the carol resounded all day long, and when rich and poor were alike welcome to enter and make merry.* "Our old games and local customs," said he, "had a great effect in making the peasant fond of his home, and the promotion of them by the gentry made him fond of his lord. They made the times merrier, and kinder, and better, and I can truly say with one of our old poets,

> " 'I like them well—the curious preciseness
> And all-pretended gravity of those
> That seek to banish hence these harmless sports,
> Have thrust away much ancient honesty.'

"The nation," continued he, "is altered; we have almost lost our simple true-hearted peasantry. They have broken asunder from the higher classes, and seem to think their interests are separate. They have become too knowing, and begin to read newspapers, listen to alehouse politicians, and talk of reform. I think one mode to keep them in good humor in these hard times would be for the nobility and gentry to pass more time on their estates, mingle more among the country people, and set the merry old English games going again."

Such was the good Squire's project for mitigating public discontent; and, indeed, he had once attempted to put his

---

* "An English gentleman at the opening of the great day, *i.e.* on Christmas day in the morning, had all his tenants and neighbors enter his hall by daybreak. The strong beer was broached, and the black jacks went plentifully about with toast, sugar, and nutmeg, and good Cheshire cheese. The Hackin (the great sausage) must be boiled by daybreak, or else two young men must take the maiden (*i.e.* the cook) by the arms and run her round the market-place till she is shamed of her laziness."—*Round about our Sea-Coal Fire.*

doctrine in practice, and a few years before had kept open house during the holydays in the old style. The country people, however, did not understand how to play their parts in the scene of hospitality; many uncouth circumstances occurred; the manor was overrun by all the vagrants of the country, and more beggars drawn into the neighborhood in one week than the parish officers could get rid of in a year. Since then he had contented himself with inviting the decent part of the neighboring peasantry to call at the hall on Christmas day, and with distributing beef, and bread, and ale, among the poor, that they might make merry in their own dwellings.

We had not been long home, when the sound of music was heard from a distance. A band of country lads, without coats, their shirt-sleeves fancifully tied with ribbons, their hats decorated with greens, and clubs in their hands, were seen advancing up the avenue, followed by a large number of villagers and peasantry. They stopped before the hall door, where the music struck up a peculiar air, and the lads performed a curious and intricate dance, advancing, retreating, and striking their clubs together, keeping exact time to the music; while one, whimsically crowned with a fox's skin, the tail of which flaunted down his back, kept capering round the skirts of the dance, and rattling a Christmas-box with many antic gesticulations.

The Squire eyed this fanciful exhibition with great interest and delight, and gave me a full account of its origin, which he traced to the times when the Romans held possession of the island; plainly proving that this was a lineal descendant of the sword-dance of the ancients. "It was now," he said, "nearly extinct, but he had accidentally met with traces of it in the neighborhood, and had encouraged its revival; though, to tell the truth, it was too apt to be followed up by rough cudgel-play and broken heads in the evening."

After the dance was concluded, the whole party was entertained with brawn and beef, and stout home-brewed. The Squire himself mingled among the rustics, and was received with awkward demonstrations of deference and regard. It is true, I perceived two or three of the younger peasants, as they were raising their tankards to their mouths, when the Squire's back was turned, making something of a grimace, and giving each other the wink; but the moment they caught my eye they pulled grave faces, and were exceedingly demure. With Master Simon, however, they all seemed more at their ease. His varied occupations and amusements had made him well known throughout the neighborhood. He was a visitor at every farmhouse and cottage; gossiped with the farmers and their wives; romped with their daughters; and, like that type of a vagrant bachelor the humble-bee, tolled the sweets from all the rosy lips of the country round.

The bashfulness of the guests soon gave way before good cheer and affability. There is something genuine and affectionate in the gayety of the lower orders when it is excited by the bounty and familiarity of those above them; the warm glow of gratitude enters into their mirth, and a kind word or a small pleasantry frankly uttered by a patron gladdens the heart of the dependent more than oil and wine. When the Squire had retired, the merriment increased, and there was much joking and laughter, particularly between Master Simon and a hale, ruddy-faced, white-headed farmer, who appeared to be the wit of the village; for I observed all his companions to wait with open mouths for his retorts, and burst into a gratuitous laugh before they could well understand them.

The whole house indeed seemed abandoned to merriment: as I passed to my room to dress for dinner, I heard the sound of music in a small court, and looking through a window that commanded it, I perceived a band of wandering musicians, with pandean pipes and tambourine; a pretty coquettish housemaid was dancing a jig with a smart country lad, while several of the other servants were looking on. In the midst of her sport, the girl caught a glimpse of my face at the window, and coloring up, ran off with an air of roguish affected confusion.

THE CHRISTMAS DINNER

"Lo, now is come our joyful'st feast!
  Let every man be jolly,
Each roome with yvie leaves is drest,
  And every post with holly.
Now all our neighbors' chimneys smoke
  And Christmas blocks are burning;
Their ovens they with bak't meats choke,
  And all their spits are turning.
    Without the door let sorrow lie,
    And if, for cold, it hap to die,
    Wee 'l bury 't in a Christmas pye,
    And evermore be merry."
                    —WITHER'S *Juvenilia*

I HAD finished my toilet, and was loitering with Frank Bracebridge in the library, when we heard a distant thwacking sound, which he informed me was a signal for the serving up of the dinner. The Squire kept up old customs in kitchen as well as hall; and the rolling-pin struck upon the dresser by the cook summoned the servants to carry in the meats.

"Just in this knick the cook knock'd thrice,
  And all the waiters in a trice
    His summons did obey;
  Each serving man, with dish in hand,
  Marched boldly up, like our train-band,
    Presented, and away." *

The dinner was served up in the great hall, where the Squire always held his Christmas banquet. A blazing crackling fire of logs had been heaped on to warm the spacious apartment, and the flame went sparkling and wreathing up the wide-mouthed chimney. The great picture of the cru-

---

* Sir John Suckling.

sader and his white horse had been profusely decorated with
greens for the occasion; and holly and ivy had likewise been
wreathed round the helmet and weapons on the opposite wall,
which I understood were the arms of the same warrior. I
must own, by the bye, I had strong doubts about the authenticity of the painting and armor as having belonged to the
crusader, they certainly having the stamp of more recent
days; but I was told that the painting had been so considered time out of mind; and that, as to the armor, it had been
found in a lumber-room, and elevated to its present situation
by the Squire, who at once determined it to be the armor of
the family hero; and as he was absolute authority on all
such subjects in his own household, the matter had passed
into current acceptation. A sideboard was set out just un
der this chivalric trophy, on which was a display of plate
that might have vied (at least in variety) with Belshazzar's
parade of the vessels of the temple; "flagons, cans, cups,
beakers, goblets, basins, and ewers"; the gorgeous utensils
of good companionship that had gradually accumulated
through many generations of jovial housekeepers. Before
these stood the two yule candles, beaming like two stars of
the first magnitude; other lights were distributed in branches,
and the whole array glittered like a firmament of silver.

We were ushered into this banqueting scene with the
sound of minstrelsy; the old harper being seated on a stool
beside the fireplace, and twanging his instrument with a vast
deal more power than melody. Never did Christmas board
display a more goodly and gracious assemblage of countenances; those who were not handsome were, at least, happy;
and happiness is a rare improver of your hard-favored visage. I always consider an old English family as well worth
studying as a collection of Holbein's portraits or Albert
Durer's prints. There is much antiquarian lore to be acquired; much knowledge of the physiognomies of former
times. Perhaps it may be from having continually before
their eyes those rows of old family portraits with which the
mansions of this country are stocked; certain it is that the

quaint features of antiquity are often most faithfully perpetuated in these ancient lines; and I have traced an old
family nose through a whole picture-gallery, legitimately
handed down from generation to generation almost from the
time of the Conquest. Something of the kind was to be observed in the worthy company around me. Many of their
faces had evidently originated in a Gothic age, and been
merely copied by succeeding generations; and there was one
little girl, in particular, of staid demeanor, with a high Roman nose, and an antique vinegar aspect, who was a great
favorite of the Squire's, being, as he said, a Bracebridge all
over, and the very counterpart of one of his ancestors who
figured in the court of Henry VIII.

The parson said grace, which was not a short familiar
one, such as is commonly addressed to the Deity in these
unceremonious days; but a long, courtly, well-worded one
of the ancient school. There was now a pause, as if something was expected; when suddenly the butler entered the
hall with some degree of bustle: he was attended by a servant on each side with a large wax-light, and bore a silver
dish, on which was an enormous pig's head, decorated with
rosemary, with a lemon in its mouth, which was placed with
great formality at the head of the table. The moment this
pageant made its appearance the harper struck up a flourish;
at the conclusion of which the young Oxonian, on receiving
a hint from the Squire, gave, with an air of the most comic
gravity, an old carol, the first verse of which was as follows:

> "Caput apri defero
> Reddens laudes Domino.
> The boar's head in hand bring I,
> With garlands gay and rosemary.
> I pray you all synge merily
> Qui estis in convivio."

Though prepared to witness many of these little eccentricities, from being apprized of the peculiar hobby of mine
host, yet, I confess, the parade with which so odd a dish was
introduced somewhat perplexed me, until I gathered from

the conversation of the Squire and the parson that it was
meant to represent the bringing in of the boar's head—a
dish formerly served up with much ceremony, and the sound
of minstrelsy and song, at great tables on Christmas day.
"I like the old custom," said the Squire, "not merely because it is stately and pleasing in itself, but because it was
observed at the college at Oxford, at which I was educated.
When I hear the old song chanted, it brings to mind the time
when I was young and gamesome—and the noble old college
hall—and my fellow-students loitering about in their black
gowns; many of whom, poor lads, are now in their graves!"

The parson, however, whose mind was not haunted by
such associations, and who was always more taken up with
the text than the sentiment, objected to the Oxonian's ver-
sion of the carol; which, he affirmed, was different from that
sung at college.   He went on, with the dry perseverance of
a commentator, to give the college reading, accompanied by
sundry annotations; addressing himself at first to the company at large; but finding their attention gradually diverted
to other talk, and other objects, he lowered his tone as his
number of auditors diminished, until he concluded his remarks in an under voice, to a fat-headed old gentleman next
him, who was silently engaged in the discussion of a huge
plateful of turkey.*

---

* The old ceremony of serving up the boar's head on Christmas day
is still observed in the hall of Queen's College, Oxford. I was favored
by the parson with a copy of the carol as now sung, and as it may be
acceptable to such of my readers as are curious in these grave and
learned matters, I give it entire:

"The boar's head in hand bear I,
    Bedeck'd with bays and rosemary;
And I pray you, my masters, be merry,
    Quot estis in convivio.
    Caput apri defero.
    Reddens laudes Domino.

"The boar's head, as I understand,
Is the rarest dish in all this land,

The table was literally loaded with good cheer, and presented an epitome of country abundance, in this season of overflowing larders. A distinguished post was allotted to "ancient sirloin," as mine host termed it; being, as he added, "the standard of old English hospitality, and a joint of goodly presence, and full of expectation." There were several dishes quaintly decorated, and which had evidently something traditional in their embellishments; but about which, as I did not like to appear overcurious, I asked no questions.

I could not, however, but notice a pie, magnificently decorated with peacocks' feathers, in imitation of the tail of that bird, which overshadowed a considerable tract of the table. This, the Squire confessed, with some little hesitation, was a pheasant pie, though a peacock pie was certainly the most authentical; but there had been such a mortality among the peacocks this season that he could not prevail upon himself to have one killed.*

Which thus bedeck'd with a gay garland
Let us servire cantico.
Caput apri defero, etc.

"Our steward hath provided this
In honor of the King of Bliss,
Which on this day to be served is
In Reginensi Atrio.
Caput apri defero," etc.

* The peacock was anciently in great demand for stately entertainments. Sometimes it was made into a pie, at one end of which the head appeared above the crust in all its plumage, with the beak richly gilt; at the other end the tail was displayed. Such pies were served up at the solemn banquets of chivalry, when knights-errant pledged themselves to undertake any perilous enterprise, whence came the ancient oath, used by Justice Shallow, "by cock and pie."

The peacock was also an important dish for the Christmas feast; and Massinger, in his "City Madam," gives some idea of the extravagance with which this, as well as other dishes, was prepared for the gorgeous revels of the olden times:

Men may talk of Country Christmasses.
Their thirty pound butter'd eggs, their pies of carps' tongues:
Their pheasants drench'd with ambergris; *the carcases of three ju*
wethers bruised for gravy to make sauce for a single peacock!

It would be tedious, perhaps, to my wiser readers, who may not have that foolish fondness for odd and obsolete things to which I am a little given, were I to mention the other makeshifts of this worthy old humorist, by which he was endeavoring to follow up, though at humble distance, the quaint customs of antiquity. I was pleased, however, to see the respect shown to his whims by his children and relatives; who, indeed, entered readily into the full spirit of them, and seemed all well versed in their parts; having doubtless been present at many a rehearsal. I was amused, too, at the air of profound gravity with which the butler and other servants executed the duties assigned them, however eccentric. They had an old-fashioned look; having, for the most part, been brought up in the household, and grown into keeping with the antiquated mansion, and the humors of its lord; and most probably looked upon all his whimsical regulations as the established laws of honorable housekeeping.

When the cloth was removed, the butler brought in a huge silver vessel of rare and curious workmanship, which he placed before the Squire. Its appearance was hailed with acclamation; being the Wassail Bowl, so renowned in Christmas festivity. The contents had been prepared by the Squire himself; for it was a beverage in the skillful mixture of which he particularly prided himself: alleging that it was too abstruse and complex for the comprehension of an ordinary servant. It was a potation, indeed, that might well make the heart of a toper leap within him; being composed of the richest and raciest wines, highly spiced and sweetened, with roasted apples bobbing about the surface.*

---

* The Wassail Bowl was sometimes composed of ale instead of wine; with nutmeg, sugar, toast, ginger, and roasted crabs; in this way the nut-brown beverage is still prepared in some old families, and round the hearth of substantial farmers at Christmas. It is also called Lamb's Wool, and it is celebrated by Herrick in his "Twelfth Night":

"Next crowne the bowle full
With gentle Lamb's Wool,

The old gentleman's whole countenance beamed with a serene look of indwelling delight, as he stirred this mighty bowl. Having raised it to his lips, with a hearty wish of a merry Christmas to all present, he sent it brimming round the board, for every one to follow his example according to the primitive style; pronouncing it "the ancient fountain of good feeling, where all hearts met together." *

There was much laughing and rallying, as the honest emblem of Christmas joviality circulated, and was kissed rather coyly by the ladies. But when it reached Master Simon, he raised it in both hands, and, with the air of a boon companion, struck up an old Wassail Chanson:

> "The brown bowle,
>   The merry brown bowle,
>   As it goes round about-a,
>   Fill
>   Still,
>   Let the world say what it will,
>   And drink your fill all out-a.

> "The deep canne,
>   The merry deep canne,
>   As thou dost freely quaff-a,
>   Sing
>   Fling,
>   Be as merry as a king,
>   And sound a lusty laugh-a."†

Much of the conversation during dinner turned upon family topics, to which I was a stranger. There was, however, a great deal of rallying of Master Simon about some

---

> Add sugar, nutmeg, and ginger,
>   With store of ale too;
>   And thus ye must doe
> To make the Wassaile a swinger."

* "The custom of drinking out of the same cup gave place to each having his cup. When the steward came to the doore with the Wassel, he was to cry three times, *Wassel, Wassel, Wassel*, and then the chappell (chaplain) was to answer with a song."—*Archæologia*.

† From Poor Robin's Almanack.

gay widow, with whom he was accused of having a flirtation. This attack was commenced by the ladies; but it was continued throughout the dinner by the fat-headed old gentleman next the parson, with the persevering assiduity of a slow hound; being one of those long-winded jokers who, though rather dull at starting game, are unrivaled for their talents in hunting it down. At every pause in the general conversation he renewed his bantering in pretty much the same terms; winking hard at me with both eyes whenever he gave Master Simon what he considered a home thrust. The latter, indeed, seemed fond of being teased on the subject, as old bachelors are apt to be; and he took occasion to inform me, in an undertone, that the lady in question was a prodigiously fine woman and drove her own curricle.

The dinner-time passed away in this flow of innocent hilarity, and though the old hall may have resounded in its time with many a scene of broader rout and revel, yet I doubt whether it ever witnessed more honest and genuine enjoyment. How easy it is for one benevolent being to diffuse pleasure around him; and how truly is a kind heart a fountain of gladness, making everything in its vicinity to freshen into smiles! The joyous disposition of the worthy Squire was perfectly contagious; he was happy himself, and disposed to make all the world happy; and the little eccentricities of his humor did but season, in a manner, the sweetness of his philanthropy.

When the ladies had retired, the conversation, as usual, became still more animated: many good things were broached which had been thought of during dinner, but which would not exactly do for a lady's ear; and though I cannot positively affirm that there was much wit uttered, yet I have certainly heard many contests of rare wit produce much less laughter. Wit, after all, is a mighty tart, pungent ingredient, and much too acid for some stomachs; but honest good-humor is the oil and wine of a merry meeting, and there is no jovial companionship equal to that, where the jokes are rather small, and the laughter abundant.

The Squire told several long stories of early college pranks
and adventures, in some of which the parson had been a
sharer; though, in looking at the latter, it required some
effort of imagination to figure such a little dark anatomy of
a man into the perpetrator of a madcap gambol.   Indeed,
the two college chums presented pictures of what men may
be made by their different lots in life: the Squire had left
the university to live lustily on his paternal domains, in the
vigorous enjoyment of prosperity and sunshine, and had
flourished on to a hearty and florid old age; while the poor
parson, on the contrary, had dried and withered away,
among dusty tomes, in the silence and shadows of his study.
Still there seemed to be a spark of almost extinguished fire
feebly glimmering in the bottom of his soul; and, as the Squire
hinted at a sly story of the parson and a pretty milkmaid whom
they once met on the banks of the Isis, the old gentleman made
an "alphabet of faces," which, as far as I could decipher his
physiognomy, I verily believe was indicative of laughter;
indeed, I have rarely met with an old gentleman that took
absolute offense at the imputed gallantries of his youth.

I found the tide of wine and wassail fast gaining on the
dry land of sober judgment.   The company grew merrier
and louder, as their jokes grew duller.   Master Simon was
in as chirping a humor as a grasshopper filled with dew; his
old songs grew of a warmer complexion, and he began to
talk maudlin about the widow.   He even gave a long song
about the wooing of a widow, which he informed me he had
gathered from an excellent black-letter work entitled "Cupid's
Solicitor for Love"; containing store of good advice for
bachelors, and which he promised to lend me; the first verse
was to this effect:

> "He that will woo a widow must not dally,
>   He must make hay while the sun doth shine;
>   He must not stand with her, shall I, shall I,
>   But boldly say, Widow, thou must be mine."

This song inspired the fat-headed old gentleman, who
made several attempts to tell a rather broad story of Joe

Miller, that was pat to the purpose; but he always stuck in the middle, everybody recollecting the latter part excepting himself. The parson, too, began to show the effects of good cheer, having gradually settled down into a doze, and his wig sitting most suspiciously on one side. Just at this juncture, we were summoned to the drawing-room, and, I suspect, at the private instigation of mine host, whose joviality seemed always tempered with a proper love of decorum.

After the dinner-table was removed, the hall was given up to the younger members of the family, who, prompted to all kind of noisy mirth by the Oxonian and Master Simon, made its old walls ring with their merriment, as they played at romping games. I delight in witnessing the gambols of children, and particularly at this happy holyday season, and could not help stealing out of the drawing-room on hearing one of their peals of laughter. I found them at the game of blind-man's-buff. Master Simon, who was the leader of their revels, and seemed on all occasions to fulfill the office of that ancient potentate, the Lord of Misrule,* was blinded in the midst of the hall. The little beings were as busy about him as the mock fairies about Falstaff; pinching him, plucking at the skirts of his coat, and tickling him with straws. One fine blue-eyed girl of about thirteen, with her flaxen hair all in beautiful confusion, her frolic face in a glow, her frock half torn off her shoulders, a complete picture of a romp, was the chief tormentor; and from the slyness with which Master Simon avoided the smaller game, and hemmed this wild little nymph in corners, and obliged her to jump shrieking over chairs, I suspected the rogue of being not a whit more blinded than was convenient.

When I returned to the drawing-room, I found the company seated round the fire, listening to the parson, who was deeply ensconced in a high-backed oaken chair, the work of

---

* "At Christmasse there was in the Kinges house, wheresoever hee was lodged, a lorde of misrule, or mayster of merie disportes, and the like had ye in the house of every nobleman of honor; or good worshippe, were he spirituall or temporall."—Stow.

some cunning artificer of yore, which had been brought from the library for his particular accommodation. From this venerable piece of furniture, with which his shadowy figure and dark weazen face so admirably accorded, he was dealing forth strange accounts of the popular superstitions and legends of the surrounding country, with which he had become acquainted in the course of his antiquarian researches. I am half inclined to think that the old gentleman was himself somewhat tinctured with superstition, as men are very apt to be who live a recluse and studious life in a sequestered part of the country, and pore over black-letter tracts, so often filled with the marvelous and supernatural. He gave us several anecdotes of the fancies of the neighboring peasantry, concerning the effigy of the crusader, which lay on the tomb by the church altar. As it was the only monument of the kind in that part of the country, it had always been regarded with feelings of superstition by the good wives of the village. It was said to get up from the tomb and walk the rounds of the churchyard in stormy nights, particularly when it thundered; and one old woman whose cottage bordered on the churchyard had seen it through the windows of the church, when the moon shone, slowly pacing up and down the aisles. It was the belief that some wrong had been left unredressed by the deceased, or some treasure hidden, which kept the spirit in a state of trouble and restlessness. Some talked of gold and jewels buried in the tomb, over which the specter kept watch; and there was a story current of a sexton, in old times, who endeavored to break his way to the coffin at night; but just as he reached it, received a violent blow from the marble hand of the effigy, which stretched him senseless on the pavement. These tales were often laughed at by some of the sturdier among the rustics; yet, when night came on, there were many of the stoutest unbelievers that were shy of venturing alone in the footpath that led across the churchyard.

From these and other anecdotes that followed, the crusader appeared to be the favorite hero of ghost stories throughout the vicinity. His picture, which hung up in the hall, was thought by the servants to have something supernatural about it; for they remarked that, in whatever part of the hall you went, the eyes of the warrior were still fixed on you. The old porter's wife, too, at the lodge, who had been born and brought up in the family, and was a great gossip among the maid-servants, affirmed, that in her young days she had often heard say that on Midsummer eve, when it was well known all kinds of ghosts, goblins, and fairies, become visible and walk abroad, the crusader used to mount his horse, come down from his picture, ride about the house, down the avenue, and so to the church to visit the tomb; on which occasion the church door most civilly swung open of itself; not that he needed it—for he rode through closed gates and even stone walls, and had been seen by one of the dairy-maids to pass between two bars of the great park gate, making himself as thin as a sheet of paper.

All these superstitions I found had been very much countenanced by the Squire, who, though not superstitious himself, was very fond of seeing others so. He listened to every goblin tale of the neighboring gossips with infinite gravity, and held the porter's wife in high favor on account of her talent for the marvelous. He was himself a great reader of old legends and romances, and often lamented that he could not believe in them; for a superstitious person, he thought, must live in a kind of fairy land.

While we were all attention to the parson's stories, our ears were suddenly assailed by a burst of heterogeneous sounds from the hall, in which were mingled something like the clang of rude minstrelsy, with the uproar of many small voices and girlish laughter. The door suddenly flew open, and a train came trooping into the room that might almost have been mistaken for the breaking up of the court of Fairy. That indefatigable spirit, Master Simon, in the faithful discharge of his duties as lord of misrule, had conceived the idea of a Christmas mummery, or masking; and having called in to his assistance the Oxonian and the young officer, who were equally ripe for anything that should occasion romping and merriment, they had carried it into instant effect. The old housekeeper had been consulted; the antique clothes-presses and wardrobes rummaged, and made to yield up the relics of finery that had not seen the light for several generations; the younger part of the company had been privately convened from parlor and hall, and the whole had been bedizened out into a burlesque imitation of an antique mask.*

Master Simon led the van as "Ancient Christmas," quaintly appareled in a ruff, a short cloak, which had very much the aspect of one of the old housekeeper's petticoats, and a hat that might have served for a village steeple, and must indubitably have figured in the days of the Covenanters. From under this, his nose curved boldly forth, flushed with a frost bitten bloom that seemed the very trophy of a December blast. He was accompanied by the blue-eyed romp, dished up as "Dame Mince Pie," in the venerable magnificence of faded brocade, long stomacher, peaked heart, and high-heeled shoes.

The young officer appeared as Robin Hood, in a sporting dress of Kendal green, and a foraging cap with a gold tassel.

The costume, to be sure, did not bear testimony to deep research, and there was an evident eye to the picturesque, natural to a young gallant in presence of his mistress. The fair Julia hung on his arm in a pretty rustic dress, as "Maid Marian." The rest of the train had been metamorphosed in various ways; the girls trussed up in the finery of the ancient belles of the Bracebridge line, and the striplings bewhiskered with burned cork, and gravely clad in broad skirts, hanging sleeves, and full-bottomed wigs, to represent the characters of Roast Beef, Plum Pudding, and other worthies

* Maskings or mummeries were favorite sports at Christmas, in old times; and the wardrobes at halls and manor-houses were often laid under contribution to furnish dresses and fantastic disguisings. I strongly suspect Master Simon to have taken the idea of his from Ben Jonson's "Masque of Christmas."

celebrated in ancient maskings. The whole was under the
control of the Oxonian, in the appropriate character of Misrule; and I observed that he exercised rather a mischievous
sway with his wand over the smaller personages of the
pageant.

The irruption of this motley crew, with beat of drum, ac·
cording to ancient custom, was the consummation of uproar
and merriment. Master Simon covered himself with glory
by the stateliness with which, as Ancient Christmas, he
walked a minuet with the peerless, though giggling, Dame
Mince Pie. It was followed by a dance from all the characters, which, from its medley of costumes, seemed as though
the old family portraits had skipped down from their frames
to join in the sport. Different centuries were figuring at
cross-hands and right and left; the dark ages were cutting
pirouettes and rigadoons; and the days of Queen Bess jig-
ging merrily down the middle, through a line of succeeding
generations.

The worthy Squire contemplated these fantastic sports,
and this resurrection of his old wardrobe, with the simple
relish of childish delight. He stood chuckling and rubbing
his hands, and scarcely hearing a word the parson said, notwithstanding that the latter was discoursing most authenti-
cally on the ancient and stately dance of the Pavon, or peacock, from which he conceived the minuet to be derived.*
For my part, I was in a continual excitement from the varied
scenes of whim and innocent gayety passing before me. It
was inspiring to see wild-eyed frolic and warm-hearted hospitality breaking out from among the chills and glooms of
winter, and old age throwing off his apathy, and catching
once more the freshness of youthful enjoyment. I felt also

---

* Sir John Hawkins, speaking of the dance called the Pavon, from
pavo, a peacock, says: "It is a grave and majestic dance; the method
of dancing it anciently was by gentlemen dressed with caps and swords,
by those of the long robe in their gowns, by the peers in their mantles,
and by the ladies in gowns with long trains, the motion whereof in
dancing resembled that of a peacock."—History of Music.

an interest in the scene, from the consideration that these fleeting customs were posting fast into oblivion, and that this was, perhaps, the only family in England in which the whole of them were still punctiliously observed. There was a quaintness, too, mingled with all this revelry, that gave it a peculiar zest: it was suited to the time and place; and as the old manor-house almost reeled with mirth and wassail, it seemed echoing back the joviality of long-departed years.

But enough of Christmas and its gambols: it is time for me to pause in this garrulity. Methinks I hear the question asked by my graver readers, "To what purpose is all this—how is the world to be made wiser by this talk?" Alas! is there not wisdom enough extant for the instruction of the world? And if not, are there not thousands of abler pens laboring for its improvement?—It is so much pleasanter to please than to instruct—to play the companion rather than the preceptor.

What, after all, is the mite of wisdom that I could throw into the mass of knowledge; or how am I sure that my sagest deductions may be safe guides for the opinions of others? But in writing to amuse, if I fail the only evil is my own disappointment. If, however, I can by any lucky chance, in these days of evil, rub out one wrinkle from the brow of care, or beguile the heavy heart of one moment of sorrow—if I can now and then penetrate through the gathering film of misanthropy, prompt a benevolent view of human nature, and make my reader more in good humor with his fellow-beings and himself, surely, surely, I shall not then have written entirely in vain.

[THE following modicum of local history was lately put into my hands by an odd-looking old gentleman in a small brown wig and snuff-colored coat, with whom I became ac-

quainted in the course of one of my tours of observation
through the center of that great wilderness, the City. I
confess that I was a little dubious, at first, whether it was
not one of those apocryphal tales often passed off upon inquiring travelers like myself; and which have brought our
general character for veracity into such unmerited reproach.
On making proper inquiries, however, I have received the
most satisfactory assurances of the author's probity; and, indeed, have been told that he is actually engaged in a full
and particular account of the very interesting region in
which he resides, of which the following may be considered
merely as a foretaste.]

LITTLE BRITAIN

"What I write is most true . . . . I have a whole booke of cases
lying by me, which if I should sette foorth, some grave auntients
(within the hearing of Bow bell) would be out of charity with me."
—NASH

IN the center of the great City of London lies a small
neighborhood, consisting of a cluster of narrow streets and
courts, of very venerable and debilitated houses, which goes
by the name of Little Britain.   Christ Church school and St.
Bartholomew's hospital bound it on the west; Smithfield and
Long Lane on the north; Aldersgate Street, like an arm of
the sea, divides it from the eastern part of the city; while
the yawning gulf of Bull-and-Mouth Street separates it from
Butcher Lane, and the regions of New Gate.   Over this little territory, thus bounded and designated, the great dome
of St. Paul's, swelling above the intervening houses of Paternoster Row, Amen Corner, and Ave-Maria Lane, looks
down with an air of motherly protection.

This quarter derives its appellation from having been, in
ancient times, the residence of the Dukes of Brittany.   As
London increased, however, rank and fashion rolled off to

the west, and trade, creeping on at their heels, took possession of their deserted abodes.   For some time, Little Britain
became the great mart of learning, and was peopled by the
busy and prolific race of booksellers: these also gradually
deserted it, and emigrating beyond the great strait of New
Gate Street, settled down in Paternoster Row and St. Paul's
Churchyard; where they continue to increase and multiply,
even at the present day.

But though thus fallen into decline, Little Britain still
bears traces of its former splendor.   There are several houses,
ready to tumble down, the fronts of which are magnificently
enriched with old oaken carvings of hideous faces, unknown
birds, beasts, and fishes; and fruits and flowers which it
would perplex a naturalist to classify.   There are also, in
Aldersgate Street, certain remains of what were once spacious and lordly family mansions, but which have in latter
days been subdivided into several tenements.   Here may
often be found the family of a petty tradesman, with its
trumpery furniture, burrowing among the relics of antiquated finery, in great rambling time-stained apartments,
with fretted ceilings, gilded cornices, and enormous marble
fireplaces.   The lanes and courts also contain many smaller
houses, not on so grand a scale; but, like your small ancient
gentry, sturdily maintaining their claims to equal antiquity.
These have their gable-ends to the street; great bow-win-
dows, with diamond panes set in lead; grotesque carvings;
and low-arched doorways.*

In this most venerable and sheltered little nest have I
passed several quiet years of existence, comfortably lodged
in the second floor of one of the smallest, but oldest edifices.
My sitting-room is an old wainscoted chamber, with small
panels, and set off with a miscellaneous array of furniture.
I have a particular respect for three or four high-backed,

* It is evident that the author of this interesting communication
has included, in his general title of Little Britain, many of those little
lanes and courts that belong immediately to Cloth Fair.

claw-footed chairs, covered with tarnished brocade, which bear the marks of having seen better days, and have doubtless figured in some of the old palaces of Little Britain. They seem to me to keep together, and to look down with sovereign contempt upon their leathern-bottomed neighbors; as I have seen decayed gentry carry a high head among the plebeian society with which they were reduced to associate. The whole front of my sitting-room is taken up with a bow-window; on the panes of which are recorded the names of previous occupants for many generations; mingled with scraps of very indifferent gentleman-like poetry, written in characters which I can scarcely decipher; and which extol the charms of many a beauty of Little Britain, who has long, long since bloomed, faded, and passed away. As I am an idle personage, with no apparent occupation, and pay my bill regularly every week, I am looked upon as the only independent gentleman of the neighborhood; and being curious to learn the internal state of a community so apparently shut up within itself, I have managed to work my way into all the concerns and secrets of the place.

Little Britain may truly be called the heart's-core of the city; the stronghold of true John Bullism. It is a fragment of London as it was in its better days, with its antiquated folks and fashions. Here flourish in great preservation many of the holyday games and customs of yore. The inhabitants most religiously eat pancakes on Shrove-Tuesday; hot-cross-buns on Good Friday, and roast goose at Michaelmas; they send love-letters on Valentine's Day; burn the Pope on the Fifth of November, and kiss all the girls under the mistletoe at Christmas. Roast beef and plum-pudding are also held in superstitious veneration, and port and sherry maintain their grounds as the only true English wines—all others being considered vile outlandish beverages.

Little Britain has its long catalogue of city wonders, which its inhabitants consider the wonders of the world: such as the great bell of St. Paul's, which sours all the beer when it tolls; the figures that strike the hours at St. Dunstan's clock; the Monument; the lions in the Tower; and the wooden giants in Guildhall. They still believe in dreams and fortune-telling; and an old woman that lives in Bull-and-Mouth Street makes a tolerable subsistence by detecting stolen goods, and promising the girls good husbands. They are apt to be rendered uncomfortable by comets and eclipses; and if a dog howls dolefully at night, it is looked upon as a sure sign of a death in the place. There are even many ghost stories current, particularly concerning the old mansion-houses; in several of which it is said strange sights are sometimes seen. Lords and ladies, the former in full-bottomed wigs, hanging sleeves, and swords, the latter in lappets, stays, hoops, and brocade, have been seen walking up and down the great waste chambers, on moonlight nights; and are supposed to be the shades of the ancient proprietors in their court-dresses.

Little Britain has likewise its sages and great men. One of the most important of the former is a tall dry old gentleman of the name of Skryme, who keeps a small apothecary's shop. He has a cadaverous countenance, full of cavities and projections; with a brown circle round each eye, like a pair of horn spectacles. He is much thought of by the old women, who consider him as a kind of conjurer, because he has two or three stuffed alligators hanging up in his shop, and several snakes in bottles. He is a great reader of almanacs and newspapers, and is much given to poring over alarming accounts of plots, conspiracies, fires, earthquakes, and volcanic eruptions; which last phenomena he considers as signs of the times. He has always some dismal tale of the kind to deal out to his customers, with their doses; and thus at the same time puts both soul and body into an uproar. He is a great believer in omens and predictions; and has the prophecies of Robert Nixon and Mother Shipton by heart. No man can make so much out of an eclipse, or even an unusually dark day; and he shook the tail of the last comet over the heads of his customers and disciples, until they were nearly frightened out of their wits. He has lately got hold of a popular legend or prophecy, on which he has been unusually eloquent. There has been a saying current among the ancient Sybils, who treasure up these things, that when the grasshopper on the top of the Exchange shook hands with the dragon on the top of Bow Church steeple, fearful events would take place. This strange conjunction, it seems, has as strangely come to pass. The same architect has been engaged lately on the repairs of the cupola of the Exchange, and the steeple of Bow Church; and, fearful to relate, the dragon and the grasshopper actually lie, cheek by jowl, in the yard of his workshop.

"Others," as Mr. Skryme is accustomed to say, "may go star-gazing, and look for conjunctions in the heavens, but here is a conjunction on the earth, near at home, and under our own eyes, which surpasses all the signs and calculations of astrologers." Since these portentous weathercocks have thus laid their heads together, wonderful events had already occurred. The good old king, notwithstanding that he had lived eighty-two years, had all at once given up the ghost; another king had mounted the throne; a royal duke had died suddenly—another, in France, had been murdered; there had been radical meetings in all parts of the kingdom; the bloody scenes at Manchester—the great plot in Cato Street; —and, above all, the Queen had returned to England! All these sinister events are recounted by Mr. Skryme with a mysterious look and a dismal shake of the head; and being taken with his drugs, and associated in the minds of his auditors with stuffed sea-monsters, bottled serpents, and his own visage, which is a title page of tribulation, they have spread great gloom through the minds of the people in Little Britain. They shake their heads whenever they go by Bow Church, and observe that they never expected any good to come of taking down that steeple, which, in old times, told nothing but glad tidings, as the history of Whittington and his cat bears witness.

The rival oracle of Little Britain is a substantial cheese-monger, who lives in a fragment of one of the old family mansions, and is as magnificently lodged as a round-bellied mite in the midst of one of his own Cheshires. Indeed, he is a man of no little standing and importance; and his renown extends through Huggin Lane, and Lad Lane, and even unto Aldermanbury. His opinion is very much taken in the affairs of state, having read the Sunday papers for the last half century, together with the "Gentleman's Magazine," Rapin's "History of England," and the "Naval Chronicle." His head is stored with invaluable maxims which have borne the test of time and use for centuries. It is his firm opinion that "it is a moral impossible," so long as England is true to herself, that anything can shake her: and he has much to say on the subject of the national debt; which, somehow or other, he proves to be a great national bulwark and blessing. He passed the greater part of his life in the purlieus of Little Britain, until of late years, when, having become rich, and grown into the dignity of a Sunday cane, he begins to take his pleasure and see the world. He has therefore made several excursions to Hampstead, Highgate, and other neighboring towns, where he has passed whole afternoons in looking back upon the metropolis through a telescope, and endeavoring to descry the steeple of St. Bartholomew's. Not a stage-coachman of Bull-and-Mouth Street but touches his hat as he passes; and he is considered quite a patron at the coach-office of the Goose and Gridiron, St. Paul's Churchyard. His family have been very urgent for him to make an expedition to Margate, but he has great doubts of these new gimcracks the steamboats, and indeed thinks himself too advanced in life to undertake sea-voyages.

Little Britain has occasionally its factions and divisions, and party spirit ran very high at one time, in consequence of two rival "Burial Societies" being set up in the place. One held its meeting at the Swan and Horseshoe, and was patronized by the cheesemonger; the other at the Cock and Crown, under the auspices of the apothecary: it is needless to say that the latter was the most flourishing. I have passed an evening or two at each, and have acquired much

valuable information as to the best mode of being buried;
the comparative merits of churchyards; together with divers
hints on the subject of patent iron coffins.   I have heard the
question discussed in all its bearings, as to the legality of pro-
hibiting the latter on account of their durability.   The feuds
occasioned by these societies have happily died away of late;
but they were for a long time prevailing themes of controversy, the people of Little Britain being extremely solicitous of funeral honors, and of lying comfortably in their
graves.

Besides these two funeral societies, there is a third of
quite a different cast, which tends to throw the sunshine
of good-humor over the whole neighborhood.   It meets once
a week at a little old-fashioned house, kept by a jolly pub-
lican of the name of Wagstaff, and bearing for insignia a resplendent half-moon, with a most seductive bunch of grapes.
The whole edifice is covered with inscriptions to catch the
eye of the thirsty wayfarer; such as "Truman, Hanbury
and Co.'s Entire," "Wine, Rum, and Brandy Vaults," "Old
Tom, Rum, and Compounds," etc.   This, indeed, has been
a temple of Bacchus and Momus, from time immemorial.
It has always been in the family of the Wagstaffs, so that
its history is tolerably preserved by the present landlord.   It
was much frequented by the gallants and cavalieros of the
reign of Elizabeth, and was looked into now and then by the
wits of Charles the Second's day.   But what Wagstaff principally prides himself upon, is, that Henry the Eighth, in
one of his nocturnal rambles, broke the head of one of his
ancestors with his famous walking-staff.   This, however, is
considered as rather a dubious and vainglorious boast of the
landlord.

The club which now holds its weekly sessions here goes
by the name of "The Roaring Lads of Little Britain."   They
abound in all catches, glees, and choice stories that are traditional in the place, and not to be met with in any other part
of the metropolis.   There is a madcap undertaker, who is inimitable at a merry song; but the life of the club, and indeed

the prime wit of Little Britain, is bully Wagstaff himself. His ancestors were all wags before him, and he has inherited with the inn a large stock of songs and jokes, which go with it from generation to generation as heirlooms. He is a dapper little fellow, with bandy legs and pot belly, a red face with a moist merry eye, and a little shock of gray hair behind. At the opening of every club night, he is called in to sing his "Confession of Faith," which is the famous old drinking trowl from Gammer Gurton's needle. He sings it, to be sure, with many variations, as he received it from his father's lips; for it had been a standing favorite at the Half-Moon and Bunch of Grapes ever since it was written; nay, he affirms that his predecessors have often had the honor of singing it before the nobility and gentry at Christmas mummeries, when Little Britain was in all its glory.*

---

* As mine host of the Half-Moon's Confession of Faith may not be familiar to the majority of readers, and as it is a specimen of the current songs of Little Britain, I subjoin it in its original orthography. I would observe, that the whole club always join in the chorus with a fearful thumping on the table and clattering of pewter pots.

"I cannot eate but lytle meate,
   My stomacke is not good,
But sure I thinke that I can drinke
   With him that weares a hood.
Though I go bare take ye no care,
   I nothing am a colde,
I stuff my skyn so full within,
   Of joly good ale and olde.

Chorus.—"Back and syde go bare, go bare,
   Both foot and hand go colde,
But belly, God send thee good ale ynoughe,
   Whether it be new or olde.

"I have no rost, but a nut brown toste
   And a crab laid in the fyre;
A little breade shall do me steade,
   Much breade I not desyre.
No frost nor snow, nor winde I trowe,
   Can hurt me if I wolde,

It would do one's heart good to hear on a club-night the shouts of merriment, the snatches of song, and now and then the choral bursts of half a dozen discordant voices, which issue from this jovial mansion. At such times the street is lined with listeners, who enjoy a delight equal to that of gazing into a confectioner's window, or snuffing up the steams of a cook-shop.

There are two annual events which produce great stir and sensation in Little Britain; these are St. Bartholomew's Fair, and the Lord Mayor's day. During the time of the Fair, which is held in the adjoining regions of Smithfield, there is nothing going on but gossiping and gadding about. The late quiet streets of Little Britain are overrun with an irruption of strange figures and faces; every tavern is a scene of rout and revel. The fiddle and the song are heard from the taproom, morning, noon, and night; and at each

---

> I am so wrapt and throwly lapt
> Of joly good ale and olde.

Chorus.—"Back and syde go bare, go bare, etc.

> "And Tyb my wife, that, as her lyfe,
> Loveth well good ale to seeke,
> Full oft drynkes she, tyll ye may see
> The teares run down her cheeke.
> Then doth shee trowle to me the bowle,
> Even as a maulte-worme sholde,
> And sayth, sweete harte, I tooke my parte
> Of this joly good ale and olde.

Chorus.—"Back and syde go bare, go bare, etc.

> "Now let them drynke, tyll they nod and winke
> Even as goode fellowes sholde doe,
> They shall not mysse to have the blisse,
> Good ale doth bring men to.
> And all poor soules that have scowred bowles,
> Or have them lustily trolde,
> God save the lyves of them and their wives,
> Whether they be yonge or olde.

Chorus.—"Back and syde go bare, go bare, etc."

window may be seen some group of boon companions, with half-shut eyes, hats on one side, pipe in mouth, and tankard in hand, fondling and prozing, and singing maudlin songs over their liquor. Even the sober decorum of private families, which, I must say, is rigidly kept up at other times among my neighbors, is no proof against this Saturnalia. There is no such thing as keeping maid servants within doors. Their brains are absolutely set madding with Punch and the Puppet Show; the Flying Horses; Signior Polito; the Fire-Eater; the celebrated Mr. Paap; and the Irish Giant. The children, too, lavish all their holyday money in toys and gilt gingerbread, and fill the house with the Lilliputian din of drums, trumpets, and penny whistles.

But the Lord Mayor's day is the great anniversary. The Lord Mayor is looked up to by the inhabitants of Little Britain as the greatest potentate upon earth; his gilt coach with six horses as the summit of human splendor; and his procession, with all the Sheriffs and Aldermen in his train, as the grandest of earthly pageants. How they exult in the idea that the King himself dare not enter the city without first knocking at the gate of Temple Bar, and asking permission of the Lord Mayor; for if he did, heaven and earth! there is no knowing what might be the consequence. The man in armor who rides before the Lord Mayor, and is the city champion, has orders to cut down everybody that offends against the dignity of the city; and then there is the little man with a velvet porringer on his head, who sits at the window of the state coach and holds the city sword, as long as a pike-staff—Od's blood! if he once draws that sword, Majesty itself is not safe!

Under the protection of this mighty potentate, therefore, the good people of Little Britain sleep in peace. Temple Bar is an effectual barrier against all internal foes; and as to foreign invasion, the Lord Mayor has but to throw himself into the Tower, call in the train bands, and put the standing army of Beef-eaters under arms, and he may bid defiance to the world!

Thus wrapped up in its own concerns, its own habits, and

its own opinions, Little Britain has long flourished as a sound heart to this great fungus metropolis. I have pleased myself with considering it as a chosen spot, where the principles of sturdy John Bullism were garnered up, like seed-corn, to renew the national character, when it had run to waste and degeneracy. I have rejoiced also in the general spirit of harmony that prevailed throughout it; for though there might now and then be a few clashes of opinion between the adherents of the cheesemonger and the apothecary, and an occasional feud between the burial societies, yet these were but transient clouds, and soon passed away. The neighbors met with good-will, parted with a shake of the hand, and never abused each other except behind their backs.

I could give rare descriptions of snug junketing parties at which I have been present; where we played at All-Fours, Pope-Joan, Tom-come-tickle-me, and other choice old games: and where we sometimes had a good old English country dance, to the tune of Sir Roger de Coverly. Once a year also the neighbors would gather together, and go on a gypsy party to Epping Forest. It would have done any man's heart good to see the merriment that took place here, as we banqueted on the grass under the trees. How we made the woods ring with bursts of laughter at the songs of little Wagstaff and the merry undertaker! After dinner, too, the young folks would play at blindman's-buff and hide-and-seek; and it was amusing to see them tangled among the briers, and to hear a fine romping girl now and then squeak from among the bushes. The elder folks would gather round the cheesemonger and the apothecary to hear them talk politics; for they generally brought out a newspaper in their pockets to pass away time in the country. They would now and then, to be sure, get a little warm in argument; but their disputes were always adjusted by reference to a worthy old umbrella-maker in a double chin, who, never exactly comprehending the subject, managed, somehow or other, to decide in favor of both parties.

All empires, however, says some philosopher or historian,

are doomed to changes and revolutions. Luxury and innovation creep in; factions arise; and families now and then
spring up, whose ambition and intrigues throw the whole
system into confusion. Thus in latter days has the tranquillity of Little Britain been grievously disturbed, and its golden
simplicity of manners threatened with total subversion, by the
aspiring family of a retired butcher.

The family of the Lambs had long been among the most
thriving and popular in the neighborhood: the Miss Lambs
were the belles of Little Britain, and everybody was pleased
when old Lamb had made money enough to shut up shop
and put his name on a brass plate on his door. In an evil
hour, however, one of the Miss Lambs had the honor of being a lady in attendance on the Lady Mayoress, at her grand
annual ball, on which occasion she wore three towering ostrich
feathers on her head. The family never got over it; they
were immediately smitten with a passion for high life; set
up a one-horse carriage, put a bit of gold lace round the
errand-boy's hat, and have been the talk and detestation of
the whole neighborhood ever since. They could no longer
be induced to play at Pope-Joan or blindman's-buff; they
could endure no dances but quadrilles, which nobody had
ever heard of in Little Britain; and they took to reading
novels, talking bad French, and playing upon the piano.
Their brother, too, who had been articled to an attorney, set
up for a dandy and a critic, characters hitherto unknown in
these parts; and he confounded the worthy folks exceedingly by talking about Kean, the Opera, and the "Edinbro'
Review."

What was still worse, the Lambs gave a grand ball, to
which they neglected to invite any of their old neighbors;
but they had a great deal of genteel company from Theo-
bald's Road, Red-lion Square, and other parts toward the
west. There were several beaux of their brother's acquaintance from Gray's Inn Lane and Hatton Garden; and not
less than three Aldermen's ladies with their daughters. This
was not to be forgotten or forgiven. All Little Britain was

in an uproar with the smacking of whips, the lashing of miserable horses, and the rattling and jingling of hackney-coaches. The gossips of the neighborhood might be seen popping their nightcaps out at every window, watching the crazy vehicles rumble by; and there was a knot of virulent old cronies that kept a lookout from a house just opposite the retired butcher's, and scanned and criticised every one that knocked at the door.

This dance was a cause of almost open war, and the whole neighborhood declared they would have nothing more to say to the Lambs. It is true that Mrs. Lamb, when she had no engagements with her quality acquaintance, would give little humdrum tea junketings to some of her old cronies, "quite," as she would say, "in a friendly way"; and it is equally true that her invitations were always accepted, in spite of all previous vows to the contrary. Nay, the good ladies would sit and be delighted with the music of the Miss Lambs, who would condescend to thrum an Irish melody for them on the piano; and they would listen with wonderful interest to Mrs. Lamb's anecdotes of Alderman Plunket's family of Portsokenward, and the Miss Timberlakes, the rich heiresses of Crutched-Friars; but then they relieved their consciences, and averted the reproaches of their confederates, by canvassing at the next gossiping convocation everything that had passed, and pulling the Lambs and their rout all to pieces.

The only one of the family that could not be made fashionable was the retired butcher himself. Honest Lamb, in spite of the meekness of his name, was a rough hearty old fellow, with the voice of a lion, a head of black hair like a shoebrush, and a broad face mottled like his own beef. It was in vain that the daughters always spoke of him as the "old gentleman," addressed him as "papa," in tones of infinite softness, and endeavored to coax him into a dressing-gown and slippers, and other gentlemanly habits. Do what they might, there was no keeping down the butcher. His sturdy nature would break through all their glozings. He

had a hearty vulgar good-humor that was irrepressible. His
very jokes made his sensitive daughters shudder; and he
persisted in wearing his blue cotton coat of a morning, dining
at two o'clock, and having a "bit of sausage with his tea."

He was doomed, however, to share the unpopularity of
his family. He found his old comrades gradually growing
cold and civil to him; no longer laughing at his jokes; and
now and then throwing out a fling at "some people," and a
hint about "quality binding." This both nettled and perplexed the honest butcher; and his wife and daughters, with
the consummate policy of the shrewder sex, taking advantage of the circumstances, at length prevailed upon him to
give up his afternoon pipe and tankard at Wagstaff's; to sit
after dinner by himself, and take his pint of port—a liquor
he detested—and to nod in his chair, in solitary and dismal
gentility.

The Miss Lambs might now be seen flaunting along the
streets in French bonnets, with unknown beaux; and talking
and laughing so loud that it distressed the nerves of every
good lady within hearing. They even went so far as to attempt patronage, and actually induced a French dancing-
master to set up in the neighborhood; but the worthy folks
of Little Britain took fire at it, and did so persecute the poor
Gaul that he was fain to pack up fiddle and dancing-pumps,
and decamp with such precipitation that he absolutely forgot
to pay for his lodgings.

I had flattered myself, at first, with the idea that all this
fiery indignation on the part of the community was merely
the overflowing of their zeal for good old English manners,
and their horror of innovation; and I applauded the silent
contempt they were so vociferous in expressing for upstart
pride, French fashions, and the Miss Lambs. But I grieve to
say that I soon perceived the infection had taken hold; and
that my neighbors, after condemning, were beginning to follow their example. I overheard my landlady importuning
her husband to let their daughters have one quarter at French
and music, and that they might take a few lessons in qua-

drilles; I even saw, in the course of a few Sundays, no less
than five French bonnets, precisely like those of the Miss
Lambs, parading about Little Britain.

I still had my hopes that all this folly would gradually
die away; that the Lambs might move out of the neighborhood; might die, or might run away with attorneys' appren-
tices; and that quiet and simplicity might be again restored
to the community. But unluckily a rival power arose. An
opulent oil-man died, and left a widow with a large jointure
and a family of buxom daughters. The young ladies had
long been repining in secret at the parsimony of a prudent
father, which kept down all their elegant aspirings. Their
ambition being now no longer restrained, broke out into a
blaze, and they openly took the field against the family of
the butcher. It is true that the Lambs, having had the first
start, had naturally an advantage of them in the fashionable
career. They could speak a little bad French, play the piano,
dance quadrilles, and had formed high acquaintances; but the
Trotters were not to be distanced. When the Lambs appeared with two feathers in their hats, the Miss Trotters
mounted four, and of twice as fine colors. If the Lambs
gave a dance, the Trotters were sure not to be behindhand;
and though they might not boast of as good company, yet
they had double the number, and were twice as merry.

The whole community has at length divided itself into
fashionable factions, under the banners of these two families.
The old games of Pope-Joan and Tom-come-tickle-me are entirely discarded; there is no such thing as getting up an honest country-dance; and on my attempting to kiss a young
lady under the mistletoe last Christmas, I was indignantly
repulsed; the Miss Lambs having pronounced it "shocking
vulgar." Bitter rivalry has also broken out as to the most
fashionable part of Little Britain; the Lambs standing up
for the dignity of Cross-Keys Square, and the Trotters for
the vicinity of St. Bartholomew's.

Thus is this little territory torn by factions and internal
dissensions, like the great empire whose name it bears; and

what will be the result would puzzle the apothecary himself, with all his talent at prognostics, to determine; though I apprehend that it will terminate in the total downfall of genuine John Bullism.

The immediate effects are extremely unpleasant to me. Being a single man, and, as I observed before, rather an idle good-for-nothing personage, I have been considered the only gentleman by profession in the place. I stand therefore in high favor with both parties, and have to hear all their cabinet councils and mutual backbitings. As I am too civil not to agree with the ladies on all occasions, I have committed myself most horribly with both parties, by abusing their opponents. I might manage to reconcile this to my conscience, which is a truly accommodating one, but I cannot to my apprehensions—if the Lambs and Trotters ever come to a reconciliation, and compare notes, I am ruined!

I have determined, therefore, to beat a retreat in time, and am actually looking out for some other nest in this great city, where old English manners are still kept up; where French is neither eaten, drank, danced, nor spoken; and where there are no fashionable families of retired tradesmen. This found, I will, like a veteran rat, hasten away before I have an old house about my ears—bid a long, though a sorrowful adieu to my present abode—and leave the rival factions of the Lambs and the Trotters to divide the distracted empire of Little Britain.

STRATFORD-ON-AVON

"Thou soft-flowing Avon, by thy silver stream
  Of things more than mortal sweet Shakespeare would dream;
  The fairies by moonlight dance round his green bed,
  For hallowed the turf is which pillowed his head."—GARRICK

To a homeless man, who has no spot on this wide world which he can truly call his own, there is a momentary feeling of something like independence and territorial conse-

quence, when, after a weary day's travel, he kicks off his
boots, thrusts his feet into slippers, and stretches himself
before an inn fire. Let the world without go as it may; let
kingdoms rise or fall, so long as he has the wherewithal to
pay his bill, he is, for the time being, the very monarch of
all he surveys. The armchair is his throne, the poker his
scepter, and the little parlor, of some twelve feet square, his
undisputed empire. It is a morsel of certainty, snatched
from the midst of the uncertainties of life; it is a sunny moment gleaming out kindly on a cloudy day; and he who has
advanced some way on the pilgrimage of existence knows
the importance of husbanding even morsels and moments of
enjoyment. "Shall I not take mine ease in mine inn?"
thought I, as I gave the fire a stir, lolled back in my elbow-
chair, and cast a complacent look about the little parlor of
the Red Horse, at Stratford-on-Avon.

The words of sweet Shakespeare were just passing through
my mind as the clock struck midnight from the tower of the
church in which he lies buried. There was a gentle tap at
the door, and a pretty chambermaid, putting in her smiling
face, inquired, with a hesitating air, whether I had rung. I
understood it as a modest hint that it was time to retire.
My dream of absolute dominion was at an end; so abdicat-
ing my throne, like a prudent potentate, to avoid being de-
posed, and putting the Stratford Guide-Book under my arm,
as a pillow companion, I went to bed, and dreamed all night
of Shakespeare, the Jubilee, and David Garrick.

The next morning was one of those quickening mornings
which we sometimes have in early spring; for it was about
the middle of March. The chills of a long winter had suddenly given way; the north wind had spent its last gasp;
and a mild air came stealing from the west, breathing the
breath of life into nature, and wooing every bud and flower
to burst forth into fragrance and beauty.

I had come to Stratford on a poetical pilgrimage. My
first visit was to the house where Shakespeare was born, and
where, according to tradition, he was brought up to his

father's craft of wool-combing. It is a small mean-looking edifice of wood and plaster, a true nestling-place of genius, which seems to delight in hatching its offspring in by-corners. The walls of its squalid chambers are covered with names and inscriptions in every language, by pilgrims of all nations, ranks, and conditions, from the prince to the peasant; and present a simple, but striking instance of the spontaneous and universal homage of mankind to the great poet of nature.

The house is shown by a garrulous old lady, in a frosty red face, lighted up by a cold blue anxious eye, and garnished with artificial locks of flaxen hair, curling from under an exceedingly dirty cap. She was peculiarly assiduous in exhibiting the relics with which this, like all other celebrated shrines, abounds. There was the shattered stock of the very matchlock with which Shakespeare shot the deer, on his poaching exploits. There, too, was his tobacco-box; which proves that he was a rival smoker of Sir Walter Raleigh; the sword also with which he played Hamlet; and the identical lantern with which Friar Laurence discovered Romeo and Juliet at the tomb! There was an ample supply also of Shakespeare's mulberry-tree, which seems to have as extraordinary powers of self-multiplication as the wood of the true cross; of which there is enough extant to build a ship of the line.

The most favorite object of curiosity, however, is Shakespeare's chair. It stands in the chimney-nook of a small gloomy chamber, just behind what was his father's shop. Here he may many a time have sat when a boy, watching the slowly-revolving spit, with all the longing of an urchin; or of an evening, listening to the crones and gossips of Stratford, dealing forth churchyard tales and legendary anecdotes of the troublesome times of England. In this chair it is the custom of every one who visits the house to sit: whether this be done with the hope of imbibing any of the inspiration of the bard, I am at a loss to say; I merely mention the fact; and mine hostess privately assured me that, though built of soild oak, such was the fervent zeal of devotees, that the chair had to be new-bottomed at least once in three years. It is worthy of notice also, in the history of this extraordinary chair, that it partakes something of the volatile nature of the Santa Casa of Loretto, or the flying chair of the Arabian enchanter; for though sold some few years since to a northern princess, yet, strange to tell, it has found its way back again to the old chimney-corner.

I am always of easy faith in such matters, and am very willing to be deceived, where the deceit is pleasant and costs nothing. I am therefore a ready believer in relics, legends, and local anecdotes of goblins and great men; and would advise all travelers who travel for their gratification to be the same. What is it to us whether these stories be true or false, so long as we can persuade ourselves into the belief of them, and enjoy all the charm of the reality? There is nothing like resolute good-humored credulity in these matters; and on this occasion I went even so far as willingly to believe the claims of mine hostess to a lineal descent from the poet, when, unluckily for my faith, she put into my hands a play of her own composition, which set all belief in her consanguinity at defiance.

From the birthplace of Shakespeare a few paces brought me to his grave. He lies buried in the chancel of the parish church, a large and venerable pile, mouldering with age, but richly ornamented. It stands on the banks of the Avon, on an embowered point, and separated by adjoining gardens from the suburbs of the town. Its situation is quiet and retired: the river runs murmuring at the foot of the churchyard, and the elms which grow upon its banks droop their branches into its clear bosom. An avenue of limes, the boughs of which are curiously interlaced, so as to form in summer an arched way of foliage, leads up from the gate of the yard to the church porch. The graves are overgrown with grass; the gray tombstones, some of them nearly sunk into the earth, are half-covered with moss, which has likewise tinted the reverend old building. Small birds have built their nests among the cornices and fissures of the walls, and keep up a continual flutter and chirping; and rooks are sailing and cawing about its lofty gray spire.

In the course of my rambles I met with the gray-headed sexton, and accompanied him home to get the key of the church. He had lived in Stratford, man and boy, for eighty years, and seemed still to consider himself a vigorous man, with the trivial exception that he had nearly lost the use of his legs for a few years past. His dwelling was a cottage, looking out upon the Avon and its bordering meadows; and was a picture of that neatness, order, and comfort, which pervade the humblest dwellings in this country. A low whitewashed room, with a stone floor carefully scrubbed, served for parlor, kitchen, and hall. Rows of pewter and earthen dishes glittered along the dresser. On an old oaken table, well rubbed and polished, lay the family Bible and prayer-book, and the drawer contained the family library, composed of about half a score of well-thumbed volumes. An ancient clock, that important article of cottage furniture, ticked on the opposite side of the room; with a bright warming-pan hanging on one side of it, and the old man's horn-handled Sunday cane on the other. The fireplace, as usual, was wide and deep enough to admit a gossip knot within its jambs. In one corner sat the old man's granddaughter sewing, a pretty blue-eyed girl—and in the opposite corner was a superannuated crony, whom he addressed by the name of John Ange, and who, I found, had been his companion from childhood. They had played together in infancy; they had worked together in manhood; they were now tottering about and gossiping away the evening of life; and in a short time they will probably be buried together in the neighboring churchyard. It is not often that we see two streams of existence running thus evenly and tranquilly side by side; it is only in such quiet "bosom scenes" of life that they are to be met with.

I had hoped to gather some traditionary anecdotes of the bard from these ancient chroniclers; but they had nothing new to impart. The long interval, during which Shakespeare's writings lay in comparative neglect, has spread its shadow over history; and it is his good or evil lot that scarcely anything remains to his biographers but a scanty handful of conjectures.

The sexton and his companion had been employed as carpenters, on the preparations for the celebrated Stratford jubilee, and they remembered Garrick, the prime mover of the fete, who superintended the arrangements, and who, according to the sexton, was "a short punch man, very lively and bustling." John Ange had assisted also in cutting down Shakespeare's mulberry - tree, of which he had a morsel in his pocket for sale; no doubt a sovereign quickener of literary conception.

I was grieved to hear these two worthy wights speak very dubiously of the eloquent dame who shows the Shakespeare house. John Ange shook his head when I mentioned her valuable and inexhaustible collection of relics, particularly her remains of the mulberry-tree; and the old sexton even expressed a doubt as to Shakespeare having been born in her house. I soon discovered that he looked upon her mansion with an evil eye, as a rival to the poet's tomb; the latter having comparatively but few visitors. Thus it is that historians differ at the very outset, and mere pebbles make the stream of truth diverge into different channels, even at the fountain-head.

We approached the church through the avenue of limes, and entered by a Gothic porch, highly ornamented with carved doors of massive oak. The interior is spacious, and the architecture and embellishments superior to those of most country churches. There are several ancient monuments of nobility and gentry, over some of which hang funeral escutcheons, and banners dropping piecemeal from the walls. The tomb of Shakespeare is in the chancel. The place is solemn and sepulchral. Tall elms wave before the pointed windows, and the Avon, which runs at a short distance from the walls, keeps up a low perpetual murmur. A flat stone marks the

spot where the bard is buried.   There are four lines inscribed
on it, said to have been written by himself, and which have
in them something extremely awful.   If they are indeed his
own, they show that solicitude about the quiet of the grave
which seems natural to fine sensibilities and thoughtful minds:

> "Good friend, for Jesus' sake, forbeare
> To dig the dust inclosed here.
> Blessed be he that spares these stones,
> And curst be he that moves my bones."

Just over the grave, in a niche of the wall, is a bust of
Shakespeare, put up shortly after his death, and considered
as a resemblance.   The aspect is pleasant and serene, with a
finely arched forehead; and I thought I could read in it clear
indications of that cheerful, social disposition, by which he
was as much characterized among his contemporaries as by
the vastness of his genius.   The inscription mentions his age
at the time of his decease—fifty-three years; an untimely
death for the world: for what fruit might not have been expected from the golden autumn of such a mind, sheltered, as
it was, from the stormy vicissitudes of life, and flourishing
in the sunshine of popular and royal favor!

The inscription on the tombstone has not been without its
effect.   It has prevented the removal of his remains from
the bosom of his native place to Westminster Abbey, which
was at one time contemplated.   A few years since also, as
some laborers were digging to make an adjoining vault, the
earth caved in, so as to leave a vacant space almost like an
arch, through which one might have reached into his grave.
No one, however, presumed to meddle with the remains so
awfully guarded by a malediction; and lest any of the idle
or the curious, or any collector of relics, should be tempted
to commit depredations, the old sexton kept watch over the
place for two days, until the vault was finished and the
aperture closed again.   He told me that he had made bold
to look in at the hole, but could see neither coffin nor bones;
nothing but dust.   It was something, I thought, to have
seen the dust of Shakespeare.

Next to his grave are those of his wife, his favorite daughter, Mrs. Hall, and others of his family. On a tomb close by, also, is a full-length effigy of his old friend John Combe, of usurious memory; on whom he is said to have written a ludicrous epitaph. There are other monuments around, but the mind refuses to dwell on anything that is not connected with Shakespeare. His idea pervades the place—the whole pile seems but as his mausoleum. The feelings, no longer checked and thwarted by doubt, here indulge in perfect confidence: other traces of him may be false or dubious, but here is palpable evidence and absolute certainty. As I trod the sounding pavement, there was something intense and thrilling in the idea that, in very truth, the remains of Shakespeare were mouldering beneath my feet. It was a long time before I could prevail upon myself to leave the place; and as I passed through the churchyard, I plucked a branch from one of the yew-trees, the only relic that I have brought from Stratford.

I had now visited the usual objects of a pilgrim's devotion, but I had a desire to see the old family-seat of the Lucys at Charlecot, and to ramble through the park where Shakespeare, in company with some of the roisterers of Stratford, committed his youthful offense of deer-stealing. In this hare-brained exploit we are told that he was taken prisoner, and carried to the keeper's lodge, where he remained all night in doleful captivity. When brought into the presence of Sir Thomas Lucy, his treatment must have been galling and humiliating; for it so wrought upon his spirit as to produce a rough pasquinade, which was affixed to the park gate at Charlecot.*

---

* The following is the only stanza extant of this lampoon:

"A parliament member, a justice of peace,
At home a poor scarecrow, at London an asse,
If lowsie is Lucy, as some volke miscalle it,
Then Lucy is lowsie, whatever befall it.
He thinks himself great;
Yet an asse in his state,
We allow by his ears with but asses to mate.
If Lucy is lowsie, as some volke miscalle it,
Then sing lowsie Lucy, whatever befall it."

This flagitious attack upon the dignity of the Knight so incensed him that he applied to a lawyer at Warwick to put the severity of the laws in force against the rhyming deer-stalker. Shakespeare did not wait to brave the united puissance of a Knight of the Shire and a country attorney. He forthwith abandoned the pleasant banks of the Avon, and his paternal trade; wandered away to London; became a hanger-on to the theaters; then an actor; and, finally, wrote for the stage; and thus, through the persecution of Sir Thomas Lucy, Stratford lost an indifferent wool-comber, and the world gained an immortal poet. He retained, however, for a long time, a sense of the harsh treatment of the Lord of Charlecot, and revenged himself in his writings; but in the sportive way of a good-natured mind. Sir Thomas is said to be the original of Justice Shallow, and the satire is slyly fixed upon him by the Justice's armorial bearings, which, like those of the Knight, had white luces * in the quarterings.

Various attempts have been made by his biographers to soften and explain away this early transgression of the poet; but I look upon it as one of those thoughtless exploits natural to his situation and turn of mind. Shakespeare, when young, had doubtless all the wildness and irregularity of an ardent, undisciplined, and undirected genius. The poetic temperament has naturally something in it of the vagabond. When left to itself, it runs loosely and wildly, and delights in everything eccentric and licentious. It is often a turn-up of a die, in the gambling freaks of fate, whether a natural genius shall turn out a great rogue or a great poet; and had not Shakespeare's mind fortunately taken a literary bias, he might have as daringly transcended all civil, as he has all dramatic laws.

I have little doubt that, in early life, when running, like an unbroken colt, about the neighborhood of Stratford, he

---

* The luce is a pike or jack, and abounds in the Avon, about Charlecot.

was to be found in the company of all kinds of odd and
anomalous characters; that he associated with all the mad-
caps of the place, and was one of those unlucky urchins at
mention of whom old men shake their heads and predict
that they will one day come to the gallows.   To him the
poaching in Sir Thomas Lucy's park was doubtless like a
foray to a Scottish knight, and struck his eager, and as yet
untamed, imagination, as something delightfully adventurous. *

The old mansion of Charlecot and its surrounding park
still remain in the possession of the Lucy family, and are

---

* A proof of Shakespeare's random habits and associates in his
youthful days may be found in a traditionary anecdote, picked up at
Stratford by the elder Ireland, and mentioned in his "Picturesque
Views on the Avon."

About seven miles from Stratford lies the thirsty little market
town of Bedford, famous for its ale. Two societies of the village yeomanry used to meet, under the appellation of the Bedford topers, and
to challenge the lovers of good ale of the neighboring villages to a
contest of drinking. Among others, the people of Stratford were
called out to prove the strength of their heads; and in the number of
the champions was Shakespeare, who, in spite of the proverb that
"they who drink beer will think beer," was as true to his ale as Falstaff to his sack. The chivalry of Stratford was staggered at the first
onset, and sounded a retreat while they had yet legs to carry them off
the field. They had scarcely marched a mile, when, their legs failing
them, they were forced to lie down under a crab-tree, where they
passed the night. It is still standing, and goes by the name of Shakespeare's tree.

In the morning his companions awaked the bard, and proposed returning to Bedford, but he declined, saying he had had enough, having
drunk with

"Piping Pebworth, Dancing Marston,
Haunted Hilbro', Hungry Grafton,
Drudging Exhall, Papist Wicksford,
Beggarly Broom, and drunken Bedford."

"The villages here alluded to," says Ireland, "still bear the epithets
thus given them: the people of Pebworth are still famed for their skill
on the pipe and tabor; Hillborough is now called Haunted Hillborough;
and Grafton is famous for the poverty of its soil."

peculiarly interesting from being connected with this whimsical but eventful circumstance in the scanty history of the bard. As the house stood at little more than three miles' distance from Stratford, I resolved to pay it a pedestrian visit, that I might stroll leisurely through some of those scenes from which Shakespeare must have derived his earliest ideas of rural imagery.

The country was yet naked and leafless; but English scenery is always verdant, and the sudden change in the temperature of the weather was surprising in its quickening effects upon the landscape. It was inspiring and animating to witness this first awakening of spring; to feel its warm breath stealing over the senses; to see the moist mellow earth beginning to put forth the green sprout and the tender blade; and the trees and shrubs, in their reviving tints and bursting buds, giving the promise of returning foliage and flower. The cold snowdrop, that little borderer on the skirts of winter, was to be seen with its chaste white blossoms in the small gardens before the cottages. The bleating of the new-dropped lambs was faintly heard from the fields. The sparrow twittered about the thatched eaves and budding hedges; the robin threw a livelier note into his late querulous wintry strain; and the lark, springing up from the reeking bosom of the meadow, towered away into the bright fleecy cloud, pouring forth torrents of melody. As I watched the little songster, mounting up higher and higher, until his body was a mere speck on the white bosom of the cloud, while the ear was still filled with his music, it called to mind Shakespeare's exquisite little song in "Cymbeline":

> "Hark! hark! the lark at heav'n's gate sings,
>   And Phœbus 'gins arise,
> His steeds to water at those springs,
>   On chaliced flowers that lies.
>
> "And winking mary-buds begin
>   To ope their golden eyes;
> With every thing that pretty bin,
>   My lady sweet, arise."

Indeed, the whole country about here is poetic ground:
everything is associated with the idea of Shakespeare.
Every old cottage that I saw, I fancied into some resort
of his boyhood, where he had acquired his intimate knowledge of rustic life and manners, and heard those legendary
tales and wild superstitions which he has woven like witchcraft into his dramas. For in his time, we are told, it was
a popular amusement in winter evenings "to sit round the
fire, and tell merry tales of errant knights, queens, lovers,
lords, ladies, giants, dwarfs, thieves, cheaters, witches, fairies,
goblins, and friars." *

My route for a part of the way lay in sight of the Avon,
which made a variety of the most fanciful doublings and
windings through a wide and fertile valley: sometimes glittering from among willows, which fringed its borders; sometimes disappearing among groves, or beneath green banks;
and sometimes rambling out into full view, and making an
azure sweep round a slope of meadow land. This beautiful
bosom of country is called the Vale of the Red Horse. A
distant line of undulating blue hills seems to be its boundary,
while all the soft intervening landscape lies in a manner en-
chained in the silver links of the Avon.

After pursuing the road for about three miles, I turned
off into a footpath, which led along the borders of fields and
under hedgerows to a private gate of the park; there was a
stile, however, for the benefit of the pedestrian; there being
a public right of way through the grounds. I delight in these
hospitable estates, in which every one has a kind of property
—at least as far as the footpath is concerned. It in some

---

* Scot, in his "Discoverie of Witchcraft," enumerates a host of
these fireside fancies. "And they have so fraid us with bull-beggars,
spirits, witches, urchins, elves, hags, fairies, satyrs, pans, fauns, syrens,
kit with the can sticke, tritons, centaurs, dwarfes, giantes, imps, cal-
cars, conjurors, nymphes, changelings, incubus, Robin-good-fellow, the
sporne, the mare, the man in the oke, the hellwaine, the fier drake, the
puckle, Tom Thombe, hobgoblins, Tom Tumbler, boneless, and such
other bugs, that we were afraid of our own shadowes."

measure reconciles a poor man to his lot, and, what is more, to the better lot of his neighbor, thus to have parks and pleasure - grounds thrown open for his recreation. He breathes the pure air as freely, and lolls as luxuriously under the shade, as the lord of the soil; and if he has not the privilege of calling all that he sees his own, he has not, at the same time, the trouble of paying for it and keeping it in order.

I now found myself among noble avenues of oaks and elms, whose vast size bespoke the growth of centuries. The wind sounded solemnly among their branches, and the rooks cawed from their hereditary nests in the treetops. The eye ranged through a long lessening vista, with nothing to interrupt the view but a distant statue; and a vagrant deer stalking like a shadow across the opening.

There is something about these stately old avenues that has the effect of Gothic architecture, not merely from the pretended similarity of form, but from their bearing the evidence of long duration, and of having had their origin in a period of time with which we associate ideas of romantic grandeur. They betoken also the long-settled dignity and proudly concentrated independence of an ancient family; and I have heard a worthy but aristocratic old friend observe, when speaking of the sumptuous palaces of modern gentry, that "money could do much with stone and mortar, but, thank Heaven, there was no such thing as suddenly building up an avenue of oaks."

It was from wandering in early life among this rich scenery, and about the romantic solitudes of the adjoining park of Fullbroke, which then formed a part of the Lucy estate, that some of Shakespeare's commentators have supposed he derived his noble forest meditations of Jacques, and the enchanting woodland pictures in "As You Like It." It is in lonely wanderings through such scenes that the mind drinks deep but quiet draughts of inspiration, and becomes intensely sensible of the beauty and majesty of nature. The imagination kindles into reverie and rapture; vague but exquisite images and ideas keep breaking upon it; and we revel in a mute and almost incommunicable luxury of thought. It was in some such mood, and perhaps under one of those very trees before me, which threw their broad shades over the grassy banks and quivering waters of the Avon, that the poet's fancy may have sallied forth into that little song which breathes the very soul of a rural voluptuary:

> "Under the green-wood tree,
>   Who loves to lie with me,
>   And tune his merry throat
>   Unto the sweet bird's note,
>   Come hither, come hither, come hither,
>   Here shall he see
>   No enemy
>   But winter and rough weather."

I had now come in sight of the house. It is a large building of brick, with stone quoins, and is in the Gothic style of Queen Elizabeth's day, having been built in the first year of her reign. The exterior remains very nearly in its original state, and may be considered a fair specimen of the residence of a wealthy country gentleman of those days. A great gateway opens from the park into a kind of courtyard in front of the house, ornamented with a grass-plot, shrubs, and flower-beds. The gateway is in imitation of the ancient barbican; being a kind of outpost, and flanked by towers; though evidently for mere ornament, instead of defense. The front of the house is completely in the old style; with stone shafted casements, a great bow-window of heavy stone-work, and a portal with armorial bearings over it, carved in stone. At each corner of the building is an octagon tower, surmounted by a gilt ball and weathercock.

The Avon, which winds through the park, makes a bend just at the foot of a gently sloping bank, which sweeps down from the rear of the house. Large herds of deer were feeding or reposing upon its borders; and swans were sailing majestically upon its bosom. As I contemplated the vener-

able old mansion, I called to mind Falstaff's encomium on
Justice Shallow's abode, and the affected indifference and
real vanity of the latter:

"*Falstaff.* You have here a goodly dwelling and a rich.
"*Shallow.* Barren, barren, barren; beggars all, beggars all, Sir
John:—marry, good air."

Whatever may have been the joviality of the old mansion
in the days of Shakespeare, it had now an air of stillness
and solitude. The great iron gateway that opened into the
courtyard was locked; there was no show of servants bustling about the place; the deer gazed quietly at me as I
passed, being no longer harried by the moss-troopers of Stratford. The only sign of domestic life that I met with was a
white cat, stealing with wary look and stealthy pace toward
the stables, as if on some nefarious expedition. I must not
omit to mention the carcass of a scoundrel crow which I saw
suspended against the barn wall, as it shows that the Lucys
still inherit that lordly abhorrence of poachers, and maintain
that rigorous exercise of territorial power which was so strenu-
ously manifested in the case of the bard.

After prowling about for some time, I at length found
my way to a lateral portal, which was the everyday entrance
to the mansion. I was courteously received by a worthy old
housekeeper, who, with the civility and communicativeness of
her order, showed me the interior of the house. The greater
part has undergone alterations, and been adapted to modern
tastes and modes of living: there is a fine old oaken staircase; and the great hall, that noble feature in an ancient
manor-house, still retains much of the appearance it must
have had in the days of Shakespeare. The ceiling is arched
and lofty; and at one end is a gallery, in which stands an
organ. The weapons and trophies of the chase, which formerly adorned the hall of a country gentleman, have made
way for family portraits. There is a wide hospitable fireplace, calculated for an ample old-fashioned wood fire, formerly the rallying place of winter festivity. On the opposite

side of the hall is the huge Gothic bow-window, with stone
shafts, which looks out upon the courtyard. Here are emblazoned in stained glass the armorial bearings of the Lucy
family for many generations, some being dated in 1558. I
was delighted to observe in the quarterings the three *white
luces* by which the character of Sir Thomas was first iden-
tified with that of Justice Shallow. They are mentioned in
the first scene of the "Merry Wives of Windsor," where the
Justice is in a rage with Falstaff for having "beaten his men,
killed his deer, and broken into his lodge." The poet had,
no doubt, the offenses of himself and his comrades in mind
at the time, and we may suppose the family pride and vindictive threats of the puissant Shallow to be a caricature of
the pompous indignation of Sir Thomas.

"*Shallow.* Sir Hugh, persuade me not: I will make a Star-Chamber
matter of it; if he were twenty Sir John Falstaffs, he shall not abuse
Robert Shallow, Esq.

"*Slender.* In the county of Gloster, justice of peace, and *coram*.

"*Shallow.* Ay, cousin Slender, and *custalorum*.

"*Slender.* Ay, and *ratalorum* too, and a gentleman born, master
parson; who writes himself *Armigero* in any bill, warrant, quittance,
or obligation, *Armigero*.

"*Shallow.* Ay, that I do; and have done any time these three hundred years.

"*Slender.* All his successors gone before him have done't, and all
his ancestors that come after him may; they may give the dozen *white
luces* in their coat.

"*Shallow.* The council shall hear it; it is a riot.

"*Evans.* It is not meet the council hear of a riot; there is no fear
of Got in a riot: the council, hear you, shall desire to hear the fear of
Got, and not to hear a riot; take your vizaments in that.

"*Shallow.* Ha! o' my life, if I were young again, the sword should
end it!"

Near the window thus emblazoned hung a portrait by Sir
Peter Lely of one of the Lucy family, a great beauty of the
time of Charles the Second: the old housekeeper shook her
head as she pointed to the picture, and informed me that this
lady had been sadly addicted to cards, and had gambled
away a great portion of the family estate, among which was

that part of the park where Shakespeare and his comrades had killed the deer. The lands thus lost have not been entirely regained by the family, even at the present day. It is but justice to this recreant dame to confess that she had a surpassingly fine hand and arm.

The picture which most attracted my attention was a great painting over the fireplace, containing likenesses of Sir Thomas Lucy and his family, who inhabited the hall in the latter part of Shakespeare's lifetime. I at first thought that it was the vindictive knight himself, but the housekeeper assured me that it was his son; the only likeness extant of the former being an effigy upon his tomb in the church of the neighboring hamlet of Charlecot. The picture gives a lively idea of the costume and manners of the time. Sir Thomas is dressed in ruff and doublet; white shoes with roses in them; and has a peaked yellow, or, as Master Slender would say, "a cane-colored beard." His lady is seated on the opposite side of the picture in wide ruff and long stomacher, and the children have a most venerable stiffness and formality of dress. Hounds and spaniels are mingled in the family group; a hawk is seated on his perch in the foreground, and one of the children holds a bow; all intimating the knight's skill in hunting, hawking, and archery—so indispensable to an accomplished gentleman in those days.*

I regretted to find that the ancient furniture of the hall had disappeared; for I had hoped to meet with the stately

---

* Bishop Earle, speaking of the country gentleman of his time, observes: "His housekeeping is seen much in the different families of dogs, and serving-men attendant on their kennels; and the deepness of their throats is the depth of his discourse. A hawk he esteems the true burden of nobility, and is exceedingly ambitious to seem delighted with the sport, and have his fist gloved with his jesses." And Gilpin, in his description of a Mr. Hastings, remarks: "He kept all sorts of hounds that run, buck, fox, hare, otter, and badger; and had hawks of all kinds both long and short winged. His great hall was commonly strewed with marrow-bones, and full of hawk perches, hounds, spaniels, and terriers. On a broad hearth, paved with brick, lay some of the choicest of terriers, hounds, and spaniels."

elbow-chair of carved oak, in which the country Squire of
former days was wont to sway the scepter of empire over his
rural domains; and in which it might be presumed the re-
doubted Sir Thomas sat enthroned in awful state, when the
recreant Shakespeare was brought before him. As I like to
deck out pictures for my own entertainment, I pleased myself with the idea that this very hall had been the scene of
the unlucky bard's examination on the morning after his
captivity in the lodge. I fancied to myself the rural potentate, surrounded by his body-guard of butler, pages, and
blue-coated serving-men with their badges; while the luck-
less culprit was brought in, forlorn and chapfallen, in the
custody of game-keepers, huntsmen and whippers-in, and followed by a rabble rout of country clowns. I fancied bright
faces of curious housemaids peeping from the half-opened
doors; while from the gallery the fair daughters of the
Knight leaned gracefully forward eying the youthful
prisoner with that pity "that dwells in womanhood."—
Who would have thought that this poor varlet, thus trembling before the brief authority of a country Squire, and the
sport of rustic boors, was soon to become the delight of
princes; the theme of all tongues and ages; the dictator to
the human mind; and was to confer immortality on his oppressor by a caricature and a lampoon!

I was now invited by the butler to walk into the garden,
and I felt inclined to visit the orchard and arbor where the
Justice treated Sir John Falstaff and Cousin Slender "to a last
year's pippen of his own graffing, with a dish of carraways";
but I had already spent so much of the day in my rambling
that I was obliged to give up any further investigations.
When about to take my leave, I was gratified by the civil entreaties of the housekeeper and butler that I would take some
refreshment—an instance of good old hospitality, which, I
grieve to say, we castle-hunters seldom meet with in modern days. I make no doubt it is a virtue which the present
representative of the Lucys inherits from his ancestors; for
Shakespeare, even in his caricature, makes Justice Shallow

importunate in this respect, as witness his pressing instances to Falstaff.

"By cock and pye, Sir, you shall not away to-night. . . . I will not excuse you; you shall not be excused; excuses shall not be admitted; there is no excuse shall serve; you shall not be excused. . . . Some pigeons, Davy; a couple of short-legged hens; a joint of mutton; and any pretty little tiny kickshaws, tell 'William Cook.'"

I now bade a reluctant farewell to the old hall. My mind had become so completely possessed by the imaginary scenes and characters connected with it that I seemed to be actually living among them. Everything brought them, as it were, before my eyes; and as the door of the dining-room opened, I almost expected to hear the feeble voice of Master Slender quavering forth his favorite ditty:

"'Tis merry in hall, when beards wag all,
And welcome merry Shrove-tide!"

On returning to my inn, I could not but reflect on the singular gift of the poet; to be able thus to spread the magic of his mind over the very face of nature; to give to things and places a charm and character not their own, and to turn this "working-day world" into a perfect fairyland. He is indeed the true enchanter, whose spell operates, not upon the senses, but upon the imagination and the heart. Under the wizard influence of Shakespeare I had been walking all day in a complete delusion. I had surveyed the landscape through the prism of poetry, which tinged every object with the hues of the rainbow. I had been surrounded with fancied beings; with mere airy nothings, conjured up by poetic power; yet which, to me, had all the charm of reality. I had heard Jacques soliloquize beneath his oak; had beheld the fair Rosalind and her companion adventuring through the woodlands; and, above all, had been once more present in spirit with fat Jack Falstaff and his contemporaries, from the august Justice Shallow down to the gentle Master Slender, and the sweet Anne Page. Ten thousand honors and blessings on the bard who has thus gilded the dull realities of life with innocent illusions; who has spread exquisite and unbought pleasures in my checkered path; and beguiled my spirit in many a lonely hour with all the cordial and cheerful sympathies of social life!

As I crossed the bridge over the Avon on my return, I paused to contemplate the distant church in which the poet lies buried, and could not but exult in the malediction which has kept his ashes undisturbed in its quiet and hallowed vaults. What honor could his name have derived from being mingled in dusty companionship with the epitaphs and escutcheons and venal eulogiums of a titled multitude? What would a crowded corner in Westminster Abbey have been, compared with this reverend pile, which seems to stand in beautiful loneliness as his sole mausoleum! The solicitude about the grave may be but the offspring of an overwrought sensibility; but human nature is made up of foibles and prejudices; and its best and tenderest affections are mingled with these factitious feelings. He who has sought renown about the world, and has reaped a full harvest of worldly favor, will find, after all, that there is no love, no admiration, no applause so sweet to the soul as that which springs up in his native place. It is there that he seeks to be gathered in peace and honor, among his kindred and his early friends. And when the weary heart and failing head begin to warn him that the evening of life is drawing on, he turns as fondly as does the infant to the mother's arms, to sink to sleep in the bosom of the scene of his childhood.

How would it have cheered the spirit of the youthful bard, when, wandering forth in disgrace upon a doubtful world, he cast back a heavy look upon his paternal home, could he have foreseen that, before many years, he should return to it covered with renown; that his name should become the boast and glory of his native place; that his ashes should be religiously guarded as its most precious treasure; and that its lessening spire, on which his eyes were fixed in tearful contemplation, should one day become the beacon, towering amid the gentle landscape, to guide the literary pilgrim of every nation to his tomb!

TRAITS OF INDIAN CHARACTER

"I appeal to any white man if ever he entered Logan's cabin hungry, and he gave him not to eat; if ever he came cold and naked, and he clothed him not."—Speech of an Indian Chief

THERE is something in the character and habits of the North American savage, taken in connection with the scenery over which he is accustomed to range, its vast lakes, boundless forests, majestic rivers, and trackless plains, that is, to my mind, wonderfully striking and sublime. He is formed for the wilderness, as the Arab is for the desert. His nature is stern, simple, and enduring; fitted to grapple with difficulties, and to support privations. There seems but little soil in his heart for the growth of the kindly virtues; and yet, if we would but take the trouble to penetrate through that proud stoicism and habitual taciturnity, which look up his character from casual observation, we should find him linked to his fellowman of civilized life by more of those sympathies and affections than are usually ascribed to him.

It has been the lot of the unfortunate aborigines of America, in the early periods of colonization, to be doubly wronged by the white men. They have been dispossessed of their hereditary possessions by mercenary and frequently wanton warfare; and their characters have been traduced by bigoted and interested writers. The colonist has often treated them like beasts of the forest; and the author has endeavored to justify him in his outrages. The former found it easier to exterminate than to civilize—the latter to vilify than to discriminate. The appellations of savage and pagan were deemed sufficient to sanction the hostilities of both; and thus the poor wanderers of the forest were persecuted and defamed, not because they were guilty, but because they were ignorant.

The rights of the savage have seldom been properly appreciated or respected by the white man. In peace, he has too often been the dupe of artful traffic; in war, he has been regarded as a ferocious animal, whose life or death was a question of mere precaution and convenience. Man is cruelly wasteful of life when his own safety is endangered, and he is sheltered by impunity; and little mercy is to be expected from him when he feels the sting of the reptile, and is conscious of the power to destroy.

The same prejudices which were indulged thus early, exist in common circulation at the present day. Certain learned societies have, it is true, with laudable diligence, endeavored to investigate and record the real characters and manners of the Indian tribes; the American government, too, has wisely and humanely exerted itself to inculcate a friendly and forbearing spirit toward them, and to protect them from fraud and injustice.* The current opinion of the Indian character, however, is too apt to be formed from the miserable hordes which infest the frontiers and hang on the skirts of the settlements. These are too commonly composed of degenerate beings, corrupted and enfeebled by the vices of society, without being benefited by its civilization. That proud independence, which formed the main pillar of savage virtue, has been shaken down, and the whole moral fabric lies in ruins. Their spirits are humiliated and debased by a sense of inferiority, and their native courage cowed and daunted by the superior knowledge and power of their enlightened neighbors. Society has advanced upon them like one of those

---

* The American government has been indefatigable in its exertions to meliorate the situation of the Indians, and to introduce among them the arts of civilization, and civil and religious knowledge. To protect them from the frauds of the white traders, no purchase of land from them by individuals is permitted; nor is any person allowed to receive lands from them as a present, without the express sanction of government. These precautions are strictly enforced.

withering airs that will sometimes breathe desola'ion over
a whole region of fertility. It has enervated their strength,
multiplied their diseases, and superinduced upon their original barbarity the low vices of artificial life. It has given
them a thousand superfluous wants, while it has diminished
their means of mere existence. It has driven before it the
animals of the chase, who fly from the sound of the ax and
the smoke of the settlement, and seek refuge in the depths
of remoter forests and yet untrodden wilds. Thus do we too
often find the Indians on our frontiers to be mere wrecks and
remnants of once powerful tribes, who have lingered in the
vicinity of the settlements, and sunk into precarious and
vagabond existence. Poverty, repining and hopeless poverty, a canker of the mind unknown in savage life, corrodes
their spirits and blights every free and noble quality of their
natures. They become drunken, indolent, feeble, thievish,
and pusillanimous. They loiter like vagrants about the settlements, among spacious dwellings, replete with elaborate
comforts, which only render them sensible of the comparative wretchedness of their own condition. Luxury spreads its
ample board before their eyes; but they are excluded from
the banquet. Plenty revels over the fields; but they are
starving in the midst of its abundance: the whole wilderness
has blossomed into a garden; but they feel as reptiles that
infest it.

How different was their state, while yet the undisputed
lords of the soil! Their wants were few, and the means of
gratification within their reach. They saw every one round
them sharing the same lot, enduring the same hardships, feeding on the same aliments, arrayed in the same rude garments. No roof then rose but was open to the homeless
stranger; no smoke curled among the trees but he was welcome to sit down by its fire and join the hunter in his repast.
"For," says an old historian of New England, "their life is
so void of care, and they are so loving also, that they make
use of those things they enjoy as common goods, and are
therein so compassionate, that rather than one should starve

through want, they would starve all; thus do they pass their time merrily, not regarding our pomp, but are better content with their own, which some men esteem so meanly of."
Such were the Indians, while in the pride and energy of their primitive natures; they resemble those wild plants which thrive best in the shades of the forest, but shrink from the hand of cultivation, and perish beneath the influence of the sun.

In discussing the savage character, writers have been too prone to indulge in vulgar prejudice and passionate exaggeration, instead of the candid temper of true philosophy. They have not sufficiently considered the peculiar circumstances in which the Indians have been placed, and the peculiar principles under which they have been educated. No being acts more rigidly from rule than the Indian. His whole conduct is regulated according to some general maxims early implanted in his mind. The moral laws that govern him are, to be sure, but few; but then he conforms to them all—the white man abounds in laws of religion, morals, and manners, but how many does he violate!

A frequent ground of accusation against the Indians is their disregard of treaties, and the treachery and wantonness with which, in time of apparent peace, they will suddenly fly to hostilities. The intercourse of the white men with the Indians, however, is too apt to be cold, distrustful, oppressive, and insulting. They seldom treat them with that confidence and frankness which are indispensable to real friendship; nor is sufficient caution observed not to offend against those feelings of pride or superstition which often prompt the Indian to hostility quicker than mere considerations of interest. The solitary savage feels silently, but acutely. His sensibilities are not diffused over so wide a surface as those of the white man; but they run in steadier and deeper channels. His pride, his affections, his superstitions, are all directed toward fewer objects; but the wounds inflicted on them are proportionably severe, and furnish motives of hostility which we cannot sufficiently appreciate. Where a community is also limited in number, and forms one great patriarchal family, as in an Indian tribe, the injury of an individual is the injury of the whole; and the sentiment of vengeance is almost instantaneously diffused. One council-fire is sufficient for the discussion and arrangement of a plan of hostilities. Here all the fighting men and sages assemble. Eloquence and superstition combine to inflame the minds of the warriors. The orator awakens their martial ardor, and they are wrought up to a kind of religious desperation, by the visions of the prophet and the dreamer.

An instance of one of those sudden exasperations, arising from a motive peculiar to the Indian character, is extant in an old record of the early settlement of Massachusetts. The planters of Plymouth had defaced the monuments of the dead at Passonagessit, and had plundered the grave of the Sachem's mother of some skins with which it had been decorated. The Indians are remarkable for the reverence which they enter-tain for the sepulchers of their kindred. Tribes that have passed generations exiled from the abodes of their ancestors, when by chance they have been traveling in the vicinity, have been known to turn aside from the highway, and, guided by wonderfully accurate tradition, have crossed the country for miles to some tumulus, buried perhaps in woods, where the bones of their tribe were anciently deposited; and there have passed hours in silent meditation. Influenced by this sublime and holy feeling, the Sachem, whose mother's tomb had been violated, gathered his men together, and ad-dressed them in the following beautifully simple and pathetic harangue; a curious specimen of Indian eloquence, and an affecting instance of filial piety in a savage.

"When last the glorious light of all the sky was under-neath this globe, and birds grew silent, I began to settle, as my custom is, to take repose. Before mine eyes were fast closed, methought I saw a vision, at which my spirit was much troubled; and trembling at that doleful sight, a spirit cried aloud, 'Behold, my son, whom I have cherished, see the breasts that gave thee suck, the hands that lapped thee

warm, and fed thee oft. Canst thou forget to take revenge
of those wild people, who have defaced my monument in a
despiteful manner, disdaining our antiquities and honorable
customs? See, now, the Sachem's grave lies like the common people, defaced by an ignoble race. Thy mother doth
complain, and implores thy aid against this thievish people,
who have newly intruded on our land. If this be suffered,
I shall not rest quiet in my everlasting habitation.' This
said, the spirit vanished, and I, all in a sweat, not able scarce
to speak, began to get some strength, and recollected my
spirits that were fled, and determined to demand your counsel and assistance."

I have adduced this anecdote at some length, as it tends
to show how these sudden acts of hostility, which have been
attributed to caprice and perfidy, may often arise from deep
and generous motives, which our inattention to Indian character and customs prevents our properly appreciating.

Another ground of violent outcry against the Indians is
their barbarity to the vanquished. This had its origin partly
in policy and partly in superstition. The tribes, though
sometimes called nations, were never so formidable in their
numbers but that the loss of several warriors was sensibly
felt; this was particularly the case when they had been frequently engaged in warfare; and many an instance occurs
in Indian history, where a tribe, that had long been formidable to its neighbors, has been broken up and driven away
by the capture and massacre of its principal fighting men.
There was a strong temptation, therefore, to the victor to
be merciless; not so much to gratify any cruel revenge as
to provide for future security. The Indians had also the
superstitious belief, frequent among barbarous nations, and
prevalent also among the ancients, that the manes of their
friends who had fallen in battle were soothed by the blood
of the captives. The prisoners, however, who are not thus
sacrificed, are adopted into their families in the place of the
slain, and are treated with the confidence and affection of
relatives and friends; nay, so hospitable and tender is their

entertainment, that when the alternative is offered them, they will often prefer to remain with their adopted brethren, rather than return to the home and the friends of their youth.

The cruelty of the Indians toward their prisoners has been heightened since the colonization of the whites. What was formerly a compliance with policy and superstition, has been exasperated into a gratification of vengeance. They cannot but be sensible that the white men are the usurpers of their ancient dominion, the cause of their degradation, and the gradual destroyers of their race. They go forth to battle, smarting with injuries and indignities which they have individually suffered, and they are driven to madness and despair by the wide-spreading desolation and the overwhelming ruin of European warfare. The whites have too frequently set them an example of violence, by burning their villages and laying waste their slender means of subsistence; and yet they wonder that savages do not show moderation and magnanimity toward those who have left them nothing but mere existence and wretchedness.

We stigmatize the Indians, also, as cowardly and treacherous, because they use stratagem in warfare, in preference to open force; but in this they are fully justified by their rude code of honor. They are early taught that stratagem is praiseworthy: the bravest warrior thinks it no disgrace to lurk in silence, and take every advantage of his foe: he triumphs in the superior craft and sagacity by which he has been enabled to surprise and destroy an enemy. Indeed, man is naturally more prone to subtilty than open valor, owing to his physical weakness in comparison with other animals. They are endowed with natural weapons of defense: with horns, with tusks, with hoofs, and talons; but man has to depend on his superior sagacity. In all his encounters with these, his proper enemies, he resorts to stratagem; and when he perversely turns his hostility against his fellow man, he at first continues the same subtle mode of warfare.

The natural principle of war is to do the most harm to

our enemy, with the least harm to ourselves; and this of course is to be effected by stratagem. That chivalrous courage which induces us to despise the suggestions of prudence, and to rush in the face of certain danger, is the off-spring of society, and produced by education. It is honor-able, because it is in fact the triumph of lofty sentiment over an instinctive repugnance to pain, and over those yearnings after personal ease and security, which society has con-demned as ignoble. It is kept alive by pride and the fear of shame; and thus the dread of real evil is overcome by the superior dread of an evil which exists but in the imagination. It has been cherished and stimulated also by various means. It has been the theme of spirit-stirring song and chivalrous story. The poet and minstrel have delighted to shed round it the splendors of fiction; and even the historian has for-gotten the sober gravity of narration, and broken forth into enthusiasm and rhapsody in its praise. Triumphs and gorgeous pageants have been its reward: monuments, on which art has exhausted its skill and opulence its treasures, have been erected to perpetuate a nation's gratitude and ad-miration. Thus artificially excited, courage has risen to an extraordinary and factitious degree of heroism; and, arrayed in all the glorious "pomp and circumstance of war," this turbulent quality has ever been able to eclipse many of those quiet, but invaluable virtues, which silently ennoble the human character, and swell the tide of human happiness.

But if courage intrinsically consists in the defiance of danger and pain, the life of the Indian is a continual exhibi-tion of it. He lives in a state of perpetual hostility and risk. Peril and adventure are congenial to his nature; or rather seem necessary to arouse his faculties and to give an interest to his existence. Surrounded by hostile tribes, whose mode of warfare is by ambush and surprisal, he is always prepared for fight, and lives with his weapons in his hands. As the ship careers in fearful singleness through the solitudes of ocean—as the bird mingles among clouds and storms, and wings its way, a mere speck, across the pathless fields of

air; so the Indian holds his course, silent, solitary, but un-
daunted, through the boundless bosom of the wilderness.
His expeditions may vie in distance and danger with the
pilgrimage of the devotee, or the crusade of the knight-errant.
He traverses vast forests, exposed to the hazards of lonely
sickness, of lurking enemies, and pining famine.   Stormy
lakes, those great inland seas, are no obstacles to his wanderings: in his light canoe of bark, he sports like a feather on
their waves, and darts with the swiftness of an arrow down
the roaring rapids of the rivers.   His very subsistence is
snatched from the midst of toil and peril.   He gains his food
by the hardships and dangers of the chase; he wraps himself
in the spoils of the bear, the panther, and the buffalo; and
sleeps among the thunders of the cataract.

No hero of ancient or modern days can surpass the Indian
in his lofty contempt of death, and the fortitude with which
he sustains its cruelest affliction.   Indeed, we here behold
him rising superior to the white man, in consequence of his
peculiar education.   The latter rushes to glorious death at
the cannon's mouth; the former calmly contemplates its
approach, and triumphantly endures it, amid the varied
torments of surrounding foes, and the protracted agonies of
fire.   He even takes a pride in taunting his persecutors, and
provoking their ingenuity of torture; and as the devouring
flames prey on his very vitals, and the flesh shrinks from the
sinews, he raises his last song of triumph, breathing the
defiance of an unconquered heart, and invoking the spirits of
his fathers to witness that he dies without a groan.

Notwithstanding the obloquy with which the early historians have overshadowed the characters of the unfortunate
natives, some bright gleams occasionally break through,
which throw a degree of melancholy luster on their memories.
Facts are occasionally to be met with in the rude annals of
the eastern provinces, which, though recorded with the coloring of prejudice and bigotry, yet speak for themselves; and
will be dwelt on with applause and sympathy when prejudice
shall have passed away.

In one of the homely narratives of the Indian wars in New England, there is a touching account of the desolation carried into the tribe of the Pequod Indians. Humanity shrinks from the cold-blooded detail of indiscriminate butchery. In one place we read of the surprisal of an Indian fort in the night, when the wigwams were wrapped in flames, and the miserable inhabitants shot down and slain in attempting to escape, "all being dispatched and ended in the course of an hour." After a series of similar transactions, "our soldiers," as the historian piously observes, "being resolved by God's assistance to make a final destruction of them," the unhappy savages being hunted from their homes and fortresses, and pursued with fire and sword, a scanty but gallant band, the sad remnant of the Pequod warriors, with their wives and children, took refuge in a swamp.

Burning with indignation, and rendered sullen by despair; with hearts bursting with grief at the destruction of their tribe, and spirits galled and sore at the fancied ignominy of their defeat, they refused to ask their lives at the hands of an insulting foe, and preferred death to submission.

As the night drew on, they were surrounded in their dismal retreat, so as to render escape impracticable. Thus situated, their enemy "plied them with shot all the time, by which means many were killed and buried in the mire." In the darkness and fog that preceded the dawn of day some few broke through the besiegers and escaped into the woods: "the rest were left to the conquerors, of which many were killed in the swamp, like sullen dogs who would rather, in their self-willedness and madness, sit still and be shot through, or cut to pieces," than implore for mercy. When the day broke upon this handful of forlorn, but dauntless spirits, the soldiers, we are told, entering the swamp, "saw several heaps of them sitting close together, upon whom they discharged their pieces, laden with ten or twelve pistol-bullets at a time; putting the muzzles of the pieces under the boughs, within a few yards of them; so as, besides those that were found dead, many more were killed and sunk into the mire, and never were minded more by friend or foe."

Can anyone read this plain unvarnished tale, without admiring the stern resolution, the unbending pride, the loftiness of spirit, that seemed to nerve the hearts of these self-taught heroes, and to raise them above the instinctive feelings of human nature? When the Gauls laid waste the city of Rome, they found the senators clothed in their robes and seated with stern tranquillity in their curule chairs; in this manner they suffered death without resistance or even supplication. Such conduct was, in them, applauded as noble and magnanimous—in the hapless Indians, it was reviled as obstinate and sullen. How truly are we the dupes of show and circumstance! How different is virtue, clothed in purple and enthroned in state, from virtue naked and destitute, and perishing obscurely in a wilderness!

But I forbear to dwell on these gloomy pictures. The eastern tribes have long since disappeared; the forests that sheltered them have been laid low, and scarce any traces remain of them in the thickly-settled States of New England, excepting here and there the Indian name of a village or a stream. And such must sooner or later be the fate of those other tribes which skirt the frontiers and have occasionally been inveigled from their forests to mingle in the wars of white men. In a little while, and they will go the way that their brethren have gone before. The few hordes which still linger about the shores of Huron and Superior, and the tributary streams of the Mississippi, will share the fate of those tribes that once spread over Massachusetts and Connecticut and lorded it along the proud banks of the Hudson; of that gigantic race said to have existed on the borders of the Susquehanna; and of those various nations that flourished about the Potowmac and the Rappahanoc, and that peopled the forests of the vast valley of Shenandoah. They will vanish like a vapor from the face of the earth; their very history will be lost in forgetfulness; and "the places that now know them will know them no more forever." Or if, perchance, some dubious memorial of them should survive, it may be in the romantic dreams of the poet, to people in imagination his glades and groves, like the fauns and satyrs and sylvan deities of antiquity. But should he venture upon the dark story of their wrongs and wretchedness; should he tell how they were invaded, corrupted, despoiled; driven from their native abodes and the sepulchers of their fathers; hunted like wild beasts about the earth, and sent down with violence and butchery to the grave—posterity will either turn with horror and incredulity from the tale, or blush with indignation at the inhumanity of their forefathers.—"We are driven back," said an old warrior, "until we can retreat no further—our hatchets are broken, our bows are snapped, our fires are nearly extinguished—a little longer and the white man will cease to persecute us—for we shall cease to exist."

PHILIP OF POKANOKET

AN INDIAN MEMOIR

"As monumental bronze unchanged his look:
A soul that pity touch'd, but never shook;
Train'd, from his tree-rock'd cradle to his bier,
The fierce extremes of good and ill to brook
Impassive—fearing but the shame of fear—
A stoic of the woods—a man without a fear."

—CAMPBELL

IT is to be regretted that those early writers who treated of the discovery and settlement of America have not given us more particular and candid accounts of the remarkable characters that flourished in savage life. The scanty anecdotes which have reached us are full of peculiarity and interest; they furnish us with nearer glimpses of human nature, and show what man is in a comparatively primitive state and what he owes to civilization. There is something of the

charm of discovery in lighting upon these wild and unex-
plored tracts of human nature; in witnessing, as it were, the
native growth of moral sentiment; and perceiving those generous and romantic qualities which have been artificially
cultivated by society, vegetating in spontaneous hardihood
and rude magnificence.

In civilized life, where the happiness, and indeed almost
the existence, of man depends so much upon the opinion of
his fellow men, he is constantly acting a studied part. The
bold and peculiar traits of native character are refined away,
or softened down by the leveling influence of what is termed
good breeding; and he practices so many petty deceptions,
and affects so many generous sentiments, for the purposes of
popularity, that it is difficult to distinguish his real from his
artificial character. The Indian, on the contrary, free from
the restraints and refinements of polished life, and, in a great
degree, a solitary and independent being, obeys the impulses
of his inclination or the dictates of his judgment; and thus
the attributes of his nature, being freely indulged, grow
singly great and striking. Society is like a lawn, where
every roughness is smoothed, every bramble eradicated, and
where the eye is delighted by the smiling verdure of a velvet
surface; he, however, who would study Nature in its wildness and variety, must plunge into the forest, must explore
the glen, must stem the torrent, and dare the precipice.

These reflections arose on casually looking through a volume of early colonial history, wherein are recorded, with
great bitterness, the outrages of the Indians, and their wars
with the settlers of New England. It is painful to perceive,
even from these partial narratives, how the footsteps of civilization may be traced in the blood of the aborigines; how
easily the colonists were moved to hostility by the lust of
conquest; how merciless and exterminating was their warfare. The imagination shrinks at the idea: how many intellectual beings were hunted from the earth—how many brave
and noble hearts, of Nature's sterling coinage, were broken
down and trampled in the dust!

Such was the fate of Philip of Pokanoket, an Indian
warrior, whose name was once a terror throughout Massachusetts and Connecticut.   He was the most distinguished of
a number of contemporary Sachems, who reigned over the
Pequods, the Narrhagansets, the Wampanoags, and the other
eastern tribes, at the time of the first settlement of New England : a band of native untaught heroes, who made the most
generous struggle of which human nature is capable; fighting
to the last gasp in the cause of their country, without a hope
of victory or a thought of renown.   Worthy of an age of
poetry, and fit subjects for local story and romantic fiction,
they have left scarcely any authentic traces on the page of
history, but stalk, like gigantic shadows, in the dim twilight
of tradition. *

When the pilgrims, as the Plymouth settlers are called by
their descendants, first took refuge on the shores of the New
World, from the religious persecutions of the Old, their situation was to the last degree gloomy and disheartening.   Few
in number, and that number rapidly perishing away through
sickness and hardships; surrounded by a howling wilderness
and savage tribes; exposed to the rigors of an almost arctic
winter and the vicissitudes of an ever-shifting climate; their
minds were filled with doleful forebodings, and nothing preserved them from sinking into despondency but the strong
excitement of religious enthusiasm.   In this forlorn situation
they were visited by Massasoit, chief Sagamore of the Wampanoags, a powerful chief, who reigned over a great extent
of country.   Instead of taking advantage of the scanty number of the strangers, and expelling them from his territories
into which they had intruded, he seemed at once to conceive
for them a generous friendship, and extended toward them
the rites of primitive hospitality.   He came early in the
spring to their settlement of New Plymouth, attended by a

---

* While correcting the proof-sheets of this article, the author is
informed that a celebrated English poet has nearly finished a heroic
poem on the story of Philip of Pokanoket

mere handful of followers; entered into a solemn league of peace and amity; sold them a portion of the soil, and promised to secure for them the good-will of his savage allies. Whatever may be said of Indian perfidy, it is certain that the integrity and good faith of Massasoit have never been impeached. He continued a firm and magnanimous friend of the white men; suffering them to extend their possessions and to strengthen themselves in the land, and betraying no jealousy of their increasing power and prosperity. Shortly before his death he came once more to New Plymouth, with his son Alexander, for the purpose of renewing the covenant of peace and of securing it to his posterity.

At this conference he endeavored to protect the religion of his forefathers from the encroaching zeal of the missionaries, and stipulated that no further attempt should be made to draw off his people from their ancient faith; but, finding the English obstinately opposed to any such condition, he mildly relinquished the demand. Almost the last act of his life was to bring his two sons, Alexander and Philip (as they had been named by the English), to the residence of a principal settler, recommending mutual kindness and confidence, and entreating that the same love and amity which had existed between the white men and himself might be continued afterward with his children. The good old Sachem died in peace, and was happily gathered to his fathers before sorrow came upon his tribe; his children remained behind to experience the ingratitude of white men.

His eldest son, Alexander, succeeded him. He was of a quick and impetuous temper, and proudly tenacious of his hereditary rights and dignity. The intrusive policy and dictatorial conduct of the strangers excited his indignation; and he beheld with uneasiness their exterminating wars with the neighboring tribes. He was doomed soon to incur their hostility, being accused of plotting with the Narrhagansets to rise against the English and drive them from the land. It is impossible to say whether this accusation was warranted by facts or was grounded on mere suspicions. It is evident,

however, by the violent and overbearing measures of the
settlers, that they had by this time begun to feel conscious of
the rapid increase of their power and to grow harsh and in-
considerate in their treatment of the natives. They dispatched an armed force to seize upon Alexander and to bring
him before their court. He was traced to his woodland
haunts, and surprised at a hunting house, where he was reposing with a band of his followers, unarmed, after the toils
of the chase. The suddenness of his arrest, and the outrage
offered to his sovereign dignity, so preyed upon the irascible
feelings of this proud savage as to throw him into a raging
fever; he was permitted to return home on condition of sending his son as a pledge for his reappearance; but the blow he
had received was fatal, and before he reached his home he
fell a victim to the agonies of a wounded spirit.

The successor of Alexander was Metamocet, or King
Philip, as he was called by the settlers, on account of his
lofty spirit and ambitious temper. These, together with his
well-known energy and enterprise, had rendered him an
object of great jealousy and apprehension, and he was accused of having always cherished a secret and implacable
hostility toward the whites. Such may very probably and very
naturally have been the case. He considered them as originally but mere intruders into the country, who had presumed
upon indulgence and were extending an influence baneful to
savage life. He saw the whole race of his countrymen melting before them from the face of the earth; their territories
slipping from their hands and their tribes becoming feeble,
scattered and dependent. It may be said that the soil was
originally purchased by the settlers; but who does not know
the nature of Indian purchases in the early periods of colonization? The Europeans always made thrifty bargains, through
their superior adroitness in traffic; and they gained vast ac-
cessions of territory by easily-provoked hostilities. An un-
cultivated savage is never a nice inquirer into the refinements
of law, by which an injury may be gradually and legally inflicted. Leading facts are all by which he judges; and it was

enough for Philip to know, that before the intrusion of the
Europeans his countrymen were lords of the soil and that
now they were becoming vagabonds in the land of their
fathers.

But whatever may have been his feelings of general hostility, and his particular indignation at the treatment of his
brother, he suppressed them for the present, renewed the
contract with the settlers, and resided peaceably for many
years at Pokanoket, or, as it was called by the English,
Mount Hope,* the ancient seat of dominion of his tribe.
Suspicions, however, which were at first but vague and in-
definite, began to acquire form and substance; and he was
at length charged with attempting to instigate the various
eastern tribes to rise at once, and, by a simultaneous effort,
to throw off the yoke of their oppressors. It is difficult at
this distant period to assign the proper credit due to these
early accusations against the Indians. There was a proneness to suspicion, and an aptness to acts of violence on the
part of the whites, that gave weight and importance to every
idle tale. Informers abounded, where tale-bearing met
with countenance and reward; and the sword was readily
unsheathed, when its success was certain, and it carved out
empire.

The only positive evidence on record against Philip is the
accusation of one Sausaman, a renegado Indian, whose
natural cunning had been quickened by a partial education
which he had received among the settlers. He changed his
faith and his allegiance two or three times, with a facility
that evinced the looseness of his principles. He had acted
for some time as Philip's confidential secretary and counselor,
and had enjoyed his bounty and protection. Finding, however, that the clouds of adversity were gathering round his
patron, he abandoned his service and went over to the whites;
and, in order to gain their favor, charged his former benefactor with plotting against their safety. A rigorous inves-

---

* Now Bristol, Rhode Island.

tigation took place. Philip and several of his subjects sub-
mitted to be examined, but nothing was proved against them.
The settlers, however, had now gone too far to retract; they
had previously determined that Philip was a dangerous
neighbor; they had publicly evinced their distrust, and had
done enough to insure his hostility: according, therefore, to
the usual mode of reasoning in these cases, his destruction
had become necessary to their security. Sausaman, the
treacherous informer, was shortly after found dead in a
pond, having fallen a victim to the vengeance of his tribe.
Three Indians, one of whom was a friend and counselor of
Philip, were apprehended and tried, and, on the testimony of
one very questionable witness, were condemned and executed
as murderers.

This treatment of his subjects and ignominious punish-
ment of his friend, outraged the pride and exasperated the
passions of Philip. The bolt which had fallen thus at his
very feet, awakened him to the gathering storm, and he determined to trust himself no longer in the power of the white
men. The fate of his insulted and broken-hearted brother
still rankled in his mind; and he had a further warning in
the tragical story of Miantonimo, a great Sachem of the
Narrhagansets, who, after manfully facing his accusers before a tribunal of the colonists, exculpating himself from a
charge of conspiracy, and receiving assurances of amity, had
been perfidiously dispatched at their instigation. Philip,
therefore, gathered his fighting men about him; persuaded
all strangers that he could to join his cause; sent the women
and children to the Narrhagansets for safety; and where-
ever he appeared was continually surrounded by armed
warriors.

When the two parties were thus in a state of distrust and
irritation, the least spark was sufficient to set them in a flame.
The Indians, having weapons in their hands, grew mischievous and committed various petty depredations. In one of
their maraudings a warrior was fired upon and killed by a
settler. This was the signal for open hostilities; the Indians

pressed to revenge the death of their comrade and the alarm
of war resounded through the Plymouth colony.

In the early chronicles of these dark and melancholy
times we meet with many indications of the diseased state of
the public mind. The gloom of religious abstraction, and
the wildness of their situation, among trackless forests and
savage tribes, had disposed the colonists to superstitious fancies and had filled their imaginations with the frightful
chimeras of witchcraft and spectrology. They were much
given also to a belief in omens. The troubles with Philip
and his Indians were preceded, we are told, by a variety of
those awful warnings which forerun great and public calamities. The perfect arm of an Indian bow appeared in the air
at New Plymouth, which was looked upon by the inhabitants
as a "prodigious apparition." At Hadley, Northampton,
and other towns in their neighborhood, "was heard the
report of a great piece of ordnance, with the shaking of the
earth and a considerable echo."* Others were alarmed on a
still sunshiny morning, by the discharge of guns and muskets;
bullets seemed to whistle past them and the noise of drums
resounded in the air, seeming to pass away to the westward;
others fancied that they heard the galloping of horses over
their heads; and certain monstrous births which took place
about the time filled the superstitious in some towns with
doleful forebodings. Many of these portentous sights and
sounds may be ascribed to natural phenomena; to the northern lights which occur vividly in those latitudes; the meteors
which explode in the air; the casual rushing of a blast through
the top branches of the forest; the crash of falling trees or
disrupted rocks; and to those other uncouth sounds and
echoes which will sometimes strike the ear so strangely amid
the profound stillness of woodland solitudes. These may
have startled some melancholy imaginations, may have been
exaggerated by the love for the marvelous, and listened to
with that avidity with which we devour whatever is fearful

---

* The Rev. Increase Mather's History.

and mysterious. The universal currency of these superstitious fancies and the grave record made of them by one of
the learned men of the day, are strongly characteristic of the
times.

The nature of the contest that ensued was such as too often
distinguishes the warfare between civilized men and savages.
On the part of the whites, it was conducted with superior
skill and success; but with a wastefulness of the blood and a
disregard of the natural rights of their antagonists: on the
part of the Indians it was waged with the desperation of
men fearless of death, and who had nothing to expect from
peace, but humiliation, dependence and decay.

The events of the war are transmitted to us by a worthy
clergyman of the time, who dwells with horror and indignation on every hostile act of the Indians, however justifiable,
while he mentions with applause the most sanguinary atroc-
ities of the whites. Philip is reviled as a murderer and a
traitor; without considering that he was a true-born prince,
gallantly fighting at the head of his subjects to avenge the
wrongs of his family; to retrieve the tottering power of his
line, and to deliver his native land from the oppression of
usurping strangers.

The project of a wide and simultaneous revolt, if such had
really been formed, was worthy of a capacious mind, and,
had it not been prematurely discovered, might have been
overwhelming in its consequences. The war that actually
broke out was but a war of detail; a mere succession of
casual exploits and unconnected enterprises. Still it sets forth
the military genius and daring prowess of Philip; and where-
ever, in the prejudiced and passionate narrations that have
been given of it, we can arrive at simple facts, we find him
displaying a vigorous mind; a fertility in expedients; a contempt of suffering and hardship; and an unconquerable resolution that command our sympathy and applause.

Driven from his paternal domains at Mount Hope, he
threw himself into the depths of those vast and trackless
forests that skirted the settlements, and were almost imper-

vious to anything but a wild beast or an Indian. Here he gathered together his forces, like the storm accumulating its stores of mischief in the bosom of the thunder-cloud, and would suddenly emerge at a time and place least expected, carrying havoc and dismay into the villages. There were now and then indications of these impending ravages that filled the minds of the colonists with awe and apprehension. The report of a distant gun would perhaps be heard from the solitary woodland, where there was known to be no white man; the cattle which had been wandering in the woods would sometimes return home wounded, or an Indian or two would be seen lurking about the skirts of the forests, and suddenly disappearing, as the lightning will sometimes be seen playing silently about the edge of the cloud that is brewing up the tempest.

Though sometimes pursued, and even surrounded by the settlers, yet Philip as often escaped almost miraculously from their toils, and, plunging into the wilderness, would be lost to all search or inquiry until he again emerged at some far distant quarter, laying the country desolate. Among his strongholds were the great swamps or morasses which extend in some parts of New England, composed of loose bogs of deep black mud, perplexed with thickets, brambles, rank weeds, the shattered and mouldering trunks of fallen trees, overshadowed by lugubrious hemlocks. The uncertain footing and the tangled mazes of these shaggy wilds rendered them almost impracticable to the white man, though the Indian could thread their labyrinths with the agility of a deer. Into one of these, the great swamp of Pocasset Neck, was Philip once driven with a band of his followers. The English did not dare to pursue him, fearing to venture into these dark and frightful recesses, where they might perish in fens and miry pits or be shot down by lurking foes. They therefore invested the entrance to the neck and began to build a fort, with the thought of starving out the foe; but Philip and his warriors wafted themselves on a raft over an arm of the sea, in the dead of night, leaving the women and children behind, and escaped away to the westward, kindling the flames of war among the tribes of Massachusetts and the Nipmuck country and threatening the colony of Connecticut.

In this way Philip became a theme of universal apprehension. The mystery in which he was enveloped exaggerated his real terrors. He was an evil that walked in darkness; whose coming none could foresee, and against which none knew when to be on the alert. The whole country abounded with rumors and alarms. Philip seemed almost possessed of ubiquity; for, in whatever part of the widely extended frontier an irruption from the forest took place, Philip was said to be its leader. Many superstitious notions also were circulated concerning him. He was said to deal in necromancy, and to be attended by an old Indian witch or prophetess whom he consulted, and who assisted him by her charms and incantations. This indeed was frequently the case with Indian chiefs; either through their own credulity or to act upon that of their followers: and the influence of the prophet and the dreamer over Indian superstition has been fully evidenced in recent instances of savage warfare.

At the time that Philip effected his escape from Pocasset, his fortunes were in a desperate condition. His forces had been thinned by repeated fights, and he had lost almost the whole of his resources. In this time of adversity he found a faithful friend in Canonchet, Chief Sachem of all the Narrhagansets. He was the son and heir of Miantonimo, the great Sachem, who, as already mentioned, after an honorable acquittal of the charge of conspiracy, had been privately put to death at the perfidious instigations of the settlers. "He was the heir," says the old chronicler, "of all his father's pride and insolence, as well as of his malice toward the English;" he certainly was the heir of his insults and injuries, and the legitimate avenger of his murder. Though he had forborne to take an active part in this hopeless war, yet he received Philip and his broken forces with open arms, and gave them the most generous countenance and support. This at once drew upon him the hostility of the English, and

it was determined to strike a signal blow that should involve
both the Sachems in one common ruin.   A great force was,
therefore, gathered together from Massachusetts, Plymouth
and Connecticut, and was sent into the Narrhaganset country
in the depth of winter, when the swamps, being frozen and
leafless, could be traversed with comparative facility, and
would no longer afford dark and impenetrable fastnesses to
the Indians.

Apprehensive of attack, Canonchet had conveyed the
greater part of his stores, together with the old, the infirm,
the women and children of his tribe, to a strong fortress,
where he and Philip had likewise drawn up the flower of
their forces.   This fortress, deemed by the Indians impreg-
nable, was situated upon a rising mound or kind of island, of
five or six acres, in the midst of a swamp; it was constructed
with a degree of judgment and skill vastly superior to what
is usually displayed in Indian fortification, and indicative of
the martial genius of these two chieftains.

Guided by a renegado Indian, the English penetrated,
through December snows, to this stronghold, and came upon
the garrison by surprise.   The fight was fierce and tumultuous.
The assailants were repulsed in their first attack, and several
of their bravest officers were shot down in the act of storming
the fortress, sword in hand.   The assault was renewed with
greater success.   A lodgment was effected.   The Indians
were driven from one post to another.   They disputed their
ground inch by inch, fighting with the fury of despair.   Most
of their veterans were cut to pieces; and after a long and
bloody battle, Philip and Canonchet, with a handful of surviving warriors, retreated from the fort and took refuge in
the thickets of the surrounding forest.

The victors set fire to the wigwams and the fort; the
whole was soon in a blaze; many of the old men, the women
and the children, perished in the flames.   This last outrage
overcame even the stoicism of the savage.   The neighboring
woods resounded with the yells of rage and despair, uttered
by the fugitive warriors as they beheld the destruction of

their dwellings, and heard the agonizing cries of their wives and offspring. "The burning of the wigwams," says a contemporary writer, "the shrieks and cries of the women and children, and the yelling of the warriors, exhibited a most horrible and affecting scene, so that it greatly moved some of the soldiers." The same writer cautiously adds, "they were in *much doubt* then, and afterward seriously inquired, whether burning their enemies alive could be consistent with humanity and the benevolent principles of the gospel." *

The fate of the brave and generous Canonchet is worthy of particular mention: the last scene of his life is one of the noblest instances on record of Indian magnanimity.

Broken down in his power and resources by this signal defeat, yet faithful to his ally and to the hapless cause which he had espoused, he rejected all overtures of peace, offered on condition of betraying Philip and his followers, and declared that "he would fight it out to the last man, rather than become a servant to the English." His home being destroyed, his country harassed and laid waste by the incursions of the conquerors, he was obliged to wander away to the banks of the Connecticut, where he formed a rallying point to the whole body of western Indians and laid waste several of the English settlements.

Early in the spring he departed on a hazardous expedition, with only thirty chosen men, to penetrate to Seaconck, in the vicinity of Mount Hope, and to procure seed-corn to plant for the sustenance of his troops. This little band of adventurers had passed safely through the Pequod country and were in the center of the Narrhaganset, resting at some wigwams near Pautucket River, when an alarm was given of an approaching enemy. Having but seven men by him at the time, Canonchet dispatched two of them to the top of a neighboring hill to bring intelligence of the foe.

Panicstruck by the appearance of a troop of English and Indians rapidly advancing, they fled in breathless terror past their chieftain, without stopping to inform him of the danger.

* MS. of the Rev. W. Ruggles.

Canonchet sent another scout who did the same. He then sent two more, one of whom, hurrying back in confusion and affright, told him that the whole British army was at hand. Canonchet saw there was no choice but immediate flight. He attempted to escape round the hill, but was perceived and hotly pursued by the hostile Indians and a few of the fleetest of the English. Finding the swiftest pursuer close upon his heels, he threw off, first his blanket, then his silver-laced coat and belt of peag, by which his enemies knew him to be Canonchet and redoubled the eagerness of pursuit.

At length, in dashing through the river his foot slipped upon a stone, and he fell so deep as to wet his gun. This accident so struck him with despair, that, as he afterward confessed, "his heart and his bowels turned within him, and he became like a rotten stick, void of strength."

To such a degree was he unnerved, that, being seized by a Pequod Indian within a short distance of the river, he made no resistance, though a man of great vigor of body and boldness of heart. But on being made prisoner, the whole pride of his spirit arose within him; and from that moment, we find, in the anecdotes given by his enemies, nothing but repeated flashes of elevated and prince-like heroism. Being questioned by one of the English who first came up with him, and who had not attained his twenty-second year, the proud-hearted warrior, looking with lofty contempt upon his youthful countenance, replied, "You are a child—you cannot understand matters of war—let your brother or your chief come—him will I answer."

Though repeated offers were made to him of his life, on condition of submitting with his nation to the English, yet he rejected them with disdain, and refused to send any proposals of the kind to the great body of his subjects; saying that he knew none of them would comply. Being reproached with his breach of faith toward the whites, his boast that he would not deliver up a Wampanoag, nor the parings of a Wampanoag's nail, and his threat that he would burn the English alive in their houses, he disdained to justify himself, haughtily answering that others were as forward for the war as himself, "and he desired to hear no more thereof."

So noble and unshaken a spirit, so true a fidelity to his cause and his friend, might have touched the feelings of the generous and the brave; but Canonchet was an Indian; a being toward whom war had no courtesy, humanity no law, religion no compassion—he was condemned to die. The last words of his that are recorded are worthy the greatness of his soul. When sentence of death was passed upon him, he observed, "that he liked it well, for he should die before his heart was soft, or he had spoken anything unworthy of himself." His enemies gave him the death of a soldier, for he was shot at Stoningham by three young Sachems of his own rank.

The defeat of the Narrhaganset fortress and the death of Canonchet were fatal blows to the fortunes of King Philip. He made an ineffectual attempt to raise a head of war, by stirring up the Mohawks to take arms; but though possessed of the native talents of a statesman, his arts were counteracted by the superior arts of his enlightened enemies, and the terror of their warlike skill began to subdue the resolution of the neighboring tribes. The unfortunate chieftain saw himself daily stripped of power and his ranks rapidly thinning around him. Some were suborned by the whites; others fell victims to hunger and fatigue and to the frequent attacks by which they were harassed. His stores were all captured; his chosen friends were swept away from before his eyes; his uncle was shot down by his side; his sister was carried into captivity, and in one of his narrow escapes he was compelled to leave his beloved wife and only son to the mercy of the enemy. "His ruin," says the historian, "being thus gradually carried on, his misery was not prevented, but augmented thereby; being himself made acquainted with the sense and experimental feeling of the captivity of his children, loss of friends, slaughter of his subjects, bereavement of all family relations, and being stripped of all outward comforts before his own life should be taken away."

To fill up the measure of his misfortunes, his own followers began to plot against his life, that by sacrificing him they might purchase dishonorable safety. Through treachery, a number of his faithful adherents, the subjects of Wetamoe, an Indian princess of Pocasset, a near kinswoman and confederate of Philip, were betrayed into the hands of the enemy. Wetamoe was among them at the time, and attempted to make her escape by crossing a neighboring river: either exhausted by swimming, or starved with cold and hunger, she was found dead and naked near the water-side. But persecution ceased not at the grave: even death, the refuge of the wretched, where the wicked commonly cease from troubling, was no protection to this outcast female, whose great crime was affectionate fidelity to her kinsman and her friend. Her corpse was the object of unmanly and dastardly vengeance; the head was severed from the body and set upon a pole, and was thus exposed, at Taunton, to the view of her captive subjects. They immediately recognized the features of their unfortunate queen, and were so affected at this barbarous spectacle that we are told they broke forth into the "most horrid and diabolical lamentations."

However Philip had borne up against the complicated miseries and misfortunes that surrounded him, the treachery of his followers seemed to wring his heart and reduce him to despondency. It is said that "he never rejoiced afterward, nor had success in any of his designs." The spring of hope was broken—the ardor of enterprise was extinguished: he looked around, and all was danger and darkness; there was no eye to pity, nor any arm that could bring deliverance. With a scanty band of followers, who still remained true to his desperate fortunes, the unhappy Philip wandered back to the vicinity of Mount Hope, the ancient dwelling of his fathers. Here he lurked about, like a specter, among the scenes of former power and prosperity, now bereft of home, of family and friend. There needs no better picture of his destitute and piteous situation than that furnished by the homely pen of the chronicler, who is unwarily enlisting the feelings of the reader in favor of the hapless warrior whom he reviles. "Philip," he says, "like a savage wild beast, having been hunted by the English forces through the woods above a hundred miles backward and forward, at last was driven to his own den upon Mount Hope, where he retired, with a few of his best friends, into a swamp, which proved but a prison to keep him fast till the messengers of death came by divine permission to execute vengeance upon him."

Even at this last refuge of desperation and despair a sullen grandeur gathers round his memory. We picture him to ourselves seated among his care-worn followers, brooding in silence over his blasted fortunes, and acquiring a savage sublimity from the wildness and dreariness of his lurking-place. Defeated, but not dismayed—crushed to the earth, but not humiliated—he seemed to grow more haughty beneath disaster, and to experience a fierce satisfaction in draining the last dregs of bitterness. Little minds are tamed and subdued by misfortune; but great minds rise above it. The very idea of submission awakened the fury of Philip, and he smote to death one of his followers who proposed an expedient of peace. The brother of the victim made his escape, and in revenge betrayed the retreat of his chieftain. A body of white men and Indians were immediately dispatched to the swamp where Philip lay crouched, glaring with fury and despair. Before he was aware of their approach, they had begun to surround him. In a little while he saw five of his trustiest followers laid dead at his feet; all resistance was vain; he rushed forth from his covert and made a headlong attempt at escape, but was shot through the heart by a renegado Indian of his own nation.

Such is the scanty story of the brave but unfortunate King Philip; persecuted while living, slandered and dishonored when dead. If, however, we consider even the prejudiced anecdotes furnished us by his enemies, we may perceive in them traces of amiable and lofty character, sufficient to awaken sympathy for his fate and respect for his memory. We find that, amid all the harassing cares and ferocious

passions of constant warfare, he was alive to the softer feelings of connubial love and paternal tenderness, and to the
generous sentiment of friendship.   The captivity of his "beloved wife and only son" is mentioned with exultation, as
causing him poignant misery: the death of any near friend
is triumphantly recorded as a new blow on his sensibilities;
but the treachery and desertion of many of his followers, in
whose affections he had confided, is said to have desolated
his heart, and to have bereaved him of all further comfort.
He was a patriot, attached to his native soil—a prince true to
his subjects, and indignant of their wrongs—a soldier, daring
in battle, firm in adversity, patient of fatigue, of hunger, of
every variety of bodily suffering, and ready to perish in the
cause he had espoused.   Proud of heart, and with an un-
tamable love of natural liberty, he preferred to enjoy it
among the beasts of the forests, or in the dismal and famished recesses of swamps and morasses, rather than bow his
haughty spirit to submission and live dependent and despised
in the ease and luxury of the settlements.   With heroic
qualities and bold achievements that would have graced a
civilized warrior, and have rendered him the theme of the
poet and the historian, he lived a wanderer and a fugitive in
his native land, and went down, like a lonely bark, founder-
ing amid darkness and tempest—without a pitying eye to
weep his fall, or a friendly hand to record his struggle.

JOHN BULL

"An old song, made by an aged old pate,
  Of an old worshipful gentleman who had a great estate,
  That kept a brave old house at a bountiful rate,
  And an old porter to relieve the poor at his gate.

"With an old study fill'd full of learned old books,
  With an old reverend chaplain, you might know him by
      his looks;
  With an old buttery-hatch worn quite off the hooks,
  And an old kitchen that maintained half a dozen old cooks.
              Like an old courtier," etc.
                                    —*Old Song*

THERE is no species of humor in which the English more excel than that which consists in caricaturing and giving ludicrous appellations or nicknames. In this way they have whimsically designated, not merely individuals, but nations; and in their fondness for pushing a joke, they have not spared even themselves. One would think that, in personifying itself, a nation would be apt to picture something grand, heroic and imposing; but it is characteristic of the peculiar humor of the English, and of their love for what is blunt, comic and familiar, that they have embodied their national oddities in the figure of a sturdy, corpulent old fellow, with a three-cornered hat, red waistcoat, leather breeches and stout oaken cudgel. Thus they have taken a singular delight in exhibiting their most private foibles in a laughable point of view; and have been so successful in their delineation that there is scarcely a being in actual existence more absolutely present to the public mind than that eccentric personage John Bull.

Perhaps the continual contemplation of the character thus drawn of them has contributed to fix it upon the nation, and thus to give reality to what at first may have been painted in a great measure from the imagination. Men are apt to acquire peculiarities that are continually ascribed to them. The common orders of English seem wonderfully captivated with the *beau ideal* which they have formed of John Bull, and endeavor to act up to the broad caricature that is perpetually before their eyes. Unluckily, they sometimes make their boasted Bull-ism an apology for their prejudice or grossness; and this I have especially noticed among those truly home-bred and genuine sons of the soil who have never migrated beyond the sound of Bow-bells. If one of these should be a little uncouth in speech, and apt to utter impertinent truths, he confesses that he is a real John Bull, and always speaks his mind. If he now and then flies into an unreasonable burst of passion about trifles, he observes that John Bull is a choleric old blade, but then his passion is over in a moment and he bears no malice. If he betrays a coarseness of taste, and an insensibility to foreign refinements, he thanks Heaven for his ignorance—he is a plain John Bull, and has no relish for frippery and knickknacks. His very proneness to be gulled by strangers, and to pay extravagantly for absurdities, is excused under the plea of munificence—for John is always more generous than wise.

Thus, under the name of John Bull, he will contrive to argue every fault into a merit, and will frankly convict himself of being the honestest fellow in existence.

However little, therefore, the character may have suited in the first instance, it has gradually adapted itself to the nation, or rather they have adapted themselves to each other; and a stranger who wishes to study English peculiarities may gather much valuable information from the innumerable portraits of John Bull, as exhibited in the windows of the caricature-shops. Still, however, he is one of those fertile humorists that are continually throwing out new portraits, and presenting different aspects from different points of view; and, often as he has been described, I cannot resist the temptation to give a slight sketch of him, such as he has met my eye.

John Bull, to all appearance, is a plain downright matter-of-fact fellow, with much less of poetry about him than rich prose. There is little of romance in his nature, but a vast deal of strong natural feeling. He excels in humor more than in wit; is jolly rather than gay; melancholy rather than morose; can easily be moved to a sudden tear, or surprised into a broad laugh; but he loathes sentiment and has no turn for light pleasantry. He is a boon companion, if you allow him to have his humor and to talk about himself; and he will stand by a friend in a quarrel, with life and purse, however soundly he may be cudgeled.

In this last respect, to tell the truth, he has a propensity to be somewhat too ready. He is a busy-minded personage, who thinks not merely for himself and family, but for all the country round, and is most generally disposed to be everybody's champion. He is continually volunteering his services to settle his neighbors' affairs, and takes it in great dudgeon if they engage in any matter of consequence without asking his advice; though he seldom engages in any friendly office of the kind without finishing by getting into a squabble with all parties and then railing bitterly at their ingratitude. He unluckily took lessons in his youth in the noble science of defense, and having accomplished himself in the use of his limbs and his weapons, and become a perfect master at boxing and cudgel-play, he has had a troublesome life of it ever since. He cannot hear of a quarrel between the most distant of his neighbors, but he begins incontinently to fumble with the head of his cudgel and consider whether his interest or honor does not require that he should meddle in the broil. Indeed, he has extended his relations of pride and policy so completely over the whole country that no event can take place without infringing some of his finely-spun rights and dignities. Couched in his little domain, with these filaments stretching forth in every direction, he is like some choleric, bottle-bellied old spider, who has woven his web over a whole chamber, so that a fly cannot buzz, nor a breeze blow, without startling his repose and causing him to sally forth wrathfully from his den.

Though really a good-hearted, good-tempered old fellow

at bottom, yet he is singularly fond of being in the midst of contention. It is one of his peculiarities, however, that he only relishes the beginning of an affray; he always goes into a fight with alacrity, but comes out of it grumbling even when victorious; and though no one fights with more obsti-nacy to carry a contested point, yet, when the battle is over, and he comes to the reconciliation, he is so much taken up with the mere shaking of hands that he is apt to let his antagonist pocket all that they have been quarreling about. It is not, therefore, fighting that he ought so much to be on his guard against as making friends. It is difficult to cudgel him out of a farthing; but put him in a good humor, and you may bargain him out of all the money in his pocket. He is like a stout ship, which will weather the roughest storm un-injured, but roll its masts overboard in the succeeding calm.

He is a little fond of playing the magnifico abroad; of pulling out a long purse; flinging his money bravely about at boxing-matches, horse-races, cock-fights, and carrying a high head among "gentlemen of the fancy"; but immediately after one of these fits of extravagance he will be taken with violent qualms of economy; stop short at the most trivial expenditure; talk desperately of being ruined and brought upon the parish; and in such moods will not pay the smallest tradesman's bill without violent altercation. He is, in fact, the most punctual and discontented paymaster in the world; drawing his coin out of his breeches pocket with infinite reluctance; paying to the uttermost farthing, but accom-panying every guinea with a growl.

With all his talk of economy, however, he is a bountiful provider and a hospitable housekeeper. His economy is of a whimsical kind, its chief object being to devise how he may afford to be extravagant; for he will begrudge himself a beefsteak and pint of port one day that he may roast an ox whole, broach a hogshead of ale, and treat all his neighbors on the next.

His domestic establishment is enormously expensive: not so much from any great outward parade, as from the great consumption of solid beef and pudding; the vast number of followers he feeds and clothes, and his singular disposition to pay hugely for small services. He is a most kind and indulgent master, and, provided his servants humor his peculiarities, flatter his vanity a little now and then, and do not peculate grossly on him before his face, they may manage him to perfection. Everything that lives on him seems to thrive and grow fat. His house servants are well paid and pampered and have little to do. His horses are sleek and lazy and prance slowly before his state carriage, and his house-dogs sleep quietly about the door and will hardly bark at a house-breaker.

His family mansion is an old castellated manor-house, gray with age, and of a most venerable, though weather-beaten, appearance. It has been built upon no regular plan, but is a vast accumulation of parts, erected in various tastes and ages. The center bears evident traces of Saxon architecture, and is as solid as ponderous stone and old English oak can make it. Like all the relics of that style, it is full of obscure passages, intricate mazes and dusky chambers, and, though these have been partially lighted up in modern days, yet there are many places where you must still grope in the dark. Additions have been made to the original edifice from time to time, and great alterations have taken place; towers and battlements have been erected during wars and tumults, wings built in time of peace, and outhouses, lodges and offices run up according to the whim or convenience of different generations, until it has become one of the most spacious, rambling tenements imaginable. An entire wing is taken up with the family chapel; a reverend pile, that must once have been exceedingly sumptuous, and, indeed, in spite of having been altered and simplified at various periods, has still a look of solemn religious pomp. Its walls within are storied with the monuments of John's ancestors; and it is snugly fitted up with soft cushions and well-lined chairs, where such of his family as are inclined to church services may doze comfortably in the discharge of their duties.

To keep up this chapel has cost John much money; but he is stanch in his religion and piqued in his zeal, from the circumstance that many dissenting chapels have been erected in his vicinity, and several of his neighbors, with whom he has had quarrels, are strong Papists.

To do the duties of the chapel he maintains, at a large expense, a pious and portly family chaplain. He is a most learned and decorous personage, and a truly well-bred Christian, who always backs the old gentleman in his opinions, winks discreetly at his little peccadilloes, rebukes the children when refractory, and is of great use in exhorting the tenants to read their Bibles, say their prayers, and, above all, to pay their rents punctually and without grumbling.

The family apartments are in a very antiquated taste, somewhat heavy and often inconvenient, but full of the solemn magnificence of former times; fitted up with rich, though faded tapestry, unwieldy furniture, and loads of massy, gorgeous old plate. The vast fireplaces, ample kitchens, extensive cellars and sumptuous banqueting halls—all speak of the roaring hospitality of days of yore, of which the modern festivity at the manor-house is but a shadow. There are, however, complete suites of rooms apparently deserted and time-worn, and towers and turrets that are tottering to decay, so that in high winds there is danger of their tumbling about the ears of the household.

John has frequently been advised to have the old edifice thoroughly overhauled and to have some of the useless parts pulled down and the others strengthened with their materials; but the old gentleman always grows testy on this subject. He swears the house is an excellent house—that it is tight and weather-proof and not to be shaken by tempests—that it has stood for several hundred years, and, therefore, is not likely to tumble down now—that as to its being inconvenient, his family is accustomed to the inconveniences and would not be comfortable without them—that as to its unwieldy size and irregular construction, these result from its being the growth of centuries and being improved by the wisdom of every generation—that an old family like his requires a large house to dwell in; new, upstart families may live in modern cottages and snug boxes, but an old English family should inhabit an old English manor-house. If you point out any part of the building as superfluous, he insists that it is material to the strength or decoration of the rest, and the harmony of the whole; and swears that the parts are so built into each other that if you pull down one you run the risk of having the whole about your ears.

The secret of the matter is that John has a great disposition to protect and patronize. He thinks it indispensable to the dignity of an ancient and honorable family to be bounteous in its appointments, and to be eaten up by dependents; and so, partly from pride, and partly from kind-heartedness, he makes it a rule always to give shelter and maintenance to his superannuated servants.

The consequence is that, like many other venerable family establishments, his manor is encumbered by old retainers whom he cannot turn off, and an old style which he cannot lay down. His mansion is like a great hospital of invalids, and, with all its magnitude, is not a whit too large for its inhabitants. Not a nook or corner but is of use in housing some useless personage. Groups of veteran beef-eaters, gouty pensioners, and retired heroes of the buttery and the larder, are seen lolling about its walls, crawling over its lawns, dozing under its trees, or sunning themselves upon the benches at its doors. Every office and outhouse is garrisoned by these supernumeraries and their families; for they are amazingly prolific, and, when they die off, are sure to leave John a legacy of hungry mouths to be provided for. A mattock cannot be struck against the most mouldering tumble-down tower, but out pops, from some cranny or loophole, the gray prate of some superannuated hanger-on, who has lived at John's expense all his life, and makes the most grievous outcry at their pulling down the roof from over the head of a worn-out servant of the family. This is an appeal that John's honest heart never can withstand; so that a man who has faithfully eaten his beef and pudding all his life is sure to be rewarded with a pipe and tankard in his old days.

A great part of his park, also, is turned into paddocks, where his broken-down chargers are turned loose to graze undisturbed for the remainder of their existence—a worthy example of grateful recollection, which if some of his neighbors were to imitate would not be to their discredit. Indeed, it is one of his great pleasures to point out these old steeds to his visitors, to dwell on their good qualities, extol their past services, and boast, with some little vainglory, of the perilous adventures and hardy exploits through which they have carried him.

He is given, however, to indulge his veneration for family usages, and family encumbrances, to a whimsical extent. His manor is infested by gangs of gypsies; yet he will not suffer them to be driven off, because they have infested the place time out of mind, and been regular poachers upon every generation of the family. He will scarcely permit a dry branch to be lopped from the great trees that surround the house, lest it should molest the rooks that have bred there for centuries. Owls have taken possession of the dovecote; but they are hereditary owls, and must not be disturbed. Swallows have nearly choked up every chimney with their nests; martins build in every frieze and cornice; crows flutter about the towers, and perch on every weathercock; and old gray-headed rats may be seen in every quarter of the house, running in and out of their holes undauntedly in broad daylight. In short, John has such a reverence for everything that has been long in the family that he will not hear even of abuses being reformed, because they are good old family abuses.

All these whims and habits have concurred wofully to drain the old gentleman's purse; and as he prides himself on punctuality in money matters, and wishes to maintain his credit in the neighborhood, they have caused him great perplexity in meeting his engagements. This, too, has been increased by the altercations and heart-burnings which are continually taking place in his family. His children have been brought up to different callings, and are of different ways of thinking; and as they have always been allowed to speak their minds freely, they do not fail to exercise the privilege most clamorously in the present posture of his affairs. Some stand up for the honor of the race, and are clear that the old establishment should be kept up in all its state, whatever may be the cost; others, who are more prudent and considerate, entreat the old gentleman to retrench his expenses, and to put his whole system of housekeeping on a more moderate footing. He has, indeed, at times, seemed inclined to listen to their opinions, but their wholesome advice has been completely defeated by the obstreperous conduct of one of his sons. This is a noisy rattle-pated fellow, of rather low habits, who neglects his business to frequent alehouses—is the orator of village clubs, and a complete oracle among the poorest of his father's tenants. No sooner does he hear any of his brothers mention reform or retrenchment, than up he jumps, takes the words out of their mouths, and roars out for an overturn. When his tongue is once going, nothing can stop it. He rants about the room; hectors the old man about his spendthrift practices; ridicules his tastes and pursuits; insists that he shall turn the old servants out of doors; give the broken-down horses to the hounds; send the fat chaplain packing, and take a field-preacher in his place—nay, that the whole family mansion shall be leveled with the ground, and a plain one of brick and mortar built in its place. He rails at every social entertainment and family festivity, and skulks away growling to the alehouse whenever an equipage drives up to the door. Though constantly complaining of the emptiness of his purse, yet he scruples not to spend all his pocket-money in these tavern convocations, and even runs up scores for the liquor over which he preaches about his father's extravagance.

It may readily be imagined how little such thwarting agrees with the old cavalier's fiery temperament. He has become so irritable, from repeated crossings, that the mere mention of retrenchment or reform is a signal for a brawl between him and the tavern oracle. As the latter is too sturdy and refractory for paternal discipline, having grown out of all fear of the cudgel, they have frequent scenes of wordy warfare, which at times run so high that John is fain to call in the aid of his son Tom, an officer who has served abroad, but is at present living at home on half-pay. This last is sure to stand by the old gentleman, right or wrong; likes nothing so much as a racketing roistering life; and is ready, at a wink or nod, to out saber, and flourish it over the orator's head, if he dares to array himself against paternal authority.

These family dissensions, as usual, have got abroad, and are rare food for scandal in John's neighborhood. People begin to look wise, and shake their heads, whenever his affairs are mentioned. They all "hope that matters are not so bad with him as represented; but when a man's own children begin to rail at his extravagance things must be badly managed. They understand he is mortgaged over head and ears, and is continually dabbling with money-lenders. He is certainly an open-handed old gentleman, but they fear he has lived too fast; indeed, they never knew any good come of this fondness for hunting, racing, reveling, and prize-fighting. In short, Mr. Bull's estate is a very fine one, and has been in the family a long while; but for all that, they have known many finer estates come to the hammer."

What is worst of all, is the effect which these pecuniary embarrassments and domestic feuds have had on the poor man himself. Instead of that jolly round corporation, and smug rosy face, which he used to present, he has of late become as shriveled and shrunk as a frostbitten apple. His scarlet gold-laced waistcoat, which bellied out so bravely in those prosperous days when he sailed before the wind, now hangs loosely about him like a mainsail in a calm. His leather breeches are all in folds and wrinkles, and apparently have much ado to hold up the boots that yawn on both sides of his once sturdy legs.

Instead of strutting about, as formerly, with his three-cornered hat on one side; flourishing his cudgel, and bringing it down every moment with a hearty thump upon the ground; looking every one sturdily in the face, and trolling out a stave of a catch or a drinking song; he now goes about whistling thoughtfully to himself, with his head drooping down, his cudgel tucked under his arm, and his hands thrust to the bottom of his breeches pockets, which are evidently empty.

Such is the plight of honest John Bull at present; yet for all this the old fellow's spirit is as tall and as gallant as ever. If you drop the least expression of sympathy or concern he takes fire in an instant; swears that he is the richest and stoutest fellow in the country; talks of laying out large sums to adorn his house or to buy another estate; and, with a valiant swagger and grasping of his cudgel, longs exceedingly to have another bout at quarterstaff.

Though there may be something rather whimsical in all this, yet I confess I cannot look upon John's situation without strong feelings of interest. With all his odd humors and obstinate prejudices he is a sterling hearted old blade. He may not be so wonderfully fine a fellow as he thinks himself, but he is at least twice as good as his neighbors represent him. His virtues are all his own; all plain, home-bred, and unaffected. His very faults smack of the raciness of his good qualities. His extravagance savors of his generosity; his quarrelsomeness, of his courage; his credulity, of his open faith; his vanity, of his pride; and his bluntness, of his sincerity. They are all the redundancies of a rich and liberal character. He is like his own oak; rough without, but sound and solid within; whose bark abounds with excrescences in proportion to the growth and grandeur of the timber; and whose branches make a fearful groaning and murmuring in the least storm, from their very magnitude and luxuriance. There is something, too, in the appearance of his old family mansion that is extremely poetical and picturesque; and as long as it can be rendered comfortably habitable, I should

almost tremble to see it meddled with during the present conflict of tastes and opinions.   Some of his advisers are no doubt
good architects that might be of service; but many, I fear,
are mere levelers, who, when they had once got to work with
their mattocks on the venerable edifice, would never stop
until they had brought it to the ground, and perhaps buried
themselves among the ruins.   All that I wish is that John's
present troubles may teach him more prudence in future;
that he may cease to distress his mind about other people's
affairs; that he may give up the fruitless attempt to promote
the good of his neighbors, and the peace and happiness of
the world, by dint of the cudgel; that he may remain quietly
at home; gradually get his house into repair; cultivate his
rich estate according to his fancy; husband his income—if
he thinks proper; bring his unruly children into order—if he
can; renew the jovial scenes of ancient prosperity; and long
enjoy, on his paternal lands, a green, an honorable, and a
merry old age.

THE PRIDE OF THE VILLAGE

"May no wolf howle: no screech-owle stir
A wing about thy sepulcher!
No boysterous winds or stormes come hither,
          To starve or wither
Thy soft sweet earth! but, like a spring,
Love keep it ever flourishing."—HERRICK

IN the course of an excursion through one of the remote
counties of England, I had struck into one of those cross-
roads that lead through the more secluded parts of the country, and stopped one afternoon at a village, the situation of
which was beautifully rural and retired.   There was an air
of primitive simplicity about its inhabitants not to be found
in the villages which lie on the great coach-roads.   I determined to pass the night there, and having taken an early
dinner, strolled out to enjoy the neighboring scenery.

My ramble, as is usually the case with travelers, soon led me to the church, which stood at a little distance from the village. Indeed, it was an object of some curiosity, its old tower being completely overrun with ivy, so that only here and there a jutting buttress, an angle of gray wall, or a fantastically carved ornament, peered through the verdant covering. It was a lovely evening. The early part of the day had been dark and showery, but in the afternoon it had cleared up; and though sullen clouds still hung overhead, yet there was a broad tract of golden sky in the west, from which the setting sun gleamed through the dripping leaves and lighted up all nature into a melancholy smile. It seemed like the parting hour of a good Christian, smiling on the sins and sorrows of the world, and giving, in the serenity of his decline, an assurance that he will rise again in glory.

I had seated myself on a half-sunken tombstone and was musing, as one is apt to do at this sober-thoughted hour, on past scenes, and early friends—on those who were distant, and those who were dead—and indulging in that kind of melancholy fancying which has in it something sweeter even than pleasure. Every now and then the stroke of a bell from the neighboring tower fell on my ear; its tones were in unison with the scene, and instead of jarring, chimed in with my feelings; and it was some time before I recollected that it must be tolling the knell of some new tenant of the tomb.

Presently I saw a funeral train moving across the village green; it wound slowly along a lane; was lost, and reappeared through the breaks of the hedges, until it passed the place where I was sitting. The pall was supported by young girls dressed in white; and another, about the age of seventeen, walked before, bearing a chaplet of white flowers; a token that the deceased was a young and unmarried female. The corpse was followed by the parents. They were a venerable couple, of the better order of peasantry. The father seemed to repress his feelings; but his fixed eye, contracted brow, and deeply-furrowed face, showed the struggle that was passing within. His wife hung on his arm, and wept aloud with the convulsive bursts of a mother's sorrow.

I followed the funeral into the church. The bier was placed in the center aisle, and the chaplet of white flowers, with a pair of white gloves, were hung over the seat which the deceased had occupied.

Every one knows the soul-subduing pathos of the funeral service: for who is so fortunate as never to have followed some one he has loved to the tomb? but when performed over the remains of innocence and beauty, thus laid low in the bloom of existence—what can be more affecting? At that simple but most solemn consignment of the body to the grave —"Earth to earth—ashes to ashes—dust to dust!" the tears of the youthful companions of the deceased flowed unre-strained. The father still seemed to struggle with his feel-ings, and to comfort himself with the assurance that the dead are blessed which die in the Lord; but the mother only thought of her child as a flower of the field, cut down and withered in the midst of its sweetness: she was like Rachel, "mourning over her children, and would not be comforted."

On returning to the inn, I learned the whole story of the deceased. It was a simple one, and such as has often been told. She had been the beauty and pride of the village. Her father had once been an opulent farmer, but was reduced in circumstances. This was an only child, and brought up en-tirely at home, in the simplicity of rural life. She had been the pupil of the village pastor, the favorite lamb of his little flock. The good man watched over her education with pa-ternal care; it was limited, and suitable to the sphere in which she was to move; for he only sought to make her an ornament to her station in life, not to raise her above it. The tenderness and indulgence of her parents, and the exemption from all ordinary occupations, had fostered a natural grace and delicacy of character that accorded with the fragile love-liness of her form. She appeared like some tender plant of the garden, blooming accidentally amid the hardier natives of the fields.

The superiority of her charms was felt and acknowledged by her companions, but without envy; for it was surpassed by the unassuming gentleness and winning kindness of her manners. It might be truly said of her—

> "This is the prettiest low-born lass, that ever
> Ran on the greensward: nothing she does or seems,
> But smacks of something greater than herself;
> Too noble for this place."

The village was one of those sequestered spots which still retains some vestiges of old English customs. It had its rural festivals and holyday pastimes, and still kept up some faint observance of the once popular rites of May. These, indeed, had been promoted by its present pastor, who was a lover of old customs, and one of those simple Christians that think their mission fulfilled by promoting joy on earth and good will among mankind. Under his auspices the May-pole stood from year to year in the center of the village green; on May-day it was decorated with garlands and streamers; and a queen or lady of the May was appointed, as in former times, to preside at the sports, and distribute the prizes and rewards. The picturesque situation of the village, and the fancifulness of its rustic fetes, would often attract the notice of casual visitors. Among these, on one May-day, was a young officer, whose regiment had been recently quartered in the neighborhood. He was charmed with the native taste that pervaded this village pageant; but, above all, with the dawning loveliness of the queen of May. It was the village favorite who was crowned with flowers, and blushing and smiling in all the beautiful confusion of girlish diffidence and delight. The artlessness of rural habits enabled him readily to make her acquaintance; he gradually won his way into her intimacy; and paid his court to her in that unthinking way in which young officers are too apt to trifle with rustic simplicity.

There was nothing in his advances to startle or alarm. He never even talked of love; but there are modes of mak-

ing it, more eloquent than language, and which convey it
subtilely and irresistibly to the heart. The beam of the eye,
the tone of the voice, the thousand tendernesses which ema-
nate from every word, and look, and action—these form the
true eloquence of love, and can always be felt and understood, but never described. Can we wonder that they should
readily win a heart, young, guileless, and susceptible? As
to her, she loved almost unconsciously; she scarcely inquired
what was the growing passion that was absorbing every
thought and feeling, or what were to be its consequences.
She, indeed, looked not to the future. When present, his
looks and words occupied her whole attention; when absent,
she thought but of what had passed at their recent interview. She would wander with him through the green lanes
and rural scenes of the vicinity. He taught her to see new
beauties in nature; he talked in the language of polite and
cultivated life, and breathed into her ear the witcheries of
romance and poetry.

Perhaps there could not have been a passion, between the
sexes, more pure than this innocent girl's. The gallant figure of her youthful admirer, and the splendor of his military
attire, might at first have charmed her eye; but it was not
these that had captivated her heart. Her attachment had
something in it of idolatry; she looked up to him as to a
being of a superior order. She felt in his society the enthusiasm of a mind naturally delicate and poetical, and now first
awakened to a keen perception of the beautiful and grand.
Of the sordid distinctions of rank and fortune she thought
nothing; it was the difference of intellect, of demeanor, of
manners, from those of the rustic society to which she had
been accustomed, that elevated him in her opinion. She
would listen to him with charmed ear and downcast look of
mute delight, and her cheek would mantle with enthusiasm;
or if ever she ventured a shy glance of timid admiration, it
was as quickly withdrawn, and she would sigh and blush at
the idea of her comparative unworthiness.

Her lover was equally impassioned; but his passion was

mingled with feelings of a coarser nature. He had begun
the connection in levity; for he had often heard his brother
officers boast of their village conquests and thought some
triumph of the kind necessary to his reputation as a man of
spirit. But he was too full of youthful fervor. His heart
had not yet been rendered sufficiently cold and selfish by a
wandering and a dissipated life; it caught fire from the very
flame it sought to kindle, and before he was aware of the
nature of his situation he became really in love.

What was he to do? There were the old obstacles which
so incessantly occur in these heedless attachments. His rank
in life—the prejudices of titled connections—his dependence
upon a proud and unyielding father—all forbade him to think
of matrimony: but when he looked down upon this innocent being, so tender and confiding, there was a purity in her
manners, a blamelessness in her life, and a bewitching
modesty in her looks, that awed down every licentious feeling. In vain did he try to fortify himself by a thousand
heartless examples of men of fashion, and to chill the glow
of generous sentiment with that cold derisive levity with
which he had heard them talk of female virtue; whenever
he came into her presence, she was still surrounded by that
mysterious but impassive charm of virgin purity in whose
hallowed sphere no guilty thought can live.

The sudden arrival of orders for the regiment to repair to
the continent completed the confusion of his mind. He remained for a short time in a state of the most painful irreso-
lution; he hesitated to communicate the tidings until the day
for marching was at hand, when he gave her the intelligence
in the course of an evening ramble.

The idea of parting had never before occurred to her. It
broke in at once upon her dream of felicity; she looked upon
it as a sudden and insurmountable evil, and wept with the
guileless simplicity of a child. He drew her to his bosom and
kissed the tears from her soft cheek, nor did he meet with a
repulse, for there are moments of mingled sorrow and tenderness which hallow the caresses of affection. He was natur-

ally impetuous, and the sight of beauty apparently yielding
in his arms, the confidence of his power over her, and the
dread of losing her forever, all conspired to overwhelm his
better feelings—he ventured to propose that she should leave
her home and be the companion of his fortunes.

He was quite a novice in seduction, and blushed and fal-
tered at his own baseness; but so innocent of mind was his intended victim that she was at first at a loss to comprehend his
meaning, and why she should leave her native village and
the humble roof of her parents.   When at last the nature of
his proposals flashed upon her pure mind the effect was
withering. She did not weep—she did not break forth into
reproaches—she said not a word—but she shrunk back aghast
as from a viper, gave him a look of anguish that pierced to
his very soul, and, clasping her hands in agony, fled, as if
for refuge, to her father's cottage.

The officer retired, confounded, humiliated and repentant.
It is uncertain what might have been the result of the conflict
of his feelings had not his thoughts been diverted by the
bustle of departure. New scenes, new pleasures and new
companions soon dissipated his self-reproach and stifled his
tenderness. Yet, amid the stir of camps, the revelries of
garrisons, the array of armies, and even the din of battles,
his thoughts would sometimes steal back to the scenes of
rural quiet and village simplicity—the white cottage—the
footpath along the silver brook and up the hawthorn hedge,
and the little village maid loitering along it, leaning on his
arm and listening to him with eyes beaming with unconscious
affection.

The shock which the poor girl had received, in the destruction of all her ideal world, had indeed been cruel. Faintings
and hysterics had at first shaken her tender frame, and were
succeeded by a settled and pining melancholy. She had
beheld from her window the march of the departing troops.
She had seen her faithless lover borne off, as if in triumph,
amid the sound of drum and trumpet and the pomp of arms.
She strained a last aching gaze after him as the morning sun

glittered about his figure and his plume waved in the breeze; he passed away like a bright vision from her sight and left her all in darkness.

It would be trite to dwell on the particulars of her after-story. It was, like other tales of love, melancholy. She avoided society and wandered out alone in the walks she had most frequented with her lover. She sought, like the stricken deer, to weep in silence and loneliness, and brood over the barbed sorrow that rankled in her soul. Sometimes she would be seen late of an evening sitting in the porch of the village church, and the milk-maids, returning from the fields, would now and then overhear her singing some plaintive ditty in the hawthorn walk. She became fervent in her devotions at church; and as the old people saw her approach, so wasted away, yet with a hectic bloom, and that hallowed air which melancholy diffuses round the form, they would make way for her, as for something spiritual, and, looking after her, would shake their heads in gloomy foreboding.

She felt a conviction that she was hastening to the tomb, but looked forward to it as a place of rest. The silver cord that had bound her to existence was loosed, and there seemed to be no more pleasure under the sun. If ever her gentle bosom had entertained resentment against her lover, it was extinguished. She was incapable of angry passions, and in a moment of saddened tenderness she penned him a farewell letter. It was couched in the simplest language, but touching from its very simplicity. She told him that she was dying and did not conceal from him that his conduct was the cause. She even depicted the sufferings which she had experienced; but concluded with saying that she could not die in peace until she had sent him her forgiveness and her blessing.

By degrees her strength declined and she could no longer leave the cottage. She could only totter to the window, where, propped up in her chair, it was her enjoyment to sit all day and look out upon the landscape. Still she uttered no complaint, nor imparted to any one the malady that was preying on her heart. She never even mentioned her lover's name; but would lay her head on her mother's bosom and weep in silence. Her poor parents hung, in mute anxiety, over this fading blossom of their hopes, still flattering themselves that it might again revive to freshness, and that the bright unearthly bloom which sometimes flushed her cheek might be the promise of returning health.

In this way she was seated between them one Sunday afternoon; her hands were clasped in theirs, the lattice was thrown open, and the soft air that stole in brought with it the fragrance of the clustering honeysuckle, which her own hands had trained round the window.

Her father had just been reading a chapter in the Bible; it spoke of the vanity of worldly things and the joys of heaven; it seemed to have diffused comfort and serenity through her bosom. Her eye was fixed on the distant village church—the bell had tolled for the evening service—the last villager was lagging into the porch—and everything had sunk into that hallowed stillness peculiar to the day of rest. Her parents were gazing on her with yearning hearts. Sickness and sorrow, which pass so roughly over some faces, had given to hers the expression of a seraph's. A tear trembled in her soft blue eye.—Was she thinking of her faithless lover? —or were her thoughts wandering to that distant churchyard, into whose bosom she might soon be gathered?

Suddenly the clang of hoofs was heard—a horseman galloped to the cottage—he dismounted before the window—the poor girl gave a faint exclamation and sunk back in her chair: —it was her repentant lover! He rushed into the house and flew to clasp her to his bosom; but her wasted form—her death-like countenance—so wan, yet so lovely in its desolation —smote him to the soul, and he threw himself in an agony at her feet. She was too faint to rise—she attempted to extend her trembling hand—her lips moved as if she spoke, but no word was articulated—she looked down upon him with a smile of unutterable tenderness and closed her eyes forever!

Such are the particulars which I gathered of this village

story. They are but scanty, and I am conscious have but
little novelty to recommend them. In the present rage also
for strange incident and high-seasoned narrative, they may
appear trite and insignificant, but they interested me strongly
at the time; and, taken in connection with the affecting ceremony which I had just witnessed, left a deeper impression
on my mind than many circumstances of a more striking
nature. I have passed through the place since and visited
the church again from a better motive than mere curiosity.
It was a wintry evening; the trees were stripped of their
foliage, the churchyard looked naked and mournful, and the
wind rustled coldly through the dry grass. Evergreens,
however, had been planted about the grave of the village
favorite, and osiers were bent over it to keep the turf uninjured. The church door was open and I stepped in.—There
hung the chaplet of flowers and the gloves, as on the day of
the funeral: the flowers were withered, it is true, but care
seemed to have been taken that no dust should soil their
whiteness. I have seen many monuments where art has
exhausted its powers to awaken the sympathy of the spectator; but I have met with none that spoke more touchingly
to my heart than this simple but delicate memento of departed
innocence.

THE ANGLER

"This day dame Nature seem'd in love,
    The lusty sap began to move,
    Fresh juice did stir th' embracing vines,
    And birds had drawn their valentines.
    The jealous trout that low did lie,
    Rose at a well dissembled fly.
    There stood my friend, with patient skill,
    Attending of his trembling quill."
                                —Sir H. Wotton

IT is said that many an unlucky urchin is induced to run
away from his family and betake himself to a seafaring life

from reading the history of Robinson Crusoe; and I suspect
that, in like manner, many of those worthy gentlemen who
are given to haunt the sides of pastoral streams with angle-
rods in hand, may trace the origin of their passion to the
seductive pages of honest Izaak Walton.   I recollect studying
his "Complete Angler" several years since, in company with
a knot of friends in America, and, moreover, that we were
all completely bitten with the angling mania.   It was early
in the year, but as soon as the weather was auspicious, and
that the spring began to melt into the verge of summer, we
took rod in hand and sallied into the country as stark mad as
was ever Don Quixote from reading books of chivalry.

One of our party had equaled the Don in the fullness of
his equipments; being attired cap-a-pie for the enterprise.
He wore a broad-skirted fustian coat, perplexed with half a
hundred pockets; a pair of stout shoes and leathern gaiters;
a basket slung on one side for fish; a patent rod; a landing
net, and a score of other inconveniences only to be found in
the true angler's armory.   Thus harnessed for the field, he
was as great a matter of stare and wonderment among the
country folk, who had never seen a regular angler, as was
the steel-clad hero of La Mancha among the goatherds of the
Sierra Morena.

Our first essay was along a mountain brook, among the
highlands of the Hudson—a most unfortunate place for the
execution of those piscatory tactics which had been invented
along the velvet margins of quiet English rivulets.   It was
one of those wild streams that lavish, among our romantic
solitudes, unheeded beauties enough to fill the sketch-book
of a hunter of the picturesque.   Sometimes it would leap
down rocky shelves, making small cascades, over which the
trees threw their broad balancing sprays, and long nameless
weeds hung in fringes from the impending banks, dripping
with diamond drops.   Sometimes it would brawl and fret
along a ravine in the matted shade of a forest, filling it with
murmurs, and, after this termagant career, would steal
forth into open day with the most placid demure face imagi-

nable; as I have seen some pestilent shrew of a housewife, after filling her home with uproar and ill-humor, come dimpling out of doors, swimming and courtesying, and smiling upon all the world.

How smoothly would this vagrant brook glide, at such times, through some bosom of green meadow land among the mountains; where the quiet was only interrupted by the occasional tinkling of a bell from the lazy cattle among the clover, or the sound of a woodcutter's ax from the neighboring forest!

For my part, I was always a bungler at all kinds of sport that required either patience or adroitness, and had not angled above half an hour before I had completely "satisfied the sentiment," and convinced myself of the truth of Izaak Walton's opinion, that angling is something like poetry—a man must be born to it. I hooked myself instead of the fish; tangled my line in every tree; lost my bait; broke my rod; until I gave up the attempt in despair and passed the day under the trees reading old Izaak; satisfied that it was his fascinating vein of honest simplicity and rural feeling that had bewitched me, and not the passion for angling. My companions, however, were more persevering in their delusion. I have them at this moment before my eyes, stealing along the border of the brook, where it lay open to the day, or was merely fringed by shrubs and bushes. I see the bittern rising with hollow scream as they break in upon his rarely-invaded haunt; the kingfisher watching them suspiciously from his dry tree, that overhangs the deep black millpond in the gorge of the hills; the tortoise letting himself slip sidewise from off the stone or log on which he is sunning himself, and the panic-struck frog plumping in headlong as they approach and spreading an alarm throughout the watery world around.

I recollect, also, that, after toiling and watching and creeping about for the greater part of a day, with scarcely any success, in spite of all our admirable apparatus, a lubberly country urchin came down from the hills with a rod made from a branch of a tree; a few yards of twine; and, as heaven shall help me! I believe a crooked pin for a hook, baited with a vile earth-worm—and in half an hour caught more fish than we had nibbles throughout the day.

But above all, I recollect the "good, honest, wholesome, hungry" repast which we made under a beech-tree just by a spring of pure sweet water that stole out of the side of a hill; and how, when it was over, one of the party read old Izaak Walton's scene with the milkmaid, while I lay on the grass and built castles in a bright pile of clouds, until I fell asleep.   All this may appear like mere egotism; yet I cannot refrain from uttering these recollections which are passing like a strain of music over my mind, and have been called up by an agreeable scene which I witnessed not long since.

In a morning's stroll along the banks of the Alun, a beautiful little stream which flows down from the Welsh hills and throws itself into the Dee, my attention was attracted to a group seated on the margin.   On approaching, I found it to consist of a veteran angler and two rustic disciples.   The former was an old fellow with a wooden leg, with clothes very much, but very carefully, patched, betokening poverty, honestly come by, and decently maintained.   His face bore the marks of former storms, but present fair weather; its furrows had been worn into a habitual smile; his iron-gray locks hung about his ears, and he had altogether the good-humored air of a constitutional philosopher, who was disposed to take the world as it went.   One of his companions was a ragged wight, with the skulking look of an arrant poacher, and I'll warrant could find his way to any gentleman's fish-pond in the neighborhood in the darkest night. The other was a tall, awkward country lad, with a lounging gait, and apparently somewhat of a rustic beau.   The old man was busied examining the maw of a trout which he had just killed, to discover by its contents what insects were seasonable for bait; and was lecturing on the subject to his companions, who appeared to listen with infinite deference.   I have a kind feeling toward all "brothers of the angle," ever since I read Izaak Walton. They are men, he affirms, of a "mild, sweet, and peaceable spirit"; and my esteem for them has been increased since I met with an old "Tretyse of fishing with the Angle," in which are set forth many of the maxims of their inoffensive fraternity. "Take goode hede," sayth this honest little tretyse, "that in going about your disportes ye open no man's gates but that ye shet them again. Also ye shall not use this foresaid crafti disport for no covetousness to the increasing and sparing of your money only, but principally for your solace and to cause the helth of your body and specyally of your soule." *

I thought that I could perceive in the veteran angler before me an exemplification of what I had read; and there was a cheerful contentedness in his looks that quite drew me toward him. I could not but remark the gallant manner in which he stumped from one part of the brook to another; waving his rod in the air, to keep the line from dragging on the ground, or catching among the bushes; and the adroitness with which he would throw his fly to any particular place; sometimes skimming it lightly along a little rapid; sometimes casting it into one of those dark holes made by a twisted root or overhanging bank, in which the large trout are apt to lurk. In the meanwhile, he was giving instructions to his two disciples; showing them the manner in which they should handle their rods, fix their flies, and play them along the surface of the stream. The scene brought to my mind the instructions of the sage Piscator to his scholar. The country around was of that pastoral kind which Walton is fond of describing. It was a part of the great plain of

---

* From this same treatise, it would appear that angling is a more industrious and devout employment than it is generally considered. "For when ye purpose to go on your disportes in fishynge, ye will not desyre greatlye many persons with you, which might let you of your game. And that ye may serve God devoutly in sayinge effectually your customable prayers. And thus doying, ye shall eschew and also avoyde many vices, as ydleness, which is a principall cause to induce man to many other vices, as it is right well known."

Cheshire, close by the beautiful vale of Gessford, and just
where the inferior Welsh hills begin to swell up from among
fresh-smelling meadows. The day, too, like that recorded
in his work, was mild and sunshiny; with now and then a
soft dropping shower that sowed the whole earth with dia-
monds.

I soon fell into conversation with the old angler, and was
so much entertained that, under pretext of receiving instructions in his art, I kept company with him almost the whole
day; wandering along the banks of the stream, and listening
to his talk. He was very communicative, having all the easy
garrulity of cheerful old age; and I fancy was a little flattered by having an opportunity of displaying his piscatory
lore; for who does not like now and then to play the sage?

He had been much of a rambler in his day; and had passed
some years of his youth in America, particularly in Savannah,
where he had entered into trade, and had been ruined by the
indiscretion of a partner. He had afterward experienced
many ups and downs in life, until he got into the navy,
where his leg was carried away by a cannon-ball, at the battle of Camperdown. This was the only stroke of real good
fortune he had ever experienced, for it got him a pension,
which, together with some small paternal property, brought
him in a revenue of nearly forty pounds. On this he retired to his native village, where he lived quietly and inde-
pendently, and devoted the remainder of his life to the "noble
art of angling."

I found that he had read Izaak Walton attentively,
and he seemed to have imbibed all his simple frankness and
prevalent good-humor. Though he had been sorely buffeted
about the world, he was satisfied that the world, in itself,
was good and beautiful. Though he had been as roughly
used in different countries as a poor sheep that is fleeced by
every hedge and thicket, yet he spoke of every nation with
candor and kindness, appearing to look only on the good side
of things; and, above all, he was almost the only man I had
ever met with who had been an unfortunate adventurer in

America, and had honesty and magnanimity enough to take the fault to his own door and not to curse the country.

The lad that was receiving his instructions I learned was the son and heir apparent of a fat old widow, who kept the village inn, and of course a youth of some expectation, and much courted by the idle, gentleman-like personages of the place. In taking him under his care, therefore, the old man had probably an eye to a privileged corner in the tap-room, and an occasional cup of cheerful ale free of expense.

There is certainly something in angling, if we could forget, which anglers are apt to do, the cruelties and tortures inflicted on worms and insects, that tends to produce a gentleness of spirit and a pure serenity of mind. As the English are methodical even in their recreations, and are the most scientific of sportsmen, it has been reduced among them to perfect rule and system. Indeed, it is an amusement peculiarly adapted to the mild and cultivated scenery of England, where every roughness has been softened away from the landscape. It is delightful to saunter along those limpid streams which wander, like veins of silver, through the bosom of this beautiful country; leading one through a diversity of small home scenery; sometimes winding through ornamented grounds; sometimes brimming along through rich pasturage, where the fresh green is mingled with sweet-smelling flowers; sometimes venturing in sight of villages and hamlets, and then running capriciously away into shady retirements. The sweetness and serenity of nature, and the quiet watchfulness of the sport, gradually bring on pleasant fits of musing; which are now and then agreeably interrupted by the song of a bird, the distant whistle of the peasant, or perhaps the vagary of some fish, leaping out of the still water and skimming transiently about its glassy surface. "When I would beget content," says Izaak Walton, "and increase confidence in the power and wisdom and providence of Almighty God, I will walk the meadows by some gliding stream, and there contemplate the lilies that take no care, and those very many other little living creatures that are not only created, but fed (man knows not how), by the goodness of the God of nature, and therefore trust in Him."

I cannot forbear to give another quotation from one of those ancient champions of angling, which breathes the same innocent and happy spirit:

"Let me live harmlessly, and near the brink
Of Trent or Avon have a dwelling-place;
Where I may see my quill or cork down sink,
With eager bite of Pike, or Bleak, or Dace,
And on the world and my creator think:
While some men strive ill-gotten goods t' embrace;
And others spend their time in base excess
Of wine, or worse, in war or wantonness.

"Let them that will, these pastimes still pursue,
And on such pleasing fancies feed their fill,
So I the fields and meadows green may view,
And daily by fresh rivers walk at will
Among the daisies and the violets blue,
Red hyacinth and yellow daffodil." *

On parting with the old angler, I inquired after his place of abode, and happening to be in the neighborhood of the village a few evenings afterward, I had the curiosity to seek him out. I found him living in a small cottage, containing only one room, but a perfect curiosity in its method and arrangement. It was on the skirts of the village, on a green bank, a little back from the road, with a small garden in front, stocked with kitchen herbs and adorned with a few flowers. The whole front of the cottage was overrun with a honeysuckle. On the top was a ship for a weathercock. The interior was fitted up in a truly nautical style, his ideas of comfort and convenience having been acquired on the berth-deck of a man-of-war. A hammock was slung from the ceiling, which in the daytime was lashed up so as to take but little room. From the center of the chamber hung a model of a ship, of his own workmanship. Two or three chairs, a table, and a large sea-chest, formed the principal movables.

* J. Davors.

About the wall were stuck up naval ballads, such as "Admiral Hosier's Ghost," "All in the Downs," and "Tom Bowling," intermingled with pictures of sea-fights, among which the battle of Camperdown held a distinguished place. The mantel-piece was decorated with seashells; over which hung a quadrant, flanked by two woodcuts of most bitter-looking naval commanders. His implements for angling were carefully disposed on nails and hooks about the room. On a shelf was arranged his library, containing a work on angling, much worn; a Bible covered with canvas; an odd volume or two of voyages; a nautical almanack, and a book of songs.

His family consisted of a large black cat with one eye, and a parrot which he had caught and tamed, and educated himself, in the course of one of his voyages; and which uttered a variety of sea phrases, with the hoarse rattling tone of a veteran boatswain. The establishment reminded me of that of the renowned Robinson Crusoe; it was kept in neat order, everything being "stowed away" with the regularity of a ship of war; and he informed me that he "scoured the deck every morning, and swept it between meals."

I found him seated on a bench before the door, smoking his pipe in the soft evening sunshine. His cat was purring soberly on the threshold, and his parrot describing some strange evolutions in an iron ring that swung in the center of his cage. He had been angling all day, and gave me a history of his sport with as much minuteness as a general would talk over a campaign; being particularly animated in relating the manner in which he had taken a large trout, which had completely tasked all his skill and wariness, and which he had sent as a trophy to mine hostess of the inn.

How comforting it is to see a cheerful and contented old age; and to behold a poor fellow like this, after being tempest-tossed through life, safely moored in a snug and quiet harbor in the evening of his days! His happiness, however, sprung from within himself, and was independent of external circumstances; for he had that inexhaustible good-nature which is the most precious gift of Heaven; spreading itself like oil over the troubled sea of thought, and keeping the mind smooth and equable in the roughest weather.

On inquiring further about him, I learned that he was a universal favorite in the village, and the oracle of the tap-room; where he delighted the rustics with his songs, and, like Sindbad, astonished them with his stories of strange lands, and shipwrecks, and sea-fights. He was much noticed too by gentlemen sportsmen of the neighborhood; had taught several of them the art of angling, and was a privileged visitor to their kitchens. The whole tenor of his life was quiet and inoffensive, being principally passed about the neighboring streams, when the weather and season were favorable; and at other times he employed himself at home, preparing his fishing tackle for the next campaign, or manufacturing rods, nets, and flies, for his patrons and pupils among the gentry.

He was a regular attendant at church on Sundays, though he generally fell asleep during the sermon. He had made it his particular request that when he died he should be buried in a green spot, which he could see from his seat in church, and which he had marked out ever since he was a boy, and had thought of when far from home on the raging sea, in danger of being food for the fishes—it was the spot where his father and mother had been buried.

I have done, for I fear that my reader is growing weary; but I could not refrain from drawing the picture of this worthy "brother of the angle," who has made me more than ever in love with the theory, though I fear I shall never be adroit in the practice of his art; and I will conclude this rambling sketch in the words of honest Izaak Walton, by craving the blessing of St. Peter's Master upon my reader, "and upon all that are true lovers of virtue; and dare trust in His providence; and be quiet; and go a angling."

THE LEGEND OF SLEEPY HOLLOW

(FOUND AMONG THE PAPERS OF THE LATE DIEDRICH KNICKERBOCKER)

"A pleasing land of drowsy head it was,
Of dreams that wave before the half-shut eye;
And of gay castles in the clouds that pass,
Forever flushing round a summer sky."
—*Castle of Indolence*

IN the bosom of one of those spacious coves which indent the eastern shore of the Hudson, at that broad expansion of the river denominated by the ancient Dutch navigators the Tappaan Zee, and where they always prudently shortened sail and implored the protection of St. Nicholas when they crossed, there lies a small market town or rural port, which by some is called Greensburgh, but which is more generally and properly known by the name of Tarry Town. This name was given it, we are told, in former days, by the good housewives of the adjacent country, from the inveterate propensity of their husbands to linger about the village tavern on market days. Be that as it may, I do not vouch for the fact, but merely advert to it, for the sake of being precise and authentic. Not far from this village, perhaps about three miles, there is a little valley or rather lap of land among high hills, which is one of the quietest places in the whole world. A small brook glides through it, with just murmur enough to lull one to repose, and the occasional whistle of a quail, or tapping of a woodpecker, is almost the only sound that ever breaks in upon the uniform tranquillity.

I recollect that, when a stripling, my first exploit in squirrel-shooting was in a grove of tall walnut-trees that shades one side of the valley. I had wandered into it at noon-time, when all nature is peculiarly quiet, and was startled by the roar of my own gun, as it broke the sabbath stillness around and was prolonged and reverberated by the angry echoes. If ever I should wish for a retreat whither I might steal from the world and its distractions, and dream quietly away the remnant of a troubled life, I know of none more promising than this little valley.

From the listless repose of the place and the peculiar character of its inhabitants, who are descendants from the original Dutch settlers, this sequestered glen has long been known by the name of SLEEPY HOLLOW, and its rustic lads are called the Sleepy Hollow Boys throughout all the neighboring country. A drowsy, dreamy influence seems to hang over the land and to pervade the very atmosphere. Some say that the place was bewitched by a high German doctor, during the early days of the settlement; others, that an old Indian chief, the prophet or wizard of his tribe, held his powwows there before the country was discovered by Master Hendrick Hudson. Certain it is, the place still continues under the sway of some witching power that holds a spell over the minds of the good people, causing them to walk in a continual reverie. They are given to all kinds of marvelous beliefs; are subject to trances and visions, and frequently see strange sights, and hear music and voices in the air. The whole neighborhood abounds with local tales, haunted spots, and twilight superstitions; stars shoot and meteors glare oftener across the valley than in any other part of the country, and the nightmare, with her whole nine fold, seems to make it the favorite scene of her gambols.

The dominant spirit, however, that haunts this enchanted region and seems to be commander-in-chief of all the powers of the air, is the apparition of a figure on horseback without a head. It is said by some to be the ghost of a Hessian trooper, whose head had been carried away by a cannon-ball in some nameless battle during the revolutionary war, and who is ever and anon seen by the country folk, hurrying

along in the gloom of night, as if on the wings of the wind.
His haunts are not confined to the valley, but extend at times
to the adjacent roads, and especially to the vicinity of a church
that is at no great distance.   Indeed, certain of the most authentic historians of those parts, who have been careful in
collecting and collating the floating facts concerning this
specter, allege that, the body of the trooper having been
buried in the churchyard, the ghost rides forth to the scene
of battle in nightly quest of his head, and that the rushing
speed with which he sometimes passes along the hollow like
a midnight blast, is owing to his being belated, and in a hurry
to get back to the churchyard before daybreak.

Such is the general purport of this legendary superstition,
which has furnished materials for many a wild story in that
region of shadows, and the specter is known at all the country firesides by the name of The Headless Horseman of Sleepy
Hollow.

It is remarkable that the visionary propensity I have mentioned is not confined to the native inhabitants of the valley,
but is unconsciously imbibed by every one who resides there
for a time.   However wide awake they may have been before they entered that sleepy region, they are sure, in a
little time, to inhale the witching influence of the air, and
begin to grow imaginative—to dream dreams and see apparitions.

I mention this peaceful spot with all possible laud; for it
is in such little retired Dutch valleys, found here and there
embosomed in the great State of New York, that population,
manners and customs remain fixed, while the great torrent
of migration and improvement, which is making such inces-
sant changes in other parts of this restless country, sweeps
by them unobserved.   They are like those little nooks of still
water which border a rapid stream, where we may see the
straw and bubble riding quietly at anchor, or slowly revolving in their mimic harbor, undisturbed by the rush of the
passing current.   Though many years have elapsed since
I trod the drowsy shades of Sleepy Hollow, yet I question

whether I should not still find the same trees and the same families vegetating in its sheltered bosom.

In this by-place of nature there abode, in a remote period of American history, that is to say, some thirty years since, a worthy wight of the name of Ichabod Crane, who sojourned, or, as he expressed it, "tarried," in Sleepy Hollow, for the purpose of instructing the children of the vicinity. He was a native of Connecticut, a State which supplies the Union with pioneers for the mind as well as for the forest, and sends forth yearly its legions of frontier woodmen and country schoolmasters.

The cognomen of Crane was not inapplicable to his person. He was tall, but exceedingly lank, with narrow shoulders, long arms and legs, hands that dangled a mile out of his sleeves, feet that might have served for shovels, and his whole frame most loosely hung together. His head was small and flat at top, with huge ears, large green glassy eyes, and a long snipe nose, so that it looked like a weathercock perched upon his spindle neck to tell which way the wind blew. To see him striding along the profile of a hill on a windy day, with his clothes bagging and fluttering about him, one might have mistaken him for the genius of famine descending upon the earth, or some scarecrow eloped from a cornfield.

His schoolhouse was a low building of one large room, rudely constructed of logs, the windows partly glazed and partly patched with leaves of copy-books. It was most ingeniously secured at vacant hours by a withe twisted in the handle of the door, and stakes set against the window-shutters; so that, though a thief might get in with perfect ease, he would find some embarrassment in getting out—an idea most probably borrowed by the architect, Yost Van Houten, from the mystery of an eelpot. The schoolhouse stood in a rather lonely but pleasant situation, just at the foot of a woody hill, with a brook running close by and a formidable birch-tree growing at one end of it. From hence the low murmur of his pupils' voices, conning over their lessons, might be heard of a drowsy summer's day, like the hum of a beehive; interrupted now and then by the authoritative voice of the master in the tone of menace or command; or, peradventure, by the appalling sound of the birch, as he urged some tardy loiterer along the flowery path of knowledge.   Truth to say, he was a conscientious man, that ever bore in mind the golden maxim, "spare the rod and spoil the child."—Ichabod Crane's scholars certainly were not spoiled.

I would not have it imagined, however, that he was one of those cruel potentates of the school who joy in the smart of their subjects; on the contrary, he administered justice with discrimination rather than severity, taking the burden off the backs of the weak and laying it on those of the strong. Your mere puny stripling, that winced at the least flourish of the rod, was passed by with indulgence; but the claims of justice were satisfied by inflicting a double portion on some little, tough, wrong headed, broad-skirted Dutch urchin, who sulked and swelled and grew dogged and sullen beneath the birch.   All this he called "doing his duty by their parents"; and he never inflicted a chastisement without following it by the assurance, so consolatory to the smarting urchin, that "he would remember it and thank him for it the longest day he had to live."

When school hours were over, he was even the companion and playmate of the larger boys; and on holyday afternoons would convoy some of the smaller ones home, who happened to have pretty sisters, or good housewives for mothers, noted for the comforts of the cupboard.   Indeed, it behooved him to keep on good terms with his pupils.   The revenue arising from his school was small, and would have been scarcely sufficient to furnish him with daily bread, for he was a huge feeder, and, though lank, had the dilating powers of an anaconda; but to help out his maintenance, he was, according to country custom in those parts, boarded and lodged at the houses of the farmers whose children he instructed.   With these he lived successively a week at a time, thus going the rounds of the neighborhood with all his worldly effects tied up in a cotton handkerchief.

That all this might not be too onerous on the purses of his rustic patrons, who are apt to consider the costs of schooling a grievous burden and schoolmasters as mere drones, he had various ways of rendering himself both useful and agreeable. He assisted the farmers occasionally in the lighter labors of their farms; helped to make hay; mended the fences; took the horses to water; drove the cows from pasture, and cut wood for the winter fire. He laid aside, too, all the dominant dignity and absolute sway with which he lorded it in his little empire, the school, and became wonderfully gentle and ingratiating. He found favor in the eyes of the mothers, by petting the children, particularly the youngest; and like the lion bold, which whilom so magnanimously the lamb did hold, he would sit with a child on one knee and rock a cradle with his foot for whole hours together.

In addition to his other vocations, he was the singing-master of the neighborhood, and picked up many bright shillings by instructing the young folks in psalmody. It was a matter of no little vanity to him on Sundays to take his station in front of the church gallery, with a band of chosen singers; where, in his own mind, he completely carried away the palm from the parson. Certain it is, his voice resounded far above all the rest of the congregation, and there are peculiar quavers still to be heard in that church, and which may even be heard half a mile off, quite to the opposite side of the mill-pond, on a still Sunday morning, which are said to be legitimately descended from the nose of Ichabod Crane. Thus by divers little makeshifts, in that ingenious way which is commonly denominated "by hook and by crook," the worthy pedagogue got on tolerably enough, and was thought, by all who understood nothing of the labor of head-work, to have a wonderfully easy life of it.

The schoolmaster is generally a man of some importance in the female circle of a rural neighborhood; being considered a kind of idle gentleman-like personage, of vastly superior taste and accomplishments to the rough country swains, and, indeed, inferior in learning only to the parson. His appearance, therefore, is apt to occasion some little stir at the tea-table of a farmhouse and the addition of a supernumerary dish of cakes or sweetmeats, or, peradventure, the parade of a silver teapot. Our man of letters, therefore, was peculiarly happy in the smiles of all the country damsels. How he would figure among them in the churchyard, between services on Sundays! gathering grapes for them from the wild vines that overrun the surrounding trees; reciting for their amusement all the epitaphs on the tombstones, or sauntering, with a whole bevy of them, along the banks of the adjacent mill-pond; while the more bashful country bumpkins hung sheepishly back, envying his superior elegance and address.

From his half itinerant life, also, he was a kind of traveling gazette, carrying the whole budget of local gossip from house to house, so that his appearance was always greeted with satisfaction. He was, moreover, esteemed by the women as a man of great erudition, for he had read several books quite through, and was a perfect master of Cotton Mather's "History of New England Witchcraft," in which, by the way, he most firmly and potently believed.

He was, in fact, an odd mixture of small shrewdness and simple credulity. His appetite for the marvelous, and his powers of digesting it, were equally extraordinary; and both had been increased by his residence in this spell-bound region. No tale was too gross or monstrous for his capacious swallow. It was often his delight, after his school was dismissed in the afternoon, to stretch himself on the rich bed of clover, bordering the little brook that whimpered by his schoolhouse, and there con over old Mather's direful tales, until the gathering dusk of evening made the printed page a mere mist before his eyes. Then, as he wended his way, by swamp and stream and awful woodland, to the farmhouse where he happened to be quartered, every sound of nature, at that witching hour, fluttered his

excited imagination: the moan of the whip-poor-will * from
the hill-side; the boding cry of the tree-toad, that harbinger
of storm; the dreary hooting of the screech-owl, or the sudden rustling in the thicket of birds frightened from their
roost. The fire-flies, too, which sparkled most vividly in the
darkest places, now and then startled him, as one of uncommon brightness would stream across his path; and if, by
chance, a huge blockhead of a beetle came winging his blun-
dering flight against him, the poor varlet was ready to give
up the ghost, with the idea that he was struck with a witch's
token. His only resource on such occasions, either to drown
thought or drive away evil spirits, was to sing psalm tunes;
and the good people of Sleepy Hollow, as they sat by
their doors of an evening, were often filled with awe
at hearing his nasal melody, "in linked sweetness long
drawn out," floating from the distant hill, or along the
dusky road.

Another of his sources of fearful pleasure was to pass
long winter evenings with the old Dutch wives, as they sat
spinning by the fire, with a row of apples roasting and sput-
tering along the hearth, and listen to their marvelous tales of
ghosts and goblins, and haunted fields and haunted brooks,
and haunted bridges and haunted houses, and particularly of
the headless horseman, or galloping Hessian of the Hollow,
as they sometimes called him. He would delight them
equally by his anecdotes of witchcraft, and of the direful
omens and portentous sights and sounds in the air, which
prevailed in the earlier times of Connecticut; and would
frighten them wofully with speculations upon comets and
shooting stars, and with the alarming fact that the world
did absolutely turn round, and that they were half the time
topsy-turvy!

But if there was a pleasure in all this, while snugly cud-

---

* The whip-poor-will is a bird which is only heard at night. It
receives its name from its note, which is thought to resemble those
words.

dling in the chimney corner of a chamber that was all of a
ruddy glow from the crackling wood fire, and where, of
course, no specter dared to show its face, it was dearly purchased by the terrors of his subsequent walk homeward.
What fearful shapes and shadows beset his path, amid the
dim and ghastly glare of a snowy night!—With what wist-
ful look did he eye every trembling ray of light streaming
across the waste fields from some distant window!—How
often was he appalled by some shrub covered with snow,
which, like a sheeted specter, beset his very path!—How
often did he shrink with curdling awe at the sound of his
own steps on the frosty crust beneath his feet, and dread to
look over his shoulder, lest he should behold some uncouth
being tramping close behind him!—and how often was he
thrown into complete dismay by some rushing blast, howling
among the trees, in the idea that it was the galloping Hessian
on one of his nightly scourings!

All these, however, were mere terrors of the night, phan-
toms of the mind, that walk in darkness: and though he had
seen many specters in his time, and had been more than once
beset by Satan in divers shapes in his lonely perambulations,
yet daylight put an end to all these evils; and he would have
passed a pleasant life of it, in despite of the Devil and all his
works, if his path had not been crossed by a being that
causes more perplexity to mortal man than ghosts, goblins,
and the whole race of witches put together; and that was
—a woman.

Among the musical disciples who assembled, one evening
in each week, to receive his instructions in psalmody, was
Katrina Van Tassel, the daughter and only child of a substantial Dutch farmer. She was a blooming lass of fresh
eighteen; plump as a partridge, ripe and melting and rosy-
cheeked as one of her father's peaches, and universally famed,
not merely for her beauty, but her vast expectations. She
was withal a little of a coquette, as might be perceived even
in her dress, which was a mixture of ancient and modern
fashions, as most suited to set off her charms. She wore the

ornaments of pure yellow gold which her great-great-grand-
mother had brought over from Saardam; the tempting stomacher of the olden time, and withal a provokingly short petticoat, to display the prettiest foot and ankle in the country
round.

Ichabod Crane had a soft and foolish heart toward the
sex; and it is not to be wondered at that so tempting a morsel
soon found favor in his eyes, more especially after he had
visited her in her paternal mansion.   Old Baltus Van Tassel
was a perfect picture of a thriving, contented, liberal-hearted
farmer.   He seldom, it is true, sent either his eyes or his
thoughts beyond the boundaries of his own farm; but within
these, everything was snug, happy, and well-conditioned.
He was satisfied with his wealth, but not proud of it; and
piqued himself upon the hearty abundance, rather than the
style in which he lived.   His stronghold was situated on the
banks of the Hudson, in one of those green, sheltered, fertile
nooks in which the Dutch farmers are so fond of nestling.
A great elm-tree spread its broad branches over it, at the
foot of which bubbled up a spring of the softest and sweetest
water, in a little well formed of a barrel, and then stole sparkling away through the grass, to a neighboring brook that
babbled along among alders and dwarf willows.   Hard by
the farmhouse was a vast barn that might have served for a
church, every window and crevice of which seemed bursting
forth with the treasures of the farm; the flail was busily resounding within it from morning to night; swallows and
martins skimmed twittering about the eaves; and rows of
pigeons, some with one eye turned up, as if watching the
weather, some with their heads under their wings, or buried
in their bosoms, and others, swelling, and cooing, and bowing about their dames, were enjoying the sunshine on the
roof.   Sleek, unwieldy porkers were grunting in the repose
and abundance of their pens, from whence sallied forth, now
and then, troops of sucking pigs, as if to snuff the air.   A
stately squadron of snowy geese were riding in an adjoining
pond, convoying whole fleets of ducks; regiments of turkeys

were gobbling through the farmyard, and guinea-fowls fretting about it like ill-tempered housewives, with their peevish, discontented cry. Before the barn door strutted the gallant cock, that pattern of a husband, a warrior and a fine gentleman, clapping his burnished wings and crowing in the pride and gladness of his heart—sometimes tearing up the earth with his feet, and then generously calling his ever-hungry family of wives and children to enjoy the rich morsel which he had discovered.

The pedagogue's mouth watered as he looked upon this sumptuous promise of luxurious winter fare. In his devouring mind's eye, he pictured to himself every roasting pig running about, with a pudding in its belly and an apple in its mouth; the pigeons were snugly put to bed in a comfortable pie and tucked in with a coverlet of crust; the geese were swimming in their own gravy, and the ducks pairing cosily in dishes, like snug married couples, with a decent competency of onion sauce. In the porkers he saw carved out the future sleek side of bacon and juicy relishing ham; not a turkey, but he beheld daintily trussed up, with its gizzard under its wing, and, peradventure, a necklace of savory sausages; and even bright chanticleer himself lay sprawling on his back, in a side dish, with uplifted claws, as if craving that quarter which his chivalrous spirit disdained to ask while living.

As the enraptured Ichabod fancied all this, and as he rolled his great green eyes over the fat meadow lands, the rich fields of wheat, of rye, of buckwheat and Indian corn, and the orchards burdened with ruddy fruit, which surrounded the warm tenement of Van Tassel, his heart yearned after the damsel who was to inherit these domains, and his imagination expanded with the idea how they might be readily turned into cash, and the money invested in immense tracts of wild land and shingle palaces in the wilderness. Nay, his busy fancy already realized his hopes, and presented to him the blooming Katrina, with a whole family of children, mounted on the top of a wagon loaded with house-

hold trumpery, with pots and kettles dangling beneath; and
he beheld himself bestriding a pacing mare, with a colt at
her heels, setting out for Kentucky, Tennessee—or the Lord
knows where!

When he entered the house, the conquest of his heart was
complete. It was one of those spacious farmhouses, with
high-ridged, but lowly-sloping roofs, built in the style handed
down from the first Dutch settlers. The low projecting eaves
forming a piazza along the front capable of being closed up
in bad weather. Under this were hung flails, harness, various utensils of husbandry, and nets for fishing in the neighboring river. Benches were built along the sides for summer
use; and a great spinning-wheel at one end and a churn at
the other showed the various uses to which this important
porch might be devoted. From this piazza the wonderful
Ichabod entered the hall, which formed the center of the
mansion, and the place of usual residence. Here, rows of
resplendent pewter, ranged on a long dresser, dazzled his
eyes. In one corner stood a huge bag of wool, ready to be
spun; in another, a quantity of linsey-woolsey just from the
loom; ears of Indian corn and strings of dried apples and
peaches hung in gay festoons along the walls, mingled with
the gaud of red peppers; and a door left ajar gave him a
peep into the best parlor, where the claw-footed chairs, and
dark mahogany tables, shone like mirrors; andirons, with
their accompanying shovel and tongs, glistened from their
covert of asparagus tops; mock-oranges and conch shells
decorated the mantel-piece; strings of various colored birds'
eggs were suspended above it; a great ostrich egg was hung
from the center of the room, and a corner cupboard, knowingly left open, displayed immense treasures of old silver and
well-mended china.

From the moment Ichabod laid his eyes upon these regions of delight, the peace of his mind was at an end, and
his only study was how to gain the affections of the peerless
daughter of Van Tassel. In this enterprise, however, he
had more real difficulties than generally fell to the lot of a

knight-errant of yore, who seldom had anything but giants, enchanters, fiery dragons, and such like easily conquered adversaries, to contend with; and had to make his way merely through gates of iron and brass and walls of adamant to the castle-keep, where the lady of his heart was confined; all which he achieved as easily as a man would carve his way to the center of a Christmas pie, and then the lady gave him her hand as a matter of course. Ichabod, on the contrary, had to win his way to the heart of a country coquette, beset with a labyrinth of whims and caprices, which were forever presenting new difficulties and impediments, and he had to encounter a host of fearful adversaries of real flesh and blood, the numerous rustic admirers who beset every portal to her heart; keeping a watchful and angry eye upon each other, but ready to fly out in the common cause against any new competitor.

Among these, the most formidable was a burly, roaring, roistering blade, of the name of Abraham, or, according to the Dutch abbreviation, Brom Van Brunt, the hero of the country round, which rung with his feats of strength and hardihood. He was broad-shouldered and double-jointed, with short curly black hair, and a bluff, but not unpleasant countenance, having a mingled air of fun and arrogance. From his Herculean frame and great powers of limb, he had received the nickname of Brom Bones, by which he was universally known. He was famed for great knowledge and skill in horsemanship, being as dexterous on horseback as a Tartar. He was foremost at all races and cock-fights, and with the ascendency which bodily strength always acquires in rustic life, was the umpire in all disputes, setting his hat on one side, and giving his decisions with an air and tone that admitted of no gainsay or appeal. He was always ready for either a fight or a frolic; had more mischief than ill-will in his composition; and, with all his overbearing roughness, there was a strong dash of waggish good-humor at bottom. He had three or four boon companions of his own stamp, who regarded him as their model, and at the head of whom he scoured the country, attending every scene of feud or merriment for miles round. In cold weather, he was distinguished by a fur cap, surmounted with a flaunting fox's tail; and when the folks at a country gathering descried this well-known crest at a distance, whisking about among a squad of hard riders, they always stood by for a squall. Sometimes his crew would be heard dashing along past the farmhouses at midnight, with whoop and halloo, like a troop of Don Cossacks, and the old dames, startled out of their sleep, would listen for a moment till the hurry-scurry had clattered by, and then exclaim, "Ay, there goes Brom Bones and his gang!" The neighbors looked upon him with a mixture of awe, admiration, and good-will; and when any madcap prank or rustic brawl occurred in the vicinity, always shook their heads, and warranted Brom Bones was at the bottom of it.

This rantipole hero had for some time singled out the blooming Katrina for the object of his uncouth gallantries, and though his amorous toyings were something like the gentle caresses and endearments of a bear, yet it was whispered that she did not altogether discourage his hopes. Certain it is, his advances were signals for rival candidates to retire, who felt no inclination to cross a lion in his amours; insomuch, that when his horse was seen tied to Van Tassel's paling, on a Sunday night, a sure sign that his master was courting, or, as it is termed, "sparking," within, all other suitors passed by in despair and carried the war into other quarters.

Such was the formidable rival with whom Ichabod Crane had to contend, and considering all things, a stouter man than he would have shrunk from the competition, and a wiser man would have despaired. He had, however, a happy mixture of pliability and perseverance in his nature; he was in form and spirit like a supple-jack—yielding, but tough; though he bent, he never broke; and though he bowed beneath the slightest pressure, yet, the moment it was away— jerk!—he was as erect and carried his head as high as ever

To have taken the field openly against his rival would have been madness; for he was not a man to be thwarted in his amours, any more than that stormy lover, Achilles. Ichabod, therefore, made his advances in a quiet and gently-insinuating manner. Under cover of his character of sing-ing-master, he made frequent visits at the farmhouse; not that he had anything to apprehend from the meddlesome interference of parents, which is so often a stumbling-block in the path of lovers. Balt Van Tassel was an easy indul-gent soul; he loved his daughter better even than his pipe, and like a reasonable man, and an excellent father, let her have her way in everything. His notable little wife, too, had enough to do to attend to her housekeeping and manage the poultry; for, as she sagely observed, ducks and geese are foolish things, and must be looked after, but girls can take care of themselves. Thus, while the busy dame bustled about the house, or plied her spinning-wheel at one end of the piazza, honest Balt would sit smoking his evening pipe at the other, watching the achievements of a little wooden war-rior, who, armed with a sword in each hand, was most val-iantly fighting the wind on the pinnacle of the barn. In the meantime, Ichabod would carry on his suit with the daughter by the side of the spring under the great elm, or sauntering along in the twilight, that hour so favorable to the lover's eloquence.

I protest not to know how women's hearts are wooed and won. To me they have always been matters of riddle and admiration. Some seem to have but one vulnerable point, or door of access; while others have a thousand avenues, and may be captured in a thousand different ways. It is a great triumph of skill to gain the former, but a still greater proof of generalship to maintain possession of the latter, for a man must battle for his fortress at every door and window. He that wins a thousand common hearts, is therefore entitled to some renown; but he who keeps undisputed sway over the heart of a coquette, is indeed a hero. Certain it is, this was not the case with the redoubtable Brom Bones; and from the moment Ichabod Crane made his advances, the interests of the former evidently declined: his horse was no longer seen tied at the palings on Sunday nights, and a deadly feud gradually arose between him and the preceptor of Sleepy Hollow.

Brom, who had a degree of rough chivalry in his nature, would fain have carried matters to open warfare, and settled their pretensions to the lady according to the mode of those most concise and simple reasoners, the knights-errant of yore —by single combat; but Ichabod was too conscious of the superior might of his adversary to enter the lists against him; he had overheard the boast of Bones, that he would "double the schoolmaster up, and put him on a shelf"; and he was too wary to give him an opportunity. There was something extremely provoking in this obstinately pacific system; it left Brom no alternative but to draw upon the funds of rustic waggery in his disposition, and to play off boorish practical jokes upon his rival. Ichabod became the object of whimsical persecution to Bones and his gang of rough riders. They harried his hitherto peaceful domains; smoked out his singing-school, by stopping up the chimney; broke into the schoolhouse at night, in spite of its formidable fastenings of withe and window stakes, and turned everything topsy-turvy; so that the poor schoolmaster began to think all the witches in the country held their meetings there. But what was still more annoying, Brom took all opportunities of turning him into ridicule in presence of his mistress, and had a scoundrel dog whom he taught to whine in the most ludicrous manner, and introduced as a rival of Ichabod's, to instruct her in psalmody.

In this way, matters went on for some time, without producing any material effect on the relative situations of the contending powers. On a fine autumnal afternoon, Ichabod, in pensive mood, sat enthroned on the lofty stool from whence he usually watched all the concerns of his little literary realm. In his hand he swayed a ferule, that scepter of despotic power; the birch of justice reposed on three nails, behind

the throne, a constant terror to evil doers; while on the desk
before him might be seen sundry contraband articles and pro-
hibited weapons, detected upon the persons of idle urchins,
such as half-munched apples, popguns, whirligigs, fly-cages,
and whole legions of rampant little paper game-cocks. Apparently there had been some appalling act of justice recently
inflicted, for his scholars were all busily intent upon their
books, or slyly whispering behind them with one eye kept
upon the master; and a kind of buzzing stillness reigned
throughout the schoolroom. It was suddenly interrupted by
the appearance of a negro in tow-cloth jacket and trousers, a
round crowned fragment of a hat, like the cap of Mercury,
and mounted on the back of a ragged, wild, half-broken colt,
which he managed with a rope by way of halter. He came
clattering up to the school door with an invitation to Ichabod
to attend a merry-making, or "quilting frolic," to be held
that evening at Mynheer Van Tassel's; and having delivered
his message with that air of importance, and effort at fine
language, which a negro is apt to display on petty embassies
of the kind, he dashed over the brook, and was seen scampering away up the hollow, full of the importance and hurry of
his mission.

All was now bustle and hubbub in the late quiet schoolroom. The scholars were hurried through their lessons,
without stopping at trifles; those who were nimble skipped
over half with impunity, and those who were tardy had a
smart application now and then in the rear, to quicken their
speed, or help them over a tall word. Books were flung
aside, without being put away on the shelves; inkstands
were overturned, benches thrown down, and the whole school
was turned loose an hour before the usual time; bursting
forth like a legion of young imps, yelping and racketing
about the green, in joy at their early emancipation.

The gallant Ichabod now spent at least an extra half-hour
at his toilet, brushing and furbishing up his best, and indeed
only suit of rusty black, and arranging his looks by a bit
of broken looking-glass that hung up in the schoolhouse.

That he might make his appearance before his mistress in the true style of a cavalier, he borrowed a horse from the farmer with whom he was domiciliated, a choleric old Dutchman, of the name of Hans Van Ripper, and thus gallantly mounted, issued forth like a knight-errant in quest of adventures. But it is meet I should, in the true spirit of romantic story, give some account of the looks and equipments of my hero and his steed. The animal he bestrode was a broken-down plow-horse that had outlived almost everything but his viciousness. He was gaunt and shagged, with a ewe neck and a head like a hammer; his rusty mane and tail were tangled and knotted with burrs; one eye had lost its pupil, and was glaring and spectral, but the other had the gleam of a genuine devil in it. Still he must have had fire and mettle in his day, if we may judge from his name, which was Gunpowder. He had, in fact, been a favorite steed of his master's, the choleric Van Ripper, who was a furious rider, and had infused, very probably, some of his own spirit into the animal; for, old and broken-down as he looked, there was more of the lurking devil in him than in any young filly in the country.

Ichabod was a suitable figure for such a steed. He rode with short stirrups, which brought his knees nearly up to the pommel of the saddle; his sharp elbows stuck out like grasshoppers'; he carried his whip perpendicularly in his hand, like a scepter, and as the horse jogged on, the motion of his arms was not unlike the flapping of a pair of wings. A small wool hat rested on the top of his nose, for so his scanty strip of forehead might be called, and the skirts of his black coat fluttered out almost to the horse's tail. Such was the appearance of Ichabod and his steed as they shambled out of the gate of Hans Van Ripper, and it was altogether such an apparition as is seldom to be met with in broad daylight.

It was, as I have said, a fine autumnal day; the sky was clear and serene, and nature wore that rich and golden livery which we always associate with the idea of abundance. The forests had put on their sober brown and yellow, while some trees of the tenderer kind had been nipped by the frosts into brilliant dyes of orange, purple, and scarlet. Streaming files of wild ducks began to make their appearance high in the air; the bark of the squirrel might be heard from the groves of beech and hickory-nuts, and the pensive whistle of the quail at intervals from the neighboring stubble-field.

The small birds were taking their farewell banquets. In the fullness of their revelry, they fluttered, chirping and frolicking, from bush to bush and tree to tree, capricious from the very profusion and variety around them. There was the honest cock-robin, the favorite game of stripling sportsmen, with its loud querulous note, and the twittering blackbirds flying in sable clouds; and the golden-winged woodpecker, with his crimson crest, his broad black gorget and splendid plumage; and the cedar-bird, with its red-tipped wings and yellow-tipped tail, and its little monteiro cap of feathers; and the blue jay, that noisy coxcomb, in his gay light blue coat and white underclothes, screaming and chattering, nodding, and bobbing, and bowing, and pretending to be on good terms with every songster of the grove.

As Ichabod jogged slowly on his way, his eye, ever open to every symptom of culinary abundance, ranged with delight over the treasures of jolly autumn. On all sides he beheld vast store of apples, some hanging in oppressive opulence on the trees, some gathered into baskets and barrels for the market, others heaped up in rich piles for the cider-press. Further on he beheld great fields of Indian corn, with its golden ears peeping from their leafy coverts and holding out the promise of cakes and hasty-pudding; and the yellow pumpkins lying beneath them, turning up their fair round bellies to the sun, and giving ample prospects of the most luxurious of pies; and anon he passed the fragrant buckwheat fields, breathing the odor of the beehive, and as he beheld them, soft anticipations stole over his mind of dainty slap-jacks, well-buttered, and garnished with honey or treacle, by the delicate little dimpled hand of Katrina Van Tassel.

Thus feeding his mind with many sweet thoughts and "sugared suppositions," he journeyed along the sides of a range of hills which look out upon some of the goodliest scenes of the mighty Hudson. The sun gradually wheeled his broad disk down into the west. The wide bosom of the Tappaan Zee lay motionless and glassy, excepting that here and there a gentle undulation waved and prolonged the blue shadow of the distant mountain. A few amber clouds floated in the sky, without a breath of air to move them. The horizon was of a fine golden tint, changing gradually into a pure apple green, and from that into the deep blue of the mid-heaven. A slanting ray lingered on the woody crests of the precipices that overhung some parts of the river, giving greater depth to the dark gray and purple of their rocky sides. A sloop was loitering in the distance, dropping slowly down with the tide, her sail hanging uselessly against the mast; and as the reflection of the sky gleamed along the still water, it seemed as if the vessel was suspended in the air.

It was toward evening that Ichabod arrived at the castle of the Heer Van Tassel, which he found thronged with the pride and flower of the adjacent country. Old farmers, a spare leathern-faced race, in homespun coats and breeches, blue stockings, huge shoes, and magnificent pewter buckles. Their brisk, withered little dames, in close crimped caps, long-waisted gowns, homespun petticoats, with scissors and pin-cushions, and gay calico pockets hanging on the outside. Buxom lasses, almost as antiquated as their mothers, excepting where a straw hat, a fine ribbon, or perhaps a white frock, gave symptoms of city innovations. The sons, in short square-skirted coats, with rows of stupendous brass buttons, and their hair generally queued in the fashion of the times, especially if they could procure an eelskin for the purpose, it being esteemed throughout the country as a potent nourisher and strengthener of the hair.

Brom Bones, however, was the hero of the scene, having

come to the gathering on his favorite steed Daredevil, a creature, like himself, full of mettle and mischief, and which no one but himself could manage. He was, in fact, noted for preferring vicious animals, given to all kinds of tricks which kept the rider in constant risk of his neck, for he held a tractable well-broken horse as unworthy of a lad of spirit.

Fain would I pause to dwell upon the world of charms that burst upon the enraptured gaze of my hero, as he entered the state parlor of Van Tassel's mansion. Not those of the bevy of buxom lasses, with their luxurious display of red and white, but the ample charms of a genuine Dutch country tea-table, in the sumptuous time of autumn. Such heaped-up platters of cakes of various and almost indescribable kinds, known only to experienced Dutch housewives! There was the doughty doughnut, the tender oly-koek, and the crisp and crumbling cruller; sweet cakes and short cakes, ginger cakes and honey cakes, and the whole family of cakes. And then there were apple pies, and peach pies, and pumpkin pies; besides slices of ham and smoked beef; and moreover delectable dishes of preserved plums, and peaches, and pears, and quinces; not to mention broiled shad and roasted chickens; together with bowls of milk and cream, all mingled higgledy-piggledy, pretty much as I have enumerated them, with the motherly teapot sending up its clouds of vapor from the midst—Heaven bless the mark! I want breath and time to discuss this banquet as it deserves, and am too eager to get on with my story. Happily, Ichabod Crane was not in so great a hurry as his historian, but did ample justice to every dainty.

He was a kind and thankful creature, whose heart dilated in proportion as his skin was filled with good cheer, and whose spirits rose with eating, as some men's do with drink. He could not help, too, rolling his large eyes round him as he ate, and chuckling with the possibility that he might one day be lord of all this scene of almost unimaginable luxury and splendor. Then, he thought, how soon he'd turn his back upon the old schoolhouse; snap his fingers in the face of Hans Van Ripper, and every other niggardly patron, and kick any itinerant pedagogue out of doors that should dare to call him comrade!

Old Baltus Van Tassel moved about among his guests with a face dilated with content and good-humor, round and jolly as the harvest moon. His hospitable attentions were brief, but expressive, being confined to a shake of the hand, a slap on the shoulder, a loud laugh, and a pressing invitation to "fall to and help themselves."

And now the sound of the music from the common room, or hall, summoned to the dance. The musician was an old gray-headed negro, who had been the itinerant orchestra of the neighborhood for more than half a century. His instrument was as old and battered as himself. The greater part of the time he scraped away on two or three strings, accompanying every movement of the bow with a motion of the head; bowing almost to the ground, and stamping with his foot whenever a fresh couple were to start.

Ichabod prided himself upon his dancing as much as upon his vocal powers. Not a limb, not a fiber about him was idle; and to have seen his loosely hung frame in full motion, and clattering about the room, you would have thought St. Vitus himself, that blessed patron of the dance, was figuring before you in person. He was the admiration of all the negroes; who, having gathered, of all ages and sizes, from the farm and the neighborhood, stood forming a pyramid of shining black faces at every door and window, gazing with delight at the scene, rolling their white eyeballs, and showing grinning rows of ivory from ear to ear. How could the flogger of urchins be otherwise than animated and joyous?—the lady of his heart was his partner in the dance, and smiling graciously in reply to all his amorous oglings; while Brom Bones, sorely smitten with love and jealousy, sat brooding by himself in one corner.

When the dance was at an end, Ichabod was attracted to a knot of the sager folks, who, with Old Van Tassel, sat smoking at one end of the piazza, gossiping over former times, and drawling out long stories about the war.

This neighborhood, at the time of which I am speaking, was one of those highly favored places which abound with chronicle and great men. The British and American line had run near it during the war; it had, therefore, been the scene of marauding, and infested with refugees, cowboys, and all kind of border chivalry. Just sufficient time had elapsed to enable each story-teller to dress up his tale with a little becoming fiction, and, in the indistinctness of his recol·lection, to make himself the hero of every exploit.

There was the story of Doffue Martling, a large blue-bearded Dutchman, who had nearly taken a British frigate with an old iron nine-pounder from a mud breastwork, only that his gun burst at the sixth discharge. And there was an old gentleman who shall be nameless, being too rich a mynheer to be lightly mentioned, who, in the battle of White-plains, being an excellent master of defense, parried a musket-ball with a small-sword, insomuch that he absolutely felt it whiz round the blade and glance off at the hilt; in proof of which he was ready at any time to show the sword, with the hilt a little bent. There were several more that had been equally great in the field, not one of whom but was persuaded that he had a considerable hand in bringing the war to a happy termination.

But all these were nothing to the tales of ghosts and apparitions that succeeded. The neighborhood is rich in legendary treasures of the kind. Local tales and superstitions thrive best in these sheltered long-settled retreats; but are trampled under foot by the shifting throng that forms the population of most of our country places. Besides, there is no encouragement for ghosts in most of our villages, for they have scarcely had time to finish their first nap, and turn themselves in their graves, before their surviving friends have traveled away from the neighborhood: so that when they turn out at night to walk their rounds, they have no acquaintance left to call upon. This is perhaps the reason why we so seldom hear of ghosts except in our long-established Dutch communities.

The immediate cause, however, of the prevalence of supernatural stories in these parts was doubtless owing to the vicinity of Sleepy Hollow. There was a contagion in the very air that blew from that haunted region; it breathed forth an atmosphere of dreams and fancies infecting all the land. Several of the Sleepy Hollow people were present at Van Tassel's, and, as usual, were doling out their wild and wonderful legends. Many dismal tales were told about funeral trains, and mourning cries and wailings heard and seen about the great tree where the unfortunate Major Andre was taken, and which stood in the neighborhood. Some mention was made also of the woman in white, that haunted the dark glen at Raven Rock, and was often heard to shriek on winter nights before a storm, having perished there in the snow. The chief part of the stories, however, turned upon the favorite specter of Sleepy Hollow, the headless horseman, who had been heard several times of late, patroling the country, and, it is said, tethered his horse nightly among the graves in the churchyard.

The sequestered situation of this church seems always to have made it a favorite haunt of troubled spirits. It stands on a knoll, surrounded by locust trees and lofty elms, from among which its decent, whitewashed walls shine modestly forth, like Christian purity, beaming through the shades of retirement. A gentle slope descends from it to a silver sheet of water, bordered by high trees, between which peeps may be caught at the blue hills of the Hudson. To look upon its grass-grown yard, where the sunbeams seem to sleep so quietly, one would think that there at least the dead might rest in peace. On one side of the church extends a wide woody dell, along which raves a large brook among broken rocks and trunks of fallen trees. Over a deep black part of the stream, not far from the church, was formerly thrown a wooden bridge; the road that led to it, and the bridge itself, were thickly shaded by overhanging trees, which cast a gloom about it, even in the daytime; but occasioned a fearful darkness at night. Such was one of the favorite haunts of the headless horseman, and the place where he was most frequently encountered. The tale was told of old Brouwer, a most heretical disbeliever in ghosts, how he met the horseman returning from his foray into Sleepy Hollow, and was obliged to get up behind him; how they galloped over bush and brake, over hill and swamp, until they reached the bridge; when the horseman suddenly turned into a skeleton, threw old Brouwer into the brook, and sprang away over the treetops with a clap of thunder.

This story was immediately matched by a thrice marvelous adventure of Brom Bones, who made light of the galloping Hessian as an arrant jockey. He affirmed that, on re turning one night from the neighboring village of Sing Sing, he had been overtaken by this midnight trooper; that he had offered to race with him for a bowl of punch, and should have won it too, for Daredevil beat the goblin horse all hollow, but just as they came to the church bridge the Hessian bolted, and vanished in a flash of fire.

All these tales, told in that drowsy undertone with which men talk in the dark, the countenances of the listeners only now and then receiving a casual gleam from the glare of a pipe, sunk deep in the mind of Ichabod. He repaid them in kind with large extracts from his invaluable author, Cotton Mather, and added many marvelous events that had taken place in his native State of Connecticut, and fearful sights which he had seen in his nightly walks about Sleepy Hollow.

The revel now gradually broke up. The old farmers gathered together their families in their wagons, and were heard for some time rattling along the hollow roads, and over the distant hills. Some of the damsels mounted on pillions behind their favorite swains, and their light-hearted laughter, mingling with the clatter of hoofs, echoed along the silent woodlands, sounding fainter and fainter, until they gradually died away—and the late scene of noise and frolic was all silent and deserted. Ichabod only lingered behind, according to the custom of country lovers, to have a tete-a-tete with the heiress, fully convinced that he was now on the high road to success. What passed at this interview I will not pretend to say, for in fact I do not know. Something, however, I fear me, must have gone wrong, for he certainly sallied forth, after no very great interval, with an air quite desolate and chapfallen.—Oh, these women! these women! Could that girl have been playing off any of her coquettish tricks?—Was her encouragement of the poor pedagogue all a mere sham to secure her conquest of his rival?—Heaven only knows, not I!—Let it suffice to say, Ichabod stole forth with the air of one who had been sacking a hen-roost, rather than a fair lady's heart. Without looking to the right or left to notice the scene of rural wealth on which he had so often gloated, he went straight to the stable, and with several hearty cuffs and kicks roused his steed most uncourteously from the comfortable quarters in which he was soundly sleeping, dreaming of mountains of corn and oats, and whole valleys of timothy and clover.

It was the very witching time of night that Ichabod, heavy-hearted and crestfallen, pursued his travel homeward, along the sides of the lofty hills which rise above Tarry Town, and which he had traversed so cheerily in the afternoon. The hour was as dismal as himself. Far below him the Tappaan Zee spread its dusky and indistinct waste of waters, with here and there the tall mast of a sloop, riding quietly at anchor under the land. In the dead hush of midnight he could even hear the barking of the watch-dog from the opposite shore of the Hudson; but it was so vague and faint as only to give an idea of his distance from this faithful companion of man. Now and then, too, the long-drawn crowing of a cock, accidentally awakened, would sound far, far off, from some farmhouse away among the hills—but it was like a dreaming sound in his ear. No signs of life occurred near him, but occasionally the melancholy chirp of a cricket, or perhaps the guttural twang of a bullfrog from a neighboring marsh, as if sleeping uncomfortably, and turning suddenly in his bed.

All the stories of ghosts and goblins that he had heard in the afternoon now came crowding upon his recollection. The night grew darker and darker, the stars seemed to sink deeper in the sky, and driving clouds occasionally hid them from his sight. He had never felt so lonely and dismal. He was, moreover, approaching the very place where many of the scenes of the ghost stories had been laid. In the center of the road stood an enormous tulip tree, which towered like a giant above all the other trees of the neighborhood, and formed a kind of landmark. Its limbs were gnarled and fantastic, large enough to form trunks for ordinary trees, twisting down almost to the earth, and rising again into the air. It was connected with the tragical story of the unfortunate Andre, who had been taken prisoner hard by; and was universally known by the name of Major Andre's tree. The common people regarded it with a mixture of respect and superstition, partly out of sympathy for the fate of its ill-starred namesake, and partly from the tales of strange sights and doleful lamentations told concerning it.

As Ichabod approached this fearful tree he began to whistle; he thought his whistle was answered: it was but a blast sweeping sharply through the dry branches. As he approached a little nearer, he thought he saw something white hanging in the midst of the tree: he paused, and ceased whistling; but, on looking more narrowly, perceived that it was a place where the tree had been scathed by lightning and the white wood laid bare. Suddenly he heard a groan —his teeth chattered, and his knees smote against the saddle: it was but the rubbing of one huge bough upon another, as they were swayed about by the breeze. He passed the tree in safety, but new perils lay before him.

About two hundred yards from the tree a small brook crossed the road, and ran into a marshy and thickly wooded glen known by the name of Wiley's Swamp. A few rough logs, laid side by side, served for a bridge over this stream.

On that side of the road where the brook entered the wood a group of oaks and chestnuts, matted thick with wild grape-vines, threw a cavernous gloom over it. To pass this bridge was the severest trial. It was at this identical spot that the unfortunate Andre was captured, and under the covert of those chestnuts and vines were the sturdy yeomen concealed who surprised him. This has ever since been considered a haunted stream, and fearful are the feelings of a schoolboy who has to pass it alone after dark.

As he approached the stream his heart began to thump; he summoned up, however, all his resolution, gave his horse half a score of kicks in the ribs, and attempted to dash briskly across the bridge; but instead of starting forward, the per-verse old animal made a lateral movement, and ran broad-side against the fence. Ichabod, whose fears increased with the delay, jerked the reins on the other side, and kicked lustily with the contrary foot. It was all in vain; his steed started, it is true, but it was only to plunge to the opposite side of the road into a thicket of brambles and alder-bushes. The schoolmaster now bestowed both whip and heel upon the starveling ribs of old Gunpowder, who dashed forward, snuf-fling and snorting, but came to a stand just by the bridge with a suddenness that had nearly sent his rider sprawling over his head. Just at this moment a plashy tramp by the side of the bridge caught the sensitive ear of Ichabod. In the dark shadow of the grove, on the margin of the brook, he beheld something huge, misshapen, black and tower-ing. It stirred not, but seemed gathered up in the gloom, like some gigantic monster ready to spring upon the traveler.

The hair of the affrighted pedagogue rose upon his head with terror. What was to be done? To turn and fly was now too late; and besides, what chance was there of escap-ing ghost or goblin, if such it was, which could ride upon the wings of the wind? Summoning up, therefore, a show of courage, he demanded in stammering accents—"Who are you?" He received no reply. He repeated his demand in a still more agitated voice. Still there was no answer. Once more he cudgeled the sides of the inflexible Gunpowder, and shutting his eyes, broke forth with involuntary fervor into a psalm tune. Just then the shadowy object of alarm put itself in motion, and with a scramble and a bound stood at once in the middle of the road. Though the night was dark and dismal, yet the form of the unknown might now in some degree be ascertained. He appeared to be a horseman of large dimensions, and mounted on a black horse of powerful frame. He made no offer of molestation or sociability, but kept aloof on one side of the road, jogging along on the blind side of old Gunpowder, who had now got over his fright and waywardness.

Ichabod, who had no relish for this strange midnight companion, and bethought himself of the adventure of Brom Bones with the galloping Hessian, now quickened his steed, in hopes of leaving him behind. The stranger, however, quickened his horse to an equal pace. Ichabod pulled up, and fell into a walk, thinking to lag behind—the other did the same. His heart began to sink within him; he endeavored to resume his psalm tune, but his parched tongue clove to the roof of his mouth, and he could not utter a stave. There was something in the moody and dogged silence of this pertinacious companion that was mysterious and appalling. It was soon fearfully accounted for. On mounting a rising ground, which brought the figure of his fellow-traveler in relief against the sky, gigantic in height, and muffled in a cloak, Ichabod was horror-struck, on perceiving that he was headless! but his horror was still more increased, on observing that the head, which should have rested on his shoulders, was carried before him on the pommel of his saddle! His terror rose to desperation; he rained a shower of kicks and blows upon Gunpowder, hoping, by a sudden movement, to give his companion the slip—but the specter started full jump with him. Away, then, they dashed through thick and thin; stones flying and sparks flashing at every bound. Ichabod's flimsy garments fluttered in the air, as he stretched his long lank body away over his horse's head, in the eagerness of his flight.

They had now reached the road which turns off to Sleepy Hollow; but Gunpowder, who seemed possessed with a demon, instead of keeping up it, made an opposite turn, and plunged headlong downhill to the left. This road leads through a sandy hollow, shaded by trees for about a quarter of a mile, where it crosses the bridge famous in goblin story; and just beyond swells the green knoll on which stands the white-washed church.

As yet the panic of the steed had given his unskillful rider an apparent advantage in the chase; but just as he had got half-way through the hollow, the girths of the saddle gave way, and he felt it slipping from under him. He seized it by the pommel, and endeavored to hold it firm, but in vain; and had just time to save himself by clasping old Gunpowder round the neck, when the saddle fell to the earth, and he heard it trampled under foot by his pursuer. For a moment the terror of Hans Van Ripper's wrath passed across his mind —for it was his Sunday saddle; but this was no time for petty fears: the goblin was hard on his haunches; and (un-skillful rider that he was!) he had much ado to maintain his seat; sometimes slipping on one side, sometimes on another, and sometimes jolted on the high ridge of his horse's back-bone, with a violence that he verily feared would cleave him asunder.

An opening in the trees now cheered him with the hopes that the church bridge was at hand. The wavering reflec-tion of a silver star in the bosom of the brook told him that he was not mistaken. He saw the walls of the church dimly glaring under the trees beyond. He recollected the place where Brom Bones's ghostly competitor had disappeared. "If I can but reach that bridge," thought Ichabod, "I am safe." Just then he heard the black steed panting and blow-ing close behind him; he even fancied that he felt his hot breath. Another convulsive kick in the ribs, and old Gun-powder sprung upon the bridge; he thundered over the resounding planks; he gained the opposite side, and now Ichabod cast a look behind to see if his pursuer should vanish, according to rule, in a flash of fire and brimstone. Just then he saw the goblin rising in his stirrups, and in the very act of hurling his head at him. Ichabod endeavored to dodge the horrible missile, but too late. It encountered his cranium with a tremendous crash—he was tumbled headlong into the dust, and Gunpowder, the black steed, and the goblin rider, passed by like a whirlwind.

The next morning the old horse was found without his saddle, and with the bridle under his feet, soberly cropping the grass at his master's gate. Ichabod did not make his appearance at breakfast—dinner-hour came, but no Ichabod. The boys assembled at the schoolhouse, and strolled idly about the banks of the brook; but no schoolmaster. Hans Van Ripper now began to feel some uneasiness about the fate of poor Ichabod, and his saddle. An inquiry was set on foot, and after diligent investigation they came upon his traces. In one part of the road leading to the church was found the saddle trampled in the dirt; the tracks of horses' hoofs deeply dented in the road, and evidently at furious speed, were traced to the bridge, beyond which, on the bank of a broad part of the brook, where the water ran deep and black, was found the hat of the unfortunate Ichabod, and close beside it a shattered pumpkin.

The brook was searched, but the body of the schoolmaster was not to be discovered. Hans Van Ripper, as executor of his estate, examined the bundle which contained all his worldly effects. They consisted of two shirts and a half; two stocks for the neck; a pair or two of worsted stockings; an old pair of corduroy small-clothes; a rusty razor; a book of psalm tunes full of dog's ears; and a broken pitch-pipe. As to the books and furniture of the schoolhouse, they belonged to the community, excepting Cotton Mather's "History of Witchcraft," a New England Almanac, and a book of dreams and fortune-telling; in which last was a sheet of foolscap much scribbled and blotted, by several fruitless attempts to make a copy of verses in honor of the heiress of Van Tassel. These magic books and the poetic scrawl were forthwith consigned to the flames by Hans Van Ripper; who, from that time forward, determined to send his children no more to school; observing that he never knew any good come of this same reading and writing. Whatever money the schoolmaster possessed, and he had received his quarter's pay but a day or two before, he must have had about his person at the time of his disappearance.

The mysterious event caused much speculation at the church on the following Sunday. Knots of gazers and gossips were collected in the churchyard, at the bridge, and at the spot where the hat and pumpkin had been found. The stories of Brouwer, of Bones, and a whole budget of others, were called to mind; and when they had diligently considered them all, and compared them with the symptoms of the present case, they shook their heads, and came to the conclusion that Ichabod had been carried off by the galloping Hessian. As he was a bachelor, and in nobody's debt, nobody troubled his head any more about him; the school was removed to a different quarter of the Hollow, and another pedagogue reigned in his stead.

It is true, an old farmer, who had been down to New York on a visit several years after, and from whom this account of the ghostly adventure was received, brought home the intelligence that Ichabod Crane was still alive; that he had left the neighborhood partly through fear of the goblin and Hans Van Ripper, and partly in mortification at having been suddenly dismissed by the heiress; that he had changed his quarters to a distant part of the country; had kept school and studied law at the same time; had been admitted to the bar; turned politician; electioneered; written for the newspapers; and finally had been made a Justice of the Ten Pound Court. Brom Bones too, who, shortly after his rival's disappearance, conducted the blooming Katrina in triumph to the altar, was observed to look exceedingly knowing whenever the story of Ichabod was related, and always burst into a hearty laugh at the mention of the pumpkin; which led some to suspect that he knew more about the matter than he chose to tell.

The old country wives, however, who are the best judges of these matters, maintain to this day that Ichabod was spirited away by supernatural means; and it is a favorite story often told about the neighborhood round the winter evening fire. The bridge became more than ever an object of superstitious awe; and that may be the reason why the road has been altered of late years, so as to approach the church by the border of the mill-pond. The schoolhouse being deserted, soon fell to decay, and was reported to be haunted by the ghost of the unfortunate pedagogue; and the plow-boy, loitering homeward of a still summer evening, has often fancied his voice at a distance, chanting a melancholy psalm tune among the tranquil solitudes of Sleepy Hollow.

POSTSCRIPT

FOUND IN THE HANDWRITING OF MR. KNICKERBOCKER

THE preceding Tale is given, almost in the precise words in which I heard it related at a Corporation meeting of the ancient city of the Manhattoes,* at which were present many of its sagest and most illustrious burghers. The narrator was a pleasant, shabby, gentlemanly old fellow in pepper-and-salt clothes, with a sadly humorous face; and one whom I strongly suspected of being poor—he made such efforts to be entertaining. When his story was concluded there was much laughter and approbation, particularly from two or three deputy aldermen, who had been asleep the greater part of the time. There was, however, one tall, dry-looking old gentleman, with beetling eyebrows, who maintained a grave

---

* New York.

and rather severe face throughout; now and then folding his arms, inclining his head, and looking down upon the floor, as if turning a doubt over in his mind. He was one of your wary men, who never laugh but upon good grounds—when they have reason and the law on their side. When the mirth of the rest of the company had subsided, and silence was restored, he leaned one arm on the elbow of his chair, and sticking the other a-kimbo, demanded, with a slight but exceedingly sage motion of the head and contraction of the brow, what was the moral of the story, and what it went to prove.

The story-teller, who was just putting a glass of wine to his lips, as a refreshment after his toils, paused for a moment, looked at his inquirer with an air of infinite deference, and lowering the glass slowly to the table, observed that the story was intended most logically to prove:

"That there is no situation in life but has its advantages and pleasures—provided we will but take a joke as we find it;

"That, therefore, he that runs races with goblin troopers is likely to have rough riding of it;

"Ergo, for a country schoolmaster to be refused the hand of a Dutch heiress is a certain step to high preferment in the State."

The cautious old gentleman knit his brows tenfold closer after this explanation, being sorely puzzled by the ratiocination of the syllogism; while, methought, the one in pepper-and-salt eyed him with something of a triumphant leer. At length he observed, that all this was very well, but still he thought the story a little on the extravagant—there were one or two points on which he had his doubts:

"Faith, sir," replied the story-teller, "as to that matter, I don't believe one-half of it myself." D. K.

L'ENVOY

"Go, little booke, God send thee good passage,
  And specially let this be thy prayere,
  Unto them all that thee will read or hear,
  Where thou art wrong, after their help to call,
  Thee to correct, in any part or all."
             —CHAUCER'S *Bell Dame sans Mercie*

IN concluding a second volume of the Sketch-Book, the
Author cannot but express his deep sense of the indulgence
with which his first has been received, and of the liberal disposition that has been evinced to treat him with kindness as
a stranger. Even the critics, whatever may be said of them
by others, he has found to be a singularly gentle and good-
natured race; it is true that each has in turn objected to some
one or two articles, and that these individual exceptions, taken
in the aggregate, would amount almost to a total condemnation of his work; but then he has been consoled by observing
that what one has particularly censured, another has as particularly praised: and thus, the encomiums being set off
against the objections, he finds his work, upon the whole,
commended far beyond its deserts.

He is aware that he runs a risk of forfeiting much of this
kind favor by not following the counsel that has been liberally
bestowed upon him; for where abundance of valuable advice
is given gratis, it may seem a man's own fault if he should
go astray. He only can say, in his vindication, that he faithfully determined, for a time, to govern himself in his second
volume by the opinions passed upon his first; but he was soon
brought to a stand by the contrariety of excellent counsel.
One kindly advised him to avoid the ludicrous; another, to
shun the pathetic; a third assured him that he was tolerable

at description, but cautioned him to leave narrative alone;
while a fourth declared that he had a very pretty knack at
turning a story, and was really entertaining when in a pensive mood, but was grievously mistaken if he imagined himself to possess a spark of humor.

Thus perplexed by the advice of his friends, who each in
turn closed some particular path, but left him all the world
beside to range in, he found that to follow all their counsels
would, in fact, be to stand still. He remained for a time
sadly embarrassed; when, all at once, the thought struck him
to ramble on as he had begun; that his work being miscellaneous, and written for different humors, it could not be
expected that anyone would be pleased with the whole; but
that if it should contain something to suit each reader, his
end would be completely answered. Few guests sit down to
a varied table with an equal appetite for every dish. One has
an elegant horror of a roasted pig; another holds a curry or
a devil in utter abomination; a third cannot tolerate the ancient flavor of venison and wild fowl; and a fourth, of truly
masculine stomach, looks with sovereign contempt on those
knickknacks here and there dished up for the ladies Thus
each article is condemned in its turn; and yet, amid this variety of appetites, seldom does a dish go away from the table
without being tasted and relished by some one or other of the
guests.

With these considerations he ventures to serve up this
second volume in the same heterogeneous way with his first;
simply requesting the reader, if he should find here and there
something to please him, to rest assured that it was written
expressly for intelligent readers like himself; but entreating
him, should he find anything to dislike, to tolerate it, as one
of those articles which the Author has been obliged to write
for readers of a less refined taste.

To be serious.—The Author is conscious of the numerous
faults and imperfections of his work; and well aware how
little he is disciplined and accomplished in the arts of authorship. His deficiencies are also increased by a diffidence aris-

ing from his peculiar situation.   He finds himself writing in
a strange land, and appearing before a public which he has
been accustomed, from childhood, to regard with the highest
feelings of awe and reverence.   He is full of solicitude to deserve their approbation, yet finds that very solicitude continually embarrassing his powers, and depriving him of that
ease and confidence which are necessary to successful exertion.   Still the kindness with which he is treated encourages
him to go on, hoping that in time he may acquire a steadier
footing; and thus he proceeds, half-venturing, half-shrink-
ing, surprised at his own good fortune, and wondering at his
own temerity.

 END OF "THE SKETCH-BOOK"